The Early Victorian Period

The Connoisseur Period Guides

to the Houses, Decoration, Furnishing and Chattels
of the Classic Periods

Edited by Ralph Edwards & L. G. G. Ramsey

❧

The Tudor Period
1500—1603

The Stuart Period
1603—1714

The Early Georgian Period
1714—1760

The Late Georgian Period
1760—1810

The Regency Period
1810—1830

The Early Victorian Period
1830—1860

❧

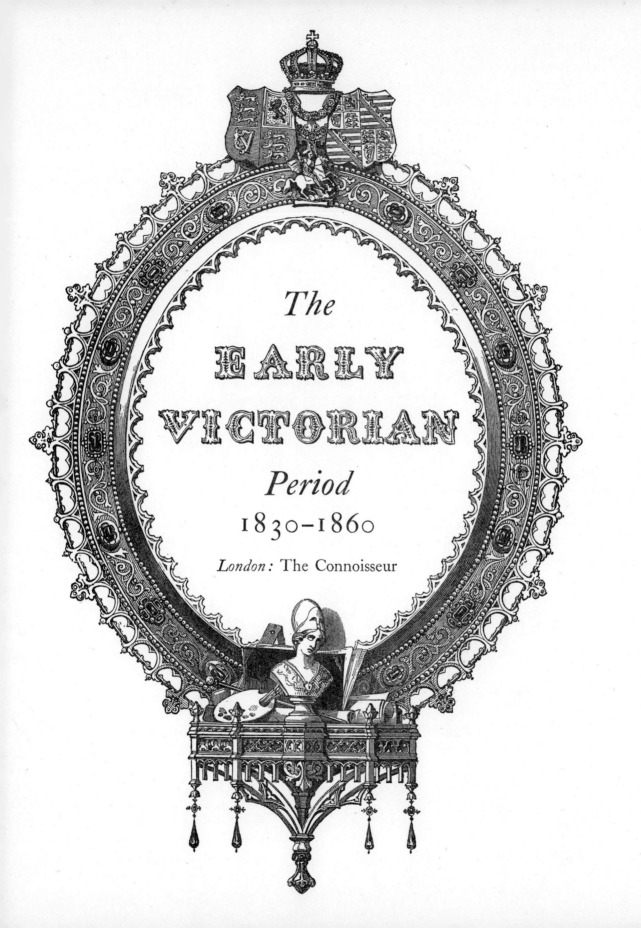

The EARLY VICTORIAN

Period
1830–1860

London: The Connoisseur

Designed and produced by Rainbird, McLean Ltd
II Charlotte Street, London W I
The text printed by Richard Clay and Company Ltd
Bungay, Suffolk
The monochrome plates printed by Robert MacLehose
Glasgow

Contents

Brunel's wrought-iron bridge over the Wye. *Illustrated Catalogue of the Great
Exhibition*, 1851.

Acknowledgments

The colour photograph used for the jacket is of Queen Victoria's sitting-room at Osborn House, Isle of Wight. The photograph was taken by A.F.Kersting.

The block on the title-page has been adapted from that on the title-page of *The Art-Journal Illustrated Catalogue*, 1851. The Coats of Arms at the top are those of Queen Victoria and Prince Albert.

For the loan of three volumes of the *Illustrated Catalogue of the Great Exhibition*, 1851, and the Wood & Sharwood type book, *c*. 1838, grateful acknowledgment is made to W.Turner Berry and the St Bride Printing Library, London.

For the loan of the original illustrated in plate 96D grateful acknowledgment is made to James Mosley, Esq., B.A.

For the loan of various books, including the one illustrated in plate 96c, grateful acknowledgment is made to Berthold Wolpe, Esq.

For the following plates acknowledgment is made to the Victoria & Albert Museum, who hold the copyright of the photographs, 26B, 49B, 53A & B, 54A, 55B, 57–61A, 62A, 63B, 64B, 69–76, 78, and 85–88. For plate 39A acknowledgment is made to the Board of Trustees, the National Galleries of Scotland.

Grateful acknowledgment is made to the Librarian and staff of the Royal Institute of British Architects Library for help and the loan of books, in particular for *The Builder*, 1843, from which the line illustrations on page 32 are taken, and also for the loan of plates 5A & B, 10–13, and 19–20.

Acknowledgment is made to P.Levene Ltd for plates 50B and 51A & B, and to the Knightsbridge Galleries for plate 55A.

For the following illustrations acknowledgment is made to the Hulton Picture Library: page xii, plates 2 and 3.

The line illustrations are by Betty Bradford, Morley Bury, Jenefer Peter and Audrey Frew.

The Index was made by the Rev. Guy Daniel, M.A.

Foreword

RALPH EDWARDS

While we are fully informed about the political, social and economic facts of the Early Victorian period, and for modern education some acquaintance with its science and literature is essential, it is strange but undeniable that in comparison we know very little of the contemporary domestic arts. On the designers and craftsmen, the producers of what formed a familiar part of the environment of the fathers and grandfathers of so many of us, 'oblivion blindly scattereth her poppy'—or in some cases has but just ceased to scatter it. A copious literature is devoted to each of the more important domestic arts from the Middle Ages down to the end of the Georgian era, but, paradoxical as it may seem, of their history in the eighteenth century far more is recorded than in a period so much nearer our own.

This omission is now being remedied, so far as the available materials allow. The vogue for Victorian art of all kinds and for Victoriana (in the sense of *trivia* that can only be labelled 'art' by an abuse of language) has already set in strongly, fostered by the growing scarcity of survivals from earlier times. We may confidently expect that it will rapidly gather momentum, and that the ineradicable, widespread instinct for collecting will seek gratification in this hitherto almost neglected field.

What has long been ignored or derided is apt on rediscovery to be greeted with excessive enthusiasm, and credited with qualities and attributes to be taken on trust rather than convincingly demonstrated. Perhaps, for this reason, a Foreword to the concluding volume of this series,

of which much of the contents represents pioneer investigations, may with advantage suggest that we should not too readily be swept away by the flowing tide, and stress the need for a critical, discriminating appraisement of the still plentiful survivals of Victorian arts and crafts.

How truly great and memorable a period in our national history the early years of Queen Victoria's reign inaugurated is vividly brought home to us in the Introduction, where its manifold activities are comprehensively surveyed; but even those most deeply imbued with the new enthusiasm will hardly maintain that its achievements in the arts – whether 'fine' or applied – have added very notably to its renown. In Architecture the 'period interest' still prejudices many people rather against, than in favour of, the more notable Early Victorian achievements. It was a time of revivals – the Gothic pre-eminently, now entering upon its later and more intensive phase – but so was the eighteenth century; and indeed revivals can be traced almost throughout the history of European architecture. Both Georgian and Victorian architects produced buildings which, despite their studious respect for precedent, cannot possibly be mistaken for those of any other age. The more unmistakably of the eighteenth century Palladian country houses are, the better we tend to like them, but only a few enthusiasts have yet managed to attach this adventitious period sentiment to *neo-cinquicento* clubs and town mansions; or to such country houses as Harlaxton – better, as it has been declared, than all but the best Elizabethan.

The Palace of Westminster, 'the most imaginatively planned and the most excellently executed major secular building anywhere in the world' (to quote Professor Pevsner), is hardly an exception. It is endeared to most people by associations which have nothing to do with 'period'. And, despite the infinite pains that Augustus Pugin took with his Gothic detail, most of the carving, which covers a vast area, is insensitive and lifeless, faithful to the designer's pattern, but lacking the individual craftsman's fancy; as is also the carved ornament both in stone and wood of innumerable churches of this phase of the Revival. Here is one of the many problems of this age of art-history – why was an age-long traditional skill, still strong and widespread in Georgian times, suddenly and so generally extinguished?

On the other hand, a strong 'period interest' now attaches to Early Victorian painting, while we find its characteristic pervading sentiment on the whole endearing. The dramatic, powerful landscapes of Constable's last years, painted in his final masterly technique, are without a hint of this sentiment – facile and often lapsing into sentimentality. And though Turner in old age continued to produce his wonderful evanescent visions, in which form is almost dissolved away or veiled in radiant light and atmosphere (and in 1840 *The Slave Ship*, according to Ruskin the greatest of all his works), only by longevity can he be counted a Victorian artist. Again, in water colour the qualities we value most in Samuel Palmer are in no way essentially Victorian, and after his departure from Shoreham in 1833 the mystic, archaic poetry that seems like a belated projection of Blake's spirit ebbs gradually away. David Cox, master of the naturalism that Palmer repudiated ('I will, God help me, never be a naturalist ...'), is a truly representative water colour artist of the time, while the drawings of Samuel Prout and other topographers faithfully reflect its enthusiasm for antiquity and the picturesque.

The appearance of the Pre-Raphaelites in 1848 was an outstanding event of this period. Cut off from the main stream of European art and largely inspired by mistaken notions of its primitive state, after a hundred years the best pictures of the Brotherhood – Millais' *Blind Girl*, for example, beautiful in design, colour and sentiment – still have the power to move us; despite the untenable doctrine of absolute realism to which the protagonists were committed. A revolt against the dreary academism of that age, the movement (literary in inspiration and dominated at the outset by D.G. Rossetti's sombre genius) must always possess for the compatriots of the artists a fascination well nigh unintelligible to foreigners.

But it is the pictures of contemporary life, a novel departure, that are a quintessential expression of the Early Victorian outlook. Many are free from any didactic intention, but others witness eloquently to the popular conviction shared by their painters, that art should tend to edification and inculcate sound morality; though some of the most extreme examples date from later in the reign. Of this line, spread throughout the country by engravers, W.P. Frith was the supreme exponent, and there can be no disputing the phenomenal skill displayed in *Derby Day* and other celebrated scenes from his hand. He was prepared on occasion to play down to his public with the most blatant preaching, but even then his instinct for marshalling his *dramatis personae* effectively seldom deserted him. The closely allied domestic *genre* and scenes derived from literature are for the most part innocent of didacticism, and what could be made of them by a painter gifted with true sensibility may be seen in Mulready's lovely little picture *The Sonnet* and in his *Choosing the Wedding Dress*, on a rather lower plane of design and imagination. Such pictures prove that an artist's individuality might reflect the spirit of the age and yet retain his individuality.

In the various domestic arts a stylistic unity prevailed throughout much the greater part of the three and a half centuries covered by these surveys, and in a previous volume that unity has been aptly described as a 'concert of styles'. Now at the beginning of Queen Victoria's reign a number of new members are added to the party, and the concert, while increasing in volume and variety, begins to get badly out of tune. The Early Victorian period was avidly eclectic, Gothic, François I, neo-Raphaelite, Elizabethan, Louis xiv, and other modes simultaneously competed, sometimes two or three of these revivalist styles being laid under contribution in the different reception rooms of a single house.

With singular unanimity the contributors note that about 1835 a decline in design begins: it gathers speed in the next twenty-five years and the end of our period marks the plunge into the abyss. During these years the faculty for producing designs which rise above mediocrity seems to have atrophied, while those of an hitherto unparalleled and unconsciously comic monstrosity were invented with lamentable ease, reaching a crescendo of pedantic absurdity in some of the 'prestige pieces' of the Great Exhibition. The eccentricities and depravities of design of which that supremely self-confident and exuberant age was capable are strikingly demonstrated in the Exhibition Catalogue; though it is essential to remember that the worst aberrations commemorated were certainly not typical of the average production.

Why these years witnessed such a general abandonment of formerly accepted standards still remains a perplexing problem. The Industrial Revolution is the orthodox explanation, but of the total output a considerable proportion—most of the fine glass, and the costly furniture—continued to be made by hand, and afford examples of Victorian craftsmanship which do not suffer by comparison with those of the Georgian era; whatever may be thought of the designs on which such craftsmanship was employed.

Moreover, all the applied or domestic arts have for centuries been largely derivative, and that designers should practise eclecticism is in itself no reproach. The authors of the sections on Porcelain, Textiles and Furniture insist (and it is undeniable) that, however derivative, the imitation is rarely so exact as to be in any way deceptive and 'not to leave scope, for the expression of a contemporary Victorian spirit'. Over a wide field these Early Victorian crafts represent the blending of derivative elements into a whole, of which the general character is so distinctive that it cannot with justice be branded as a *pastiche* or a reproduction. But unless we can claim more than that the praise is equivocal. It is the character of the interpretation and the manner of reassembling the borrowed elements that must decide the verdict. The main charge against Early Victorian design and craftsmanship is (as Mrs Morris points out) its 'equation of elaboration and beauty' – an equation made also in earlier times, but never perhaps on so extensive a scale. Contributors to this volume are not sparing of strictures on the more heinous lapses; nor were they spared by contemporary critics, as the various reports of the Commissioners on Art and Industry prove – most of them inspired by the delusive hope that 'an alliance between fine arts and manufacture would promote public taste'.

Here the sections on Furniture and Textiles may be singled out for their special value in removing misconceptions, supplying information not available before, illustrating unfamiliar examples, and establishing a reliable chronology of the sequence of styles. Much information has been irretrievably lost through neglect and indifference, and it is probable that no additions of much consequence will be made to our knowledge of these aspects of Victorian craftsmanship.

While there are many Elizabethan, Stuart and Georgian interiors complete with contemporary decoration and furniture, very few remain to represent the domestic environment of the upper and middle classes in Early Victorian times. Even a single room of the period which retains its original character is rare, and on account of its evidential value worthy of careful preservation. A reappraisal of this phase of taste is now being undertaken, and we must hope that it will be so made that a sense of proportion and a proper regard for critical standards may temper enthusiasm for rediscovery.

VICTORIA.

H.M. Queen Victoria, *c.* 1837, after an engraving by T.W.Harland.

The Age of Progress

A. J. TAYLOR

'I believe a year never opened with less cheerful prospects to a country than the present for old England; distress attending all classes of the community'. – General William Dyott's Diary: Entry for 1 January 1830.

'Never was there a year ... in which so much has been done, and such vast progress made'. – *The Times*, 1 January 1861.

Europe in 1830 was a continent in ferment. From the Netherlands to Greece, from Poland to Portugal, the fires of revolution burned or smouldered. France dethroned the last of the Bourbons; Belgians and Poles rose against their alien rulers; in Brunswick, Saxony and Hesse-Cassel, German princes conceded constitutional reform in face of imminent revolution; insurrection threatened in the Papal States; and much-troubled Portugal and Greece knew the uneasy quiet which precedes the returning storm.

Britain's troubles were small beside these; but they were not to be lightly endured. Distress drove the agricultural labourers of the southern counties to actions unprecedented since the days of Cade and Ket: ricks burned, threshing-machines were destroyed, and in some villages the tricolour was raised. In the industrial districts of the north and on the coalfields cotton-spinners and miners struck against their employers; while in the Midlands Thomas Attwood of Birmingham, in initiating the Political Union movement, expressed a discontent whose roots lay deeper than immediate distress. Nor did 1831 promise any lightening of the gloom. Trade and industry, reviving slowly in 1830, relapsed into renewed depression; a long and bitter conflict convulsed the north-eastern coalfield; riots in favour of political reform broke out at Nottingham, Derby and Bristol; and in the southern counties the agrarian revolt collapsed only in face of vindictive intimidation and repression. Nature also was playing a hostile hand. The harvests of 1830 and 1831 were the worst for a decade, and in October 1831 the cholera, already forewarned from the Continent, reached Sunderland.

Not all the omens of these years were unpropitious, however. If profits and wages were low and unemployment high, British industry in 1830 was more productive than at any previous time in its history. In that year Henry Parnell published his influential and prophetic tract *On Financial Reform* and the first railway to be wholly served by steam locomotives was opened between Liverpool and Manchester; while at Westminster the long reign of the Tories, now led by the obdurate Duke of Wellington, ended, and the Whigs, committed in letter if not in spirit to radical reform, came to power. If the forces making for distress and revolution seemed all-powerful in the black autumn of 1830, not they but economic advance and reform – the railway, Free Trade and political liberalism – were in the long run to dominate the history of the British people in the ensuing thirty years.

The Railway Age

The middle decades of the nineteenth century have been variously and paradoxically described. It was the age of reform – but also of *laissez-faire*; of Chartism – and Free Trade; a Bleak Age, yet at the last an age of prosperity. In an era of change different men and different classes had varying fortunes: yet, with all this diversity of experience, few in 1860 could deny the enormous material progress which Britain had made in three decades. As early as 1846 G.R.Porter in his aptly titled *Progress of the Nation* had written of the surging tide of advance 'working with incessant and increasing energy'. He could see before him a time 'in which the most zealous advocates of progress may see their hopes outstripped, and their most sanguine wishes brought within the reach of accomplishment'.

Nothing had done more to promote this advance than the coming of the railway. In the late 1820's the prosperity of British industry was failing not for want of capital, labour or inventiveness, but through insufficiency of markets. The railway transformed this situation. With every mile of track the opportunities of merchant and industrialist expanded as goods were conveyed greater distances and at cheaper cost, to the benefit of buyer and seller alike. The length of public railway in Britain was increased from less than 100 miles in 1830 to almost 2,000 miles by 1843, and to five times that amount seventeen years later; and the conveyance of passengers and goods multiplied even more rapidly. By the middle of the century both the stage-coach and the canal-barge had virtually given up the struggle with the locomotive. Transport by sea as well as by land was revolutionized by the twin forces of steam and iron, but the victory of steam over sail and of iron over wood was less quickly accomplished than that of rail over road and canal. Not until after 1860, when the fuel economies effected by the compound engine became apparent, did the steam-vessel finally win its way; but already in 1858 the *Great Eastern* had been launched as a brave if ill-starred prophet of the coming new era of oceanic transport.

The supreme beneficiaries of the railway age were the basic industries of coal and iron. Between 1830 and 1860 coal output expanded threefold and pig-iron production five-fold, mounting to 80 million and 10 million tons respectively by 1860. The railway itself, in construction and operation, was a voracious consumer both of coal and iron. Not only this, by the ease and cheapness with which they transported heavy goods and by their quickening influence on the whole economy, the railways of Britain and Europe increased enormously the market for the basic raw materials of industry. Iron, symbolized as much by the humble drainage-pipe as by the liner, became the raw material of the age, and was put to use with equal effectiveness in the iron-girt Crystal Palace and in the steam-engine itself. By 1860, however, iron in its turn was giving way to steel, and an era which had been ushered in by Neilson's discovery of the hot-blast method of iron-smelting moved into its successor with the patenting of the Bessemer process for the large-scale manufacture of steel.

Hand in hand with the advance of basic industry went the growth of the activities of the engineer. In the first half of the nineteenth century engineering was rich in invention and innovation. The achievement of a succession of able and resourceful pioneers like Maudslay, Whitworth and Nasmyth, together with the demands of expanding industry, had not only enhanced the status of the engineer's craft but enlarged its scale. Where £50 had sufficed to equip a modest workshop in 1825, twenty times that sum might be required to establish a business less than a quarter century later; and as the engineer's tools were transformed, so was the organization of his craft. Nowhere in these years of growth is the mounting tempo of change more apparent than at this nodal point of Britain's industrial economy.

But if the changes of these years are most readily discernible in coal, iron and engineering, the developments in manufacturing industry were little less significant. With the stimulus of an expanding market, British manufacturers were enabled to carry on the work of innovation and enterprise to which the Watts and Arkwrights of the previous century had given such vitality. The steam-engine and the factory system had already established their place in the British economy even before 1800, but as late as 1830 large areas of the industrial world were still unaffected by them. In the next thirty years the steam-engine gained ground rapidly. Although important sections of British industry – tailoring and shoe-making among them – still lay wholly outside the orbit of the factory system in 1860, the days of domestic industry were clearly numbered.

Cotton, always in the van of technical progress, had already travelled far along the road of technological and organizational change by 1830; yet it still numbered some 200,000 hand-loom weavers among its company of less than half a million workers. In the next twenty years the privations of these survivors of an older order frequently attracted the attention of Parliament. But by 1850 time had worked its own solution: the power-loom had won its victory and domestic employment had virtually disappeared from the English cotton industry. Where cotton led, other textiles followed, some, like the worsted industry, with a rapidity no less than that of cotton itself; others, like wool, at a slower but no less certain pace. With increasing mechanization came heightened productivity: in a quarter of a century the cotton industry achieved a fourfold expansion in output with a negligible increase in its labour force. Outside the textile industries, the steam-engine and the machine were also making rapid conquests. The domestic nailmakers of the Black Country were fighting their final rearguard action against factory industry in the 1850's, while a host of smaller industries likewise felt the impact of steam-power and the organizational revolution which it implied.

As significant as the transformation of old industries, however, was the advent of new products and processes. None among these was more portentous than the advance of the rubber industry, which, originating in the earlier years of the century, came to maturity in the railway age. *Macintosh* entered the English language in 1836, and a decade later the vulcanization process and the pneumatic tyre were patented. With the striking of Pennsylvanian oil in 1859, the door was already

being opened on a world where coal and the steam-engine itself would find their new-won supremacy strongly challenged.

More highly mechanized industries catering for bigger markets meant larger firms and greater demands for capital. Here, as in other things, the railway pointed the way. In its ultimate penetration of the economic life of the nation the joint-stock company with limited liability derives its example and impetus from the needs of the railway promoters. No boom did more than the railway mania of 1844–6 to extend the investing habit and increase the numbers of the shareholding public, a development for which even the speculative machinations of George Hudson, 'the Railway King', were not too high a price to pay. In 1855 general legislative sanction was finally given to the limited liability company, in advance perhaps of the immediate demands of manufacturing industry, but to its lasting benefit. Eleven years earlier, in 1844, Parliament had passed the Bank Charter Act. This, with the legislation of the previous decade, had established English banking on the twin foundation of the central Bank of England and the joint-stock banks; and thereby given to it a structure which, for all its undoubted defects of detail, was to conserve and increase the nation's financial resources and prestige in the expansionist years which lay ahead.

The corollary to industrial growth was the expansion of the export trade. Already in 1830, by accident rather than design, Britain had abandoned the form, if not the pretence, of a balanced economy. Though in good harvest years the country might still achieve a bare self-sufficiency in essential foodstuffs, she imported food and raw materials on an increasingly lavish scale in exchange for the products of her mills and workshops. Exports of British goods doubled in value between 1830 and 1850, and almost doubled again in the succeeding decade. In volume the overall increase was even greater. With the repeal of the protective Corn Laws in 1846 all pretence of maintaining balance in the economy disappeared; not only Britain's prosperity but her very existence was henceforth committed into the hands of her industrialists and merchants.

3

The fate of agriculture amid these changes and chances wore some of the marks of paradox. In 1830 farming had been more depressed than any other industry. Its sickness was of long standing, going back in the memories of some to the end of the French Wars. Yet opportunity for advancement was not lacking. A rapidly growing urban population made increasing demands for food; transport was improving; and tariff protection minimized the effects of foreign competition. Yet it was not till after 1850, with the Corn Laws repealed, that full revival came – a revival made possible by the removal of financial burdens, radical readjustment to new conditions, the advent of the railway, and a rapid improvement in urban living standards. The progress thus achieved, and measurable alike in terms of higher profits, rents and wages, should not, however, be misinterpreted. In their rate of expansion agricultural profits lagged far behind those of industry; and while the working population as a whole rose by over 1 million in the single decade 1851–61, employment in agriculture fell by almost 100,000. Agriculture, prosperous though it might be, had declined in status; and its decline had implications not only for the British economy, but for the country's social and political structure.

The mounting tide of industrial productivity brought with it a great increase in the nation's wealth. Before 1850, except in years of war, the State itself made little demand upon these growing riches, but much of the product of industry was reinvested to provide the capital assets for later generations. In the second quarter of the nineteenth century the railway was perhaps the finest outcome of this spirit of thrift, but in industry itself the constant pursuit of innovation reflects the same desire to live for tomorrow as well as today. The emphasis on long-term investment rather than on immediate consumption may explain in part the seeming poverty in the midst of plenty which clouds even the years of greatest prosperity in the two decades after 1830. Merchants and manufacturers might know increased wealth and display it not only in their expanded businesses, but also in the bricks and mortar of their town and country houses; but the economic progress of the industrial worker was less clearly marked. For the skilled craftsman, be he millwright or coal-hewer, cotton-spinner or carpenter, the rewards of an expanding economy could be measured in terms of a swelling pay-packet and an increasing command of goods and services, many of them cheapened by the cost-reductions of factory-industry. But for the less skilled, and for those employed in decaying domestic crafts – handloom-weavers, framework knitters, nailers and the like – the note of economic progress had a hollow ring. If the demand for labour was increasing, so too were the means of supply; for to the rapid natural increase of population was added the outpouring of an over-populated and famine-threatened Ireland. The high price of necessities, induced in part by the protective system, and the effects of slump following upon boom, served only further to depress the living standards of the still large numbers of the industrious poor.

To the problems which low wages, short-time and unemployment brought in their train were added those of life in the rapidly growing industrial towns. In the decades after 1830 house-building more than kept pace with population growth, but the continued low quality of construction and the neglect of earlier years laid a heavy burden on Victorian England. So rapidly had the new towns been called into being – Oldham, for example, increased its population from 12,000 to 53,000 in the first half of the nineteenth century and Manchester swelled from 77,000 to 316,000 in the same fifty years – that local authorities both before and after the Municipal Corporation Act of 1835 were unable to keep pace with the need for increased water-supply and improved sanitation. Not every town-dweller lived in a back-to-back house, devoid of running water and rudimentary sanitary provision, but such conditions were the rule rather than the exception in many of the urban areas of the new England of the North and Midlands.

From the middle of the century the life of the working-classes slowly took on a less sombre appearance. The wealth of the nation, if not more diffused, was at least so augmented as to raise the living standards of all but the poorest and least adaptable of the community. Even the farm-labourer, hitherto the most distressed member of a depressed economic group, felt the benefit of a buoyant economy. Corn, its price held firm in the midst of slow yet perceptible inflation, became of increasingly less account in working-class budgets; and rising living-standards were reflected not only in an expanding consumption of such working-class luxuries as rice, tobacco and tea, but also in the growth of the number of institutions for working-class thrift. Legislation had removed the worst of the evils attending the employment of women and children, and in the towns the new councils, increasing in strength and authority, not only built civic halls and reservoirs, but, equally significantly, appointed Medical Officers charged with the oversight of the manifold health problems of the growing urban communities. By 1860, though poverty, like disease, was far from conquered, the working man with his family could look to a future richer in wealth, leisure and the means of its enjoyment than his father could have dared to hope for thirty years earlier.

The age of reform

The spirit of reform was not born in the dark days of 1830, though economic depression in that year, as in 1842 and 1848, served to sharpen the fine edge of militant radicalism. Nor did it owe its existence wholly to the Industrial Revolution, even if the strong tide of industrialization and urbanization served to emphasize old problems and create new ones. The demand for reform was deeply rooted and sprang as much from the world of ideas as of material circumstance. There were those who, basing their views on principles of liberty developed in the seventeenth century by John Locke, sought primarily the emancipation of man's economic life. Such were the followers of Adam Smith, who extolled the virtues of international free trade and the benefits of an unfettered economic society – the Classical Economists, the Manchester School, the advocates of *laissez-faire*. Close to them in sympathy, if not in fundamental doctrine, stood the Utilitarian followers of Jeremy Bentham, believers in the principle of 'the

greatest happiness of the greatest number' as the yardstick of social behaviour and of the efficacy of social institutions. To them, unlike the extreme advocates of *laissez-faire*, the State had a limited right of intervention in the affairs of men, but its intervention must conform to the 'greatest-happiness' principle, and above all things be efficient. Both these groups approached economic and social problems with a scientific purpose and method. In others the heart seemed sometimes to speak louder than the head, a broad humanitarianism finding its rallying point in the reforming zeal of the Evangelicals, and its leader in the seventh Earl of Shaftesbury. All these movements found favourable soil for growth in mid-nineteenth-century England. Others, no less significant, were more alien to the temper of the times. The egalitarianism which in varied forms expressed itself in the writings and activities of Owen and Kingsley, of Ruskin and Marx, was in advance of its time. Similarly, that radicalism which nostalgically invited a return to a pre-industrial society ran counter to the prevailing spirit of an age exulting in the benefits which bourgeois capitalism and industrialization were bestowing. But, however much their origins and purposes might differ, the varied movements of reform shared a common dissatisfaction with men and institutions as they were, and an inquiring spirit far removed from the complacency which had characterized so much English thinking in the previous century.

When men spoke of reform in 1830, they meant the reform of Parliament. A radical revision of the system of parliamentary representation was looked upon as the key to all other reforms in society. In the eyes of utilitarians and working-class radicals alike the prevailing system of representation, with its grossly unequal electoral districts and unrepresented towns, its rotten boroughs and irrational franchises, stood condemned on grounds both of natural justice and governmental efficiency. Members of Parliament were less convinced of the validity of these strictures, but they could not resist their consequence. The Whigs were led to carry Reform in 1832 as much from motives of expediency as of principle: reform was for them a lesser evil than revolution. But it was the results, not the motives of reform which were to have lasting significance.

The Great Reform Act of 1832, the culmination of months of bitter struggle inside and outside Parliament, gave representation to large towns like Birmingham and Manchester and the vote to the wealthier sections of the middle classes in country and town alike. By design it tied the vote to property, enfranchising those, and only those, who had a 'stake in the country'. The electorate was thereby increased by about 50 per cent, but, despite this significant numerical expansion, neither the methods of electioneering nor the personnel of the House of Commons were changed overnight. Dickens' Eatanswill belongs to the decade after the Reform Act and Trollope's House of Commons still had a strongly aristocratic flavour in the 1860's. Such a limited measure of reform could not satisfy either the more extreme among the radical thinkers or the politically-conscious sections of the working-class. Hence it brought quickly in its train the People's Charter of 1838, in which pride of place was given to the demand for universal male suffrage. But in Chartism, even more than in the reform movement of 1830–2, the demand for the vote soon became merely a means to an end – the social and economic regeneration of society. Every proletarian discontent found its rallying point in Chartism – the call for factory legislation, opposition to the new Poor Law, and, particularly in 1842, blind reaction to unemployment and distress – until in 1848, that *annus mirabilis* of revolutionary activity, the movement reached its culmination with the presentation of the Great Petition. By 1851, as a potent force, it was dead, killed by ridicule and prosperity.

The combined effect of rapid industrialization and population growth – the population of England and Wales alone rose from 9 to 14 million between 1801 and 1831, and to 20 million by 1861 – had produced a variety of urgent social problems, among them those of conditions in the new factories and in the new – and older – towns; of poverty, seemingly chronic in the rural south and deep, if spasmodic, in the industrial north; and of ignorance and illiteracy among the growing numbers of the working-class. To the resolution of these problems the reformers bent their best endeavours, though by no means always with common policy or intent. Evangelicals and humanitarians like the Tory Richard Oastler welcomed any and every limitation which the legislature might impose on the working hours of factory children; the more radical disciples of Adam Smith and Ricardo, on the other hand, could not countenance the infringement of *laissez-faire* which such limitation implied; while the Benthamite Edwin Chadwick advocated a middle course which combined a clearly defined and restricted intervention with the supervisory power of an efficient inspectorate. Likewise in the Poor Law reform of 1834, while, on the one hand, Malthusians might reject all attempts at relief as interference with the operation of the laws of nature, and, on the other, a Disraeli or a Dickens assert that to restrict relief was to cheat the poor of their rightful inheritance, it was Chadwick who, again pursuing the middle way, devised the 'Workhouse Test' and the centralizing organization of the Poor Law Board.

In brief, the Evangelicals and Utilitarians were the heart and head of the movement for social reform, even if at times heart spoke against head in no uncertain fashion. The greatest single triumph of the Evangelicals was perhaps the Abolition of Slavery in 1833, that of the Utilitarians the amendment of the Poor Law a year later; but, while the humanitarianism of the Evangelicals represents an ongoing tradition in British life and thought, the methods and achievements of the Utilitarians were in their day sufficiently novel to merit further examination here. The followers of Bentham, and first among them Chadwick, made the Royal Commission the instrument of their inquiries and the parliamentary Blue Book the vehicle of their propaganda. Inquiry and propaganda paved the way to reform, and here the Benthamite weapon was the parliamentary act and the administrative Board or Inspectorate. Factory Inspectors were first appointed in 1833 and Mines Inspectors in the following decade: the permanent Poor Law Commission was established in 1834, and the Central Board of

Health in 1848. In these two last Chadwick himself played a leading part. Thus over a wide field of social policy the influence of the Benthamites ran strong and deep. The followers of Bentham were to the nineteenth century what the Fabians were to become to the twentieth – agents of purposeful and scientific inquiry and protagonists of social reform through administrative centralization – and, like the Fabians, they were assailed for allowing the precepts of social theory to overrule the deeper promptings of humanity. In so far as the charge may have substance, it can perhaps be more justly levied at the results than the motives of their policies.

Posterity, however, owes an even fuller debt to the Utilitarians and those who kept close company with them. To men like G.R.Porter at the Board of Trade, Leonard Horner in the Factory Inspectorate, and, perhaps above all, to Chadwick himself, in his manifold public administrative duties, is owed that new conception of the functions of the public official which has been one of the great legacies of early Victorian England to later generations. Patronage, nepotism and the idea of the sinecure were slow in dying in the British Civil Service. Chadwick and those like him, by their example of tireless and efficient service, paved the way for that thorough-going reform of public administration which followed from the legislation of 1855, and the acceptance of the principle of open competition which it involved.

The industrial and commercial sections of the middle class, whom the Reform Act of 1832 had enfranchized, were more concerned with economic than with social reform. For them, after 1832, reform meant the reduction of the tariff and the repeal of the Corn Laws. Their earliest and best hopes lay with the party that had given them the franchise, the party not only of Grey and Russell, the architects of '1832', but of Henry Parnell and Poulett Thomson, of Villiers, Bright and Cobden, all unequivocal advocates of Free Trade. In the event, however, it was not the Whigs but the Tory Peel and his lieutenant Gladstone who liberalized the tariff. The decisive battle may be said to have begun with the foundation of the Manchester-inspired Anti-Corn Law League

in 1838. The movement for tariff reform derived impetus from the proceedings of the Select Committee on Import Duties of 1840, before which the Free Traders deployed their arguments with such adroitness as to discomfort thoroughly the protagonists of protection; it profited from a swing of the trade cycle, which, out of depression in 1842, imposed upon the Tory administration the necessity of adopting radical measures to meet the nation's economic difficulties and, in the prosperity of 1845, gave it the opportunity to justify and consolidate them; and it gained speedy realization of its best hopes from finding in Peel a minister of flexible outlook, who drew his inspiration not only from Harrow and Christ Church, which educated him, but also from industrial Lancashire, where his deeper roots lay. Peel attempted to restore the Government's credit and to revive the nation's trade by a temporary restoration of the income-tax and a reduction of prohibitory and protective tariffs. If of his work only the income-tax now remains, this is no measure of his immediate or ultimate achievement. On his work, at least in part, rested the prosperity that was to be Britain's for a generation and more.

Peel's crowning achievement was the repeal of the Corn Laws, an action enforced upon him prematurely by the Irish Potato Famine of 1845. It ended his ministerial career, broke the party which he had re-established little more than a decade earlier, and brought down upon him the execrations of many whom he had hitherto counted as his supporters and friends; but his reward was the reputation for high statesmanship which posterity has accorded him. In the next generation the work which he had begun so experimentally in 1842 was carried boldly and logically to its conclusion. The Navigation Laws, designed initially to protect the British carrying trade, were repealed in 1849; and in the two great budgets of 1853 and 1860 Gladstone completed the structure of Free Trade, adding to the last for good measure a commercial treaty with France.

The triumph of the middle class

The repeal of the Corn Laws was a political triumph for the middle class, won in part as a

7

result of the most sustained and powerfully financed campaign in British parliamentary history. It was a victory for the interests of commerce and industry over those of the land and agriculture, gained in a parliament in which the landed interest still held a clear numerical ascendency. Such is not merely the verdict of the historian: it was the opinion of contemporaries on both sides of the argument, protectionists like Disraeli as well as Free Traders like Cobden. Where, then, one may ask, did political power reside in early Victorian England; in what institution and with what class? The question admits of no simple answer. The legalist might assert the supremacy of 'the King in Parliament' and interpret this in practical terms as the rule of the King's ministers. But whereas a century earlier the royal will had determined the fate of ministries, that authority had now passed to Parliament, and within Parliament to the House of Commons. In the thirty years between 1830 and 1860 no less than eleven distinct ministries were formed. Of these only a minority lived out their natural term of office: the rest died in parliamentary conflict, destroyed by the adverse votes of the Lower House. This was the outcome of an age where parliamentary majorities were generally small, and where party organization and party loyalty were conspicuously weak. At times, as in the crises over Reform and the Corn Law and during the Crimean War, the need for strong government asserted itself, but more often the Commons held the whip hand and made and unmade ministries almost at their pleasure, restrained only by the occupational risks – and costs – which a dissolution could bring to every member.

As within the body politic, so among classes the exact balance of power and influence is difficult to determine. Mere appearances would suggest the continuing ascendency of the aristocracy. Every administration between 1830 and 1860 drew at least half its members from the titled classes and none – Whig or Tory, Liberal or Conservative – counted less than a third of its members in the House of Lords. Palmerston's second Liberal Cabinet, formed in 1859, had three dukes, two earls, three lesser peers and three knights in its

complement of fifteen. But although the road to political office might continue to lie, as Trollope's Phineas Finn discovered, through the doors of the houses of the aristocracy – and of their ladies – and though the patronage flowing from landed wealth still acted powerfully in determining the personnel of the House of Commons, the middle classes, when their vital interests were affected in the Corn Law struggle of 1846, were able to exert an influence out of all proportion to their representation in Parliament or Cabinet. The inheritance of power was seemingly theirs whenever they should choose to claim it, but for the present they were content to busy themselves about their own affairs, and to leave politics in the hands of those whose economic primacy they had usurped, well satisfied so long as industry and commerce were allowed to go their own ways unhindered and unmolested.

The Reform Act was a turning point in the history of parties as well as of the constitution. The old names of Whig and Tory – and by 1832 they had become little more than names – had outlived their usefulness as rallying points of opinion and interest. The Tories, beaten in 1830 and again in 1832, were the first to recognize this, and in 1834 attempted to regroup their forces under the banner of Peelite Conservatism, adopting as their principle the 'careful review of institutions, civil and ecclesiastical, undertaken in a friendly temper, combining, with the firm maintenance of established rights, the correction of proved abuses and the redress of real grievances'. But parties are founded on interest as much as principle, and when in 1846 interest and principle came into conflict, it was interest – the economic interest of the landowning classes – which triumphed, and Peelite Conservatism was doomed. It was left to Derby and Disraeli to attempt a second reconstruction. They recreated the party on the basis of an appeal to the disaffected and underprivileged, to the farm-labourer as much as the landowner, the factory-worker as the agriculturalist. The fruits of such a reconstruction, however, could not be garnered until a second Reform Act in 1867 had enfranchised the urban working-class. The Whigs knew no such extreme

8

crisis as that which beset the Tories both in 1832 and 1846; but Whiggism, with its essentially aristocratic roots, was too narrowly based for the needs of a middle-class electorate in an industrial age. By 1860 the name of Whig had been exchanged for Liberal, and the party had broadened its ranks to include, not only a considerable and varied Radical element, but also the rejected of the Tory Party of 1846. The Liberals had thereby become predominantly the party of industrial England and of the middle class: Lancashire and Manchester would have none other, and Manchester's voice was prophetic of England's. But, like its opponent, the Liberal Party needed the stimulus of a widened electorate to find itself – and its organization – in fullest measure.

If parties counted for little in mid-nineteenth-century Britain, men counted for much. Grey and Wellington, Peel and Cobden, Palmerston and Bright, Russell and Derby, Gladstone and Disraeli – this roll of honour, already long, is still incomplete. It omits two prime ministers and a host of others who were rightly honoured in their generation. Grey and Wellington, the one Whig, the other Tory, represented in 1830 a dying order: for if Grey played the midwife at the birth of the new régime, he quickly retired from political life when this office was completed, and Wellington, though active in politics almost until his death in 1852, was content to tread the side-lines save when duty called him to placate a turbulent House of Lords in 1832 and 1846. If Grey and Wellington represented the past, Gladstone and Disraeli were the heralds of the future. By 1860 the star of both was clearly in the ascendent, but for neither was it fully risen. Gladstone had come a long way from his Tory beginnings in Eton and Christ Church. As a Peelite he finally crossed his Rubicon into the Liberal Party in 1859, but already under Peel's inspiration in the 'forties his deeper mercantile origins had asserted themselves, and joined Liverpool to Oxford in his mental and spiritual make-up. In two as yet brief but glorious periods at the Exchequer – between 1852 and 1855 and latterly from 1859 – the spirit of Liverpool had made itself manifest. The days of Ireland and the Midlothian Campaign – and the higher office

which they carried with them – still lay in the future, but in the emphasis on public economy which he added to that on Free Trade the heir of Peel had already made his firm mark upon the Victorian political scene. Palmerston and Russell still stood between Gladstone and the highest ministerial office in 1860. In like manner Derby barred the upward path of the ambitious Disraeli. Disraeli had prospered not by responding to the spirit of the age but by opposing it. From the wreck of Tory fortunes in 1846 he had survived as an almost lone eminence in a party deprived not only of numbers but of men of intellect by the defection of the Peelites. But in 1860, although already twice Chancellor of the Exchequer, his hour had not yet struck; nor would it until a changed electorate and a changing economic climate made possible an invocation of the spirit of empire out of place in the bourgeois England of the young Victoria.

If we seek to personify the spirit of this great age of parliamentary government, therefore, we must look neither to Grey or Wellington nor to Gladstone or Disraeli. In an era of change no other single name suggests itself. If choice be made, it must rather rest on the representatives of two conflicting traditions – the manufacturer, Richard Cobden, and the aristocrat, Viscount Palmerston. Cobden, the greatest back-bencher of the age, spoke, for all his Sussex birth, with the authentic voice of the industrial north. A whole-hearted believer in Britain's economic supremacy, he was yet an internationalist seeing in Free Trade a means to the greater end of universal understanding and peace. In him were conjoined the hard-headed realism of the business-man and the utopianism of the idealist – both ingredients in the make-up of the nineteenth-century Liberal. Palmerston has a more timeless quality. His parliamentary career (from 1807 to 1865) spans the old and the new in British politics. Secretary at War under four prime ministers before 1832, he survived to die in harness as Prime Minister – and the people's darling – in 1865. He was truly 'John Bull incarnate', pugnacious, firmly convinced of Britain's central position in the world, and willing to threaten a war to protect the life and honour of a British subject – the focal point of a nation's pride in an age when prosperity and power went hand in hand, and a Cincinnatus waiting recall when disaster threatened in the Crimean War. It was on the justice of the war with Russia that Cobden and Palmerston clashed, not for the first or last time; but, differ as they might in outlook and policy, each in his mounting confidence and vigorous optimism expressed the spirit and temper of the age. Palmerston, himself, felt the kinship and in 1859, only three years after the ending of the war, offered Cobden an honoured place in his last great administration; but Cobden, an unbending Radical to the last, refused.

Britain since the Revolution of 1688 had been but indifferently blessed in her kings and queens; and in none less than George IV, who went to an unhonoured grave in 1830. That the monarchy should have seen its power decline was perhaps inevitable, but that it should have lost a nation's respect was as unnecessary as it was unfortunate. Indeed, had republicanism been in the air in 1830 – had France preferred a President to the Orleanist Louis-Philippe – revolution, not reform, might have been the nation's choice. William IV, and still more the young Victoria, retrieved the monarchy's prestige, but they could not stem the ebbing tide of its political authority. Though both were able on occasion to use their limited powers – 'to be consulted, to encourage, to warn', in Bagehot's well-known phrase – to good effect, their capacity as creators of ministries or initiators of policy was waning and by 1860 had largely disappeared. William IV dismissed Melbourne in 1834 and five years later, in the comic opera episode of the Bedchamber Crisis, Victoria rebuffed Peel, but neither experiment was repeated. Thereafter the instances of effective royal intervention, as in the dismissal of Palmerston from the Foreign Office in 1851, are few and in sum of little importance, and when party organization strengthened, the opportunity for royal action would decline still further. Although the monarch might remain the supreme umpire in the parliamentary game, her verdict was rarely required or requested. Yet if the monarchy's political power continued to diminish, its prestige was enhanced with every

year of the young Queen's reign. The first phase of recovery was completed with the death of the Prince Consort in 1861. The Queen had then reigned for twenty-four years, and the example of her family life, her attention to her religious and political duties, her rigid moral code, high seriousness and industry, commended themselves to a nation which had grown weary of laxer standards. 'Middle-class morality' was not merely the reflected manners of a reformed Court – it grew out of the values which nonconformity and industrial growth engendered – but it responded in full measure to the changed behaviour of royalty. Looking back in 1861 to the reign of George IV, Thackeray could write: 'He is dead but thirty years, and one asks how a great society could have tolerated him? Would we bear him now? In the quarter of a century, what a silent revolution has been working! How it has separated us from old times and manners! How it has changed men themselves!' In a dynamic society in which, as the young Disraeli perceived, forces of social disintegration were threatening disaster, the reformed monarchy was a powerful binding force, reconciling in itself the institutions of the old order and the social needs of the new.

Britain and the world

A nation so busy about its own affairs had little time to look out on to a wider world. Though her citizens travelled abroad no less, Britain in the mid-nineteenth century was becoming increasingly insular in thought, culture and in foreign policy. In the troubles of the 1830's Palmerston had spoken powerfully and purposefully on the side of the liberal angels, but the exercise was not allowed to cost the life of a single British soldier; and after 1848 even the voice became less certain and effective. So long as no continental Power threatened to dominate Europe, Britain was content to stand aside. France and Russia at different times seemed likely to upset the European balance, and on each occasion the resources of Palmerstonian diplomacy were stretched to the uttermost in the attempt to contain the threatened advance. Thus France was checked first in the Netherlands, then in Spain and finally – though not with complete success – in Italy. Russia occasioned a deeper and more continuing anxiety. Here the threat was not only to the European balance, but to the United Kingdom's commercial interests in the eastern Mediterranean and beyond. In face of suspected Russian predatoriness in the Balkans, British foreign secretaries attempted to bolster up a disintegrating Ottoman Empire. As a result, in 1854 Britain tumbled into war with Russia in the Crimea, a war with but one heroine, Florence Nightingale, and one hero, the Light Brigade, and with little else to commend it to a nation disappointed by the news of military stalemates and the winter miseries of the British forces, and dismayed by the mounting evidence of bureaucratic maladministration and incompetence. But the appetite of the British public for foreign adventure, reawakened after long years of peace, survived the disenchantment of the Russian War to become the jingoism of Palmerston's declining years.

If Europe often seemed far away, the colonial empire was even more remote. This has sometimes been called an age of anti-imperialism. But perhaps these should rather be called years of imperial neglect, or more precisely of public apathy. The period of disillusionment which followed the loss of the American Colonies had passed – though memories of it were awakened when Canada flared up into rebellion in 1837; but if, as was widely believed, Free Trade and the repeal of the Navigation Laws were severing the final links of empire, few at home were disposed to wish it otherwise. The colonies, for their part, flourished on neglect. Canada, Australia and New Zealand moved forward towards self-government and dominion status; and their settlers, increased in number by the prospect of gold and the activities of Gibbon Wakefield and the Land and Emigration Board, grew not only in prosperity, but also in loyalty to the Crown. Out of apathy was born a Commonwealth: it was one of the richest if the most fortuitous of the legacies of early Victorian England to later generations.

Britain's 'other empire' – of trading-posts and commercial settlements, and less formally of economic concessions – could not be retained without conflict and expense. Between 1839 and 1842 British forces were engaged in unwanted and disastrous operations in Afghanistan to protect India's North-West Frontier. Over the same period a war, more successful in its conduct and outcome, was waged against the Chinese Empire. As a result the Chinese ceded Hong Kong, and the 'treaty ports' were opened to British trade. In 1858 the unequal struggle was renewed and by 1860 Britain had again asserted her authority in the China Seas. But the British public, diverted by happenings nearer home, could only enthuse ephemerally over such adventures.

By 1860, however, new comets were in the sky, though their portent was not yet understood. During the early years of Victoria's reign the British hold on the sub-continent of India had been gradually strengthened in part by force, in part by peaceful annexation, but always with little more than the passive acquiescence of the home Government. In 1858, however, following the Mutiny, the Crown assumed those responsibilities for the government of India which had hitherto been vested in the East India Company. Meanwhile, in Africa, David Livingstone, watched with increasing eagerness from Britain, was penetrating the heart of the unexplored continent. The stage was beginning to be set for the heady imperialism of the nineteenth century's closing years.

Though Britain might neglect her colonial empire, she was never allowed to forget Ireland. If Catholic Emancipation had assuaged a grievance, it had done nothing to feed a single Irishman; and so long as the land system remained unreformed there could be no true prospect of lasting peace in Ireland. The Potato Famine brought misery, depopulation, and, more tardily, land reform in its train. But already in the 'forties a deeper discontent had revealed itself. The Young Ireland movement paved the way not only for the fury of Fenian outrage in the 'sixties, but also for the broader political demands of the century's later decades. Ireland lay like a sullen volcano off the shores of England, never wholly quiescent, always seemingly on the point of violent eruption.

Change and tradition

No age lives by bread and politics alone; but, in the pursuit of both, men frequently reveal their deeper attitudes and values. In questions of religion the early Victorians showed that combination of adventurous advance and respect for established institutions which was so characteristic of their political life and thought. The early Victorian Age was in the broadest, if not necessarily the deepest, sense a religious age: it was certainly, by twentieth-century standards, an age of church-going. Five out of every twelve persons – young and old – in England and Wales are estimated to have attended a place of worship on 'Census Sunday' in 1851 – some on more than one occasion in the day. Only half of these worshippers were members of the Established Church. Dissent, which claimed the majority of the remainder, had won a powerful and numerous following in the industrial towns and on the coalfields; and among the sects none had achieved a larger body of adherents than the Methodists. Methodism had won its converts by the simple, evangelical appeal of Pauline Christianity, but the social and political implications of its achievement were complex. While the Wesleyan 'orthodoxy' of Jabez Bunting, for forty years 'the Premier of Methodism', enjoined an almost Tory respect for the powers-that-be within the State, the dissident Primitive wing of the movement was more radical in its social and political outlook and nurtured within itself the leaders of working-class revolt. The Established Church had been slow to respond to the needs of a growing industrial and urban society, but by 1850, under the powerful influence of the Evangelicals and the Tractarians, the work of church-building was going rapidly forward. The Tractarians, however, for all their evangelical and reforming zeal, were essentially a conservative force, attempting to revitalize the Church by recalling it to its ancient Orders and discipline. And in a wider sense the entire Christian Church in England, Catholic as well as Protestant, Nonconformist as well as Anglican, displayed a conservatism which belied the inquiring spirit of the age. Though divided in all else, Christians of differing denominations were virtually united in taking their stand upon the Bible. A narrow literalism, which only a few dared to question, was accepted by every sect. Yet this rock was soon to prove shifting sand. With the publication of Darwin's *Origin of Species* in 1859, Christian orthodoxy found itself faced by revolutionary forces no less potentially solvent than those which had disrupted the Church of Rome three centuries before.

As in religion, so in education, the forces of change and tradition went hand in hand. The established connection between religion and education was one which few Victorians would lightly challenge. In 1860 the State still held aloof from direct involvement in the provision of elementary education, preferring to give financial aid to the competing sectarian bodies already in the field; and, despite its timidity, this policy had over a quarter of a century sufficed to bring almost every working-class child within the orbit of the educational system. At the same time, under the influence of the reforming Arnold at Rugby, provision for the educational needs of the expanding middle class was being made by a growing number of public and grammar schools; and even in the field of university education, with the advent of London and Durham and an incipient Manchester, the facilities for higher learning were being slowly increased. But to extend the bounds of opportunity in education was not necessarily to deepen its content. The three 'Rs' might be considered diet enough for the new working-class, but, as the Newcastle Commission reported in 1861, many – perhaps most – children left school 'without the power of reading, writing and cyphering in an intelligent manner'. Where teaching thus failed in its most elementary objective, it is not surprising that a sight of wider intellectual horizons was denied to the children of the labouring classes. The failings in the education of their social betters lay in other directions. Notwithstanding a modest widening of the curriculum at Rugby, the reform of the public schools had touched the spirit and temper rather than the content of education. The discipline of the classics might nurture a Peel or a Gladstone, but its

(A) Charles Grey, 2nd Earl,
by SIR THOMAS LAWRENCE.
(*detail*)

(B) Sir Robert Peel, 2nd Baronet,
by HENRY WILLIAM PICKERSGILL.
(*detail*)

(C) Richard Cobden,
by L. DICKINSON.
(*detail*)

(D) Lord Palmerston, 3rd Viscount,
by F. CRUICKSHANK.

All these portraits are from the *National Portrait Gallery*.

PLATE 1

(A) The Crystal Palace, the Great Exhibition of 1851.

SPECIMENS FROM MR. PUNCH'S INDUSTRIAL EXHIBITION OF 1850.

(TO BE IMPROVED IN 1851).

(B) Cartoon from *Punch*, 1851.

PLATE 2

(A) An engraving of Lymington Iron Works on the Tyne,
by J. SANDS after Thomas Allom, 1835.

(B) A woman and child in a coal mine, 1842.

PLATE 3

The first meeting of the reformed House of Commons, 1833. *National Portrait Gallery.*

PLATE 4

adequacy in face of the changing social conditions of the nineteenth century was none the less open to question. More serious for individual and community alike was the failure to provide for the developing educational needs of the lower middle class. A society changing rapidly under the impact of the forces of science and technology was strangely blind both to the place of scientific and technical study in its schools and to the need for facilitating the further education of its leaders in industry and commerce. Well might the percipient Kay-Shuttleworth declare in 1866 that 'the education of the middle class is generally in a chaotic state. ... While a large part of Europe has been successfully preparing its entire peoples to meet the great crisis of their history with intelligence, we have refused to learn from their example and experience.' The bitter fruits of that refusal are not wholly ungathered today.[1]

Science, thus excluded from the schools, was compelled to find other channels of development. It was in societies like the British Association for the Advancement of Science and the London Statistical Society (both established in the 1830's) that a lively interest in scientific subjects was fostered and sustained; and it is against such a background that the high achievement of men of genius like Faraday, Thomson (the later Lord Kelvin), Darwin and Huxley is to be measured. Thomson was compelled to cross the Channel in 1845 to get the laboratory experience which Britain failed to give him. Twenty years later such a journey would have been unnecessary. The completion of the first laboratories at Oxford in 1861 is as momentous and pregnant an event in educational history as the opening of that university's doors to dissenters in the following decade.

The learned society was but one of the many forms of association to which the principle and practice of 'self-help' gave birth. That principle had its roots alike in resurgent puritanism and in economic liberalism; it was to be seen as much in the development of trade unions as in the lives of the entrepreneurs, as much in the emergent co-operative movement as in professional organizations like the newly-established British Medical Association. Yet though self-help might know no class frontiers, its ethos was predominantly that of the middle class. Thus by the 1850's both trade unions and co-operative societies had surrendered their earlier revolutionary positions and had reconciled themselves to the values and judgements of an essentially bourgeois society: in less than two decades Robert Owen's militant Grand National Consolidated Trades Union had given place to the respectability of the Associated Society of Engineers and of the Rochdale Pioneers.

The emergence of a powerful urban middle class also gave new significance to provincialism as a force in British social life. In the seventeenth and eighteenth centuries the increasing power of commerce had brought London to a position of overwhelming dominance both in the political and in the economic and cultural life of England; but with the growth of new industry the balance in terms of population and of wealth was readjusted. Although London continued to grow prodigiously, its rate of expansion was matched and surpassed by that of Manchester, Birmingham and a host of smaller towns; just as in Scotland, Glasgow came to outpace Edinburgh in its capacity for increase. With growth went vitality, and the provincial cities, though merely imitative in some respects – Manchester had its Piccadilly and its Athenæum – gave their own colour to the thought and culture of the age. Under the stimulus of the Municipal Corporations Act of 1835 town government was revitalized and civic pride enhanced, not the least of the fruits of this awakening being the advent of the public library and art gallery. Likewise, encouraged in part by the repeal of the Stamp Duty in 1855, but still more by the growing numbers of the literate working-class, the provincial Press entered upon its greatest age. Where in 1846 there had been 200 local newspapers, in 1865 there were 750, many of them 'dailies' like the Manchester *Guardian* and the Liverpool *Post*, exerting in the provinces an influence in politics as great as that of Delane's *Times* in the capital itself.

[1] These strictures do not wholly apply to Scotland where education up to University level was more readily obtained and more broadly based than in England.

The vigorous culture of the Manchester Man, however, carried within itself the defects of its own high qualities. No one would deny the creative power of this new provincial society; but its capacity for creative imagination or contemplation is more open to question. This was the age of the technologist rather than the scientist, the evangelist rather than the mystic. Even in literature, the crowning glory of the age, the distinction is to be sensed. The high noon of the Romantic period was passed, and notwithstanding the work of Tennyson and the Brownings, of Matthew Arnold and Swinburne, this is an age of prose rather than of poetry. In prose these are indeed years of plenty – the years of Carlyle and John Stuart Mill, of Macaulay and Froude, of Dickens and Thackeray – and in the novel, above all, years not only of abundance, but also of the highest achievement. Yet even in the novel the full depths of human experience are rarely sounded. The Brontës alone provide an outstanding exception to this generalization. With them, living out their timeless existence on the Yorkshire moors, we catch again the unreined imaginative power of a Shelley or a Keats. But in general, for the novelist at least, this was the age of the extrovert. Only at the last, with the advent of George Eliot and Meredith, does a new note of fundamental questioning and soul-searching emerge.

To say this is not to suggest that this was an uncritical age. Dickens, Mrs Gaskell, Disraeli and even Trollope explored the social and political tensions of their day and set their face against the evils of industrialism and of political jobbery which they saw around them. Outside the novel the accent of criticism is sharper and often deeper. In the essays and sermons of Carlyle and Ruskin, of Newman and Arnold, the spirit of the age – its materialism, self-satisfaction and insensitivity – is put to question and found wanting. But the abiding impression of the literature of these years remains one of assurance rather than of scepticism, of creative exuberance rather than of inward wrestling.

The Age of Progress

Wherein, then, lies the unity of this age of change? Perhaps to seek a unity deeper than

change itself is to pursue a shadow. By 1860 the idea of progress firmly held the field – the progress not only of the statistician and the Manchester merchant, but also of Macaulay's *History* and the *Origin of Species*. But this mood had been of slow growth. If it had captured the middle class by 1846 or earlier, as Porter suggests, its hold upon the proletariat was still precarious. Of a previous age – the mid-sixteenth century – it has been said that in it England turned a 'dangerous corner' in her history: such was now her experience once again. In 1848, as in 1830, Europe was torn by revolution and afflicted with cholera. In Britain, as industry languished and distress increased, the Chartists were preparing to march on London. To the mind of the comfortable there may have come at this time pictures of children dragging coal in narrow seams, of disease-ridden alleys in smoke-begrimed towns, of demoralized men in dreary workhouses. Reform had already removed the more tractable of these evils, but the Blue Books of a decade had imprinted them upon a nation's conscience. To the pessimist revolution may have seemed imminent.

But by 1851 the corner was being turned. All over Europe the tide of revolution had receded; in Britain it had never reached the full. Out of the struggles of the 'forties the nation had at last come to the high ranges of Victorian prosperity. If there had been no miraculous transformation of sickness into health, of poverty into riches, despair at least had been swallowed up in optimism. Throughout the summer of 1851 men and women of every class thronged into the great Crystal Palace. Each day Britain's new railways carried their trainloads of excursionists to the capital. Rich and poor alike were made to feel their pride and place in the story of a nation's progress. The Great Exhibition symbolized the conquering spirit of the age – brashly self-confident, blatantly materialist, yet imbued with a high seriousness of purpose and a sense of mission.

By 1860, in spite of the Crimean War, the Indian Mutiny and the economic crisis of 1857, nothing had shaken this fundamental confidence or sense of destiny. A stormy decade of war in Europe and America, and of agitation for reform at home lay ahead, but as yet these were the merest clouds upon a bright horizon. As the year closed, only a troubled Italy, striving for her unity, disturbed a continent's tranquillity. Britain, happy in her sovereign and prosperous as never before, was at peace with herself and the world. This was the age of progress, and there was no reason why it should not go on for ever.

Girders employed in the building of the Crystal Palace being tested, weighed and erected by a modification of Bramah's hydraulic press. *Illustrated Catalogue of the Great Exhibition*, 1851.

Obverse design of the Council, the Prize, and the
Jurors' medals, struck by the Royal Mint in commemoration of the Great Exhibition of 1851. Engraved
by William Wyon.

Architecture and Interior Decoration

Architecture and Interior Decoration

DENYS HINTON

Most respectable guides and histories of architecture end at or about 1830. There may be many reasons for this. Architecture before the Romantic Movement falls easily into classified groups and is therefore more popular with those who write: and those who read desire, for the most part, guides to periods which they already know. But beyond these prejudices lurks an uneasy notion, that there is something disreputable about Victorian Architecture, that in the 1830's the virtue went out of it and never came back.

The irony of this notion is that what really distinguishes Victorian architecture is its high moral purpose and what Matthew Arnold called 'excellent high seriousness'. To Pugin it appeared that virtue had been absent from architecture since the Reformation and that he was restoring it. Fifty years later William Morris prepared for a golden age of socialism by turning back the clock: and throughout both of their lifetimes their contemporaries thought, talked and wrote about beauty, goodness and progress. There was never an age that was so serious about architecture and never an architecture so earnestly repudiated by its heirs.

This wholesale rejection of the work of three-quarters of a century has been an obstacle to serious study, and accounts for the fact that Victorian architecture has become the province of a few devoted specialists. Outside the work of this select band interest has centred largely on the superficial aspects of Victorian design and decoration – those, for instance, which have lent themselves to reproduction on the stage, where the literary and dramatic – not to say melodramatic –

associations of the period have gained them a steady popularity not for several generations enjoyed by the real architecture which they represent. More recently this theatrical taste has overflowed into the stream of contemporary decoration, mixing with the counter-flood to the severe functionalism of the 1930's to create a rather precious style in which interiors are, once again, filled with *objets d'art* and where diversity, even incongruity, is preferred to unity and restraint.

All this, however, owes more to the turning of the wheel of fashion than to the advance of historical knowledge: and the cult of Victoriana reflects no more understanding of the nineteenth century than Horace Walpole's Gothick did of the Middle Ages.

The absence of serious study has furthermore obscured the fact that between 1830 and 1900 English architecture moved from the era of John Nash to that of Charles Rennie Mackintosh – a period of change, the scope and rapidity of which are probably unequalled in its history. The first thirty years of this period, forming the subject of this guide, are a transition between the last great phase of Georgian architecture and town-planning and the High Victorian period of the 'sixties and 'seventies.

In 1830, Nash and Soane were both alive and active. Although each was a great individualist, each worked in an idiom that had its roots in the use of classical orders and proportions. The stuccoed Regency villa with its low-pitched roof and elegant detailing or, on a larger scale, the terrace, crescent or Town square, are not only the typical buildings of the nineteenth century's first decade, but also the continued expression of unquestionable confidence in the Georgian view of life. The story of Early Victorian architecture is a series of questions – mostly rhetorical – to which the whole fabric of architectural thought is subjected.

This is not the place to analyse in detail the causes, which lie outside the province of architecture itself. Yet all architecture is to some extent a reflection of contemporary events, thought and habits; and nothing would have been stranger than the survival of the eighteenth-century ideal after two such cataclysmic events as the Napoleonic wars and the Industrial Revolution. Parallel to the effect of these powerful political, technical and economic forces, the Romantic Movement in literature, the Oxford Movement in religion and the growth of a social conscience all exerted a powerful influence on architectural thought.

The London club houses

Yet to the architects of the first part of the century the problem must have appeared in simpler terms. They were at the end of a great period and were conscious that the rich seam was nearly worked out. In the 1820's there were manifestations of restlessness even among the Georgians. No less than in Soane's work at the Bank of England and in his own house in Lincoln's Inn, the younger men were looking for precedents outside the English Georgian tradition. Perhaps no building illustrates this more clearly than the evolution of the London club, which, from being in the eighteenth century a conversion from a coffee-house or a private residence, acquired a new status as a building type in its own right. One of the earliest buildings designed expressly as a club house was the United Service Club of John Nash, built in Waterloo Place in 1827.[1] It was essentially a Roman building with pedimented windows, deep cornice and richly relieved frieze. A portico through two storeys with twin Doric columns be-low and Corinthian above supports a pediment whose heavy detailing recalls the robustness of the Regent's Park terraces.

The Athenæum, by Decimus Burton, on the other hand, also built on an old Carlton House site, was distinctly Greek and must have appeared even more Greek before the addition of its present attic storey. Refined, detached and crowned with a panathenaic frieze, it is the stylistic heir to a score of other large classical buildings of the eighteenth century.

To resolve the contrast came the Travellers Club, founded by Lord Castlereagh before the end of the Napoleonic wars, but without a permanent home until 1831, in which year Charles (afterwards Sir Charles) Barry's building was completed. The inspiration for this club house and for that of the Reform Club which followed it, also by Barry, was the palazzo of the Italian Renaissance; and that to which it bears the strongest resemblance is Raphael's Pandolfini in Florence. The choice of precedent is an interesting one, and Barry's dexterous handling of it set a new pattern for Victorian secular buildings. The palace built round a courtyard provides an appropriate plan for the corporate home of a new ruling class. The site is small and the building, by comparison with its neighbour the Athenæum, is modest: the plan is asymmetrical and comparatively unpretentious, but the rooms are beautifully organized and the external features and decorations are articulated in a way quite foreign to those classical buildings which rely on the use of orders.

Almost ten years later than the Travellers', Barry produced on the site adjoining it in Pall Mall the Reform Club house – a commission won in a limited competition against the formidable field of Blore, Burton, Smirke, Basevi and Cockerell. Joined to the Travellers' by a link containing an entrance to the upper floors, the Reform building is conceived on a more generous scale than its neighbour and carries an attic storey. With minor variations, however, the elements of the façade are identical in detail and handling. The plan again centres on a cortile, adapted to the London climate by the use of iron beams supporting a glass roof. The staircase is again subordinated

[1] The name had formerly belonged to Smirke's building (1816) on the corner of Regent Street and Charles II Street, subsequently the Junior United Service Club and largely rebuilt in the 1850's by Nelson and Innes.

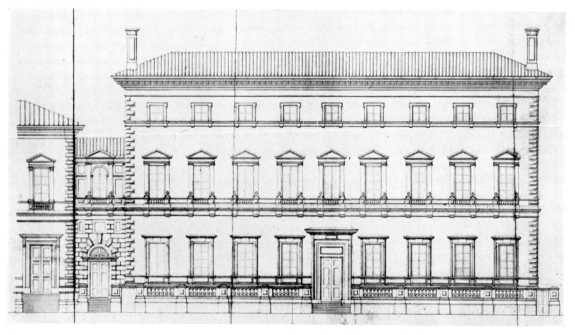

(A) SIR CHARLES BARRY. Front elevation of Reform Club House, Pall Mall, London, 1838–40.
Royal Institute of British Architects.

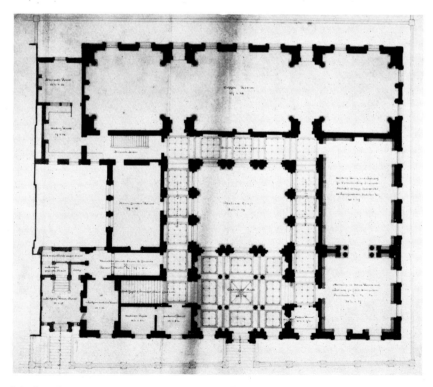

(B) SIR CHARLES BARRY. Plan of ground floor of Reform Club House, Pall
Mall, London, 1838–40. *Royal Institute of British Architects.*

PLATE 5

Sir Charles Barry. Travellers Club House, 1832, and Reform Club, 1838–40, Pall Mall, London.
National Buildings Record.

PLATE 6

(A) SIR CHARLES BARRY. Garden elevation of
Travellers Club, Pall Mall, London, 1832.
National Buildings Record.

(B) SIR CHARLES BARRY. Entrance Hall of the
Reform Club, Pall Mall, London, 1838–40.
Warburg Institute.

PLATE 7

SIR CHARLES BARRY. Bridgewater House, Westminster, 1847. *Warburg Institute.*

PLATE 8

SIR CHARLES BARRY. Gallery of Hall of Bridgewater House, Westminster, 1847. *National Buildings Record.*

PLATE 9

(A) SIR CHARLES BARRY. Drawings for alterations to Clumber House, 1857.
Royal Institute of British Architects.

(B) WILLIAM BURN. Drawing for Fonthill, Wiltshire, 1849. *Royal Institute of British Architects.*

PLATE 10

(A) ANTHONY SALVIN. Drawing for Harlaxton Hall, Lincolnshire, 1837–60.
Royal Institute of British Architects.

(B) ANTHONY SALVIN. Scotney Castle, 1837. *Royal Institute of British Architects.*

PLATE 11

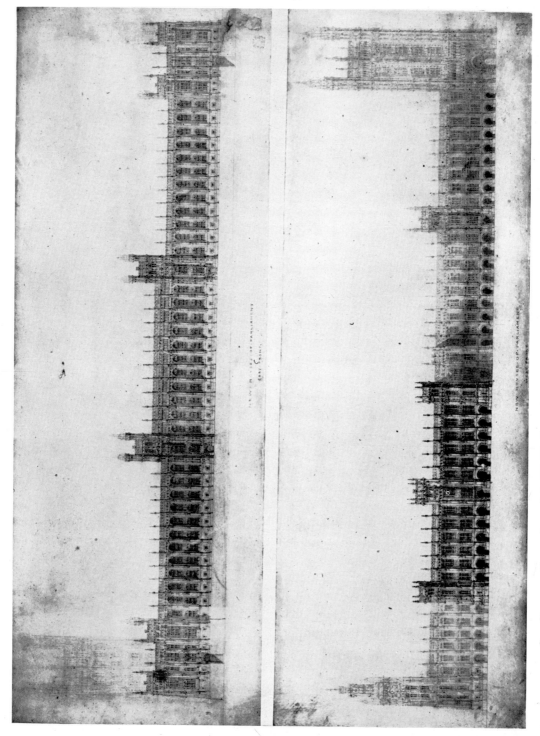

Sir Charles Barry's and A. W. N. Pugin's original design for the Westminster New Palace, 1836.
Royal Institute of British Architects.

PLATE 12

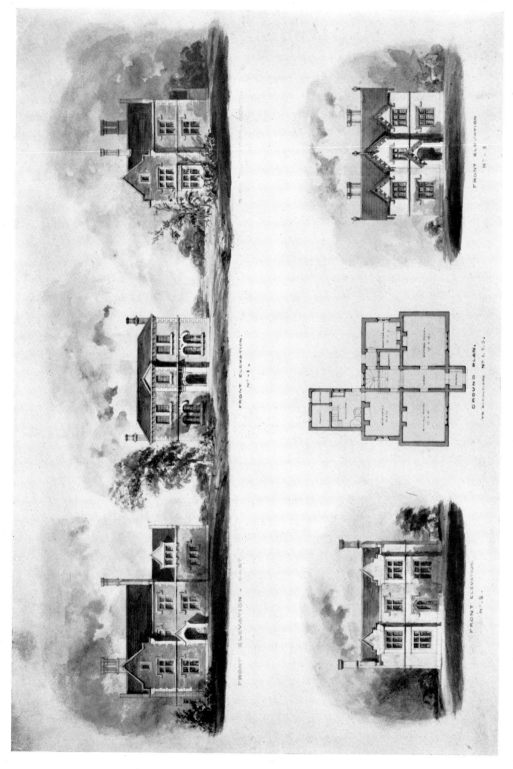

Plan with alternative elevations for Early Victorian villas, c. 1840. *Royal Institute of British Architects*

PLATE 13

A. W. N. PUGIN, 1837–52, and E. W. PUGIN's, 1860–8, remodelled Scarisbrick Hall, Lancashire.
P. Fleetwood-Hesketh, Murray's Lancashire Architectural Guide.

PLATE 14

(A) *Above left*, A. W. N. PUGIN. The King's Room at Scarisbrick Hall, Lancashire, 1836–9. *P. Fleetwood-Hesketh, Murray's Lancashire Architectural Guide.*

(B) *Above right*, A. W. N. PUGIN. The red and gold wall paper in the Red Drawing Room, hand-printed with blocks, designed for Charles Scarisbrick by A. W. Pugin, at Scarisbrick Hall, Lancashire, *c.* 1837. *P. Fleetwood-Hesketh, Murray's Lancashire Architectural Guide.*

(C) *Left*, A. W. N. PUGIN. View from the King's Room to the Red Drawing Room at Scarisbrick Hall, Lancashire, 1836–9. *P. Fleetwood-Hesketh, Murray's Lancashire Architectural Guide.*

PLATE 15

WILLIAM BUTTERFIELD. All Saints', Margaret Street, London, 1859. *National Buildings Record.*

PLATE 16

WILLIAM BUTTERFIELD. Interior of All Saints', Margaret Street, London, 1859.
National Buildings Record.

PLATE 17

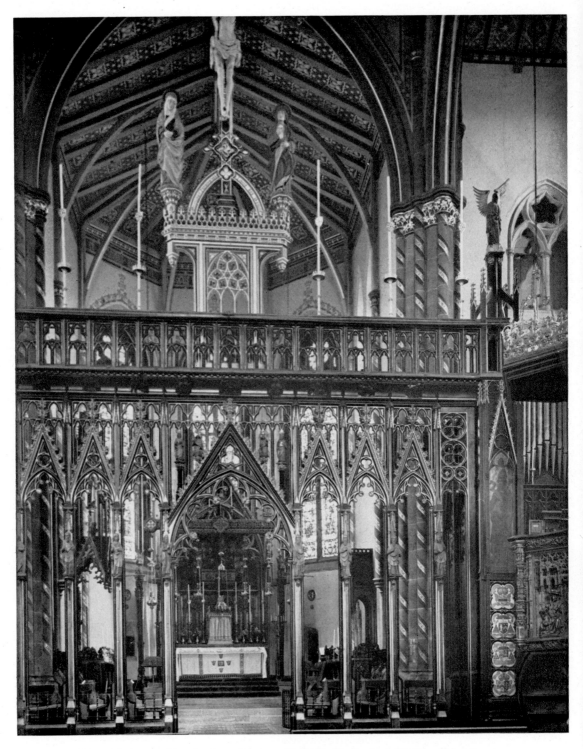

A. W. N. PUGIN. Birmingham Roman Catholic Cathedral (St Chad's), 1839–41.
National Buildings Record.

PLATE 18

PHILIP and P. C. HARDWICK. The Great Hall at Euston Station, London.
Royal Institute of British Architects.

PLATE 19

P. C. HARDWICK. The Coffee Room at Paddington Station, London. *Royal Institute of British Architects.*

PLATE 20

but, having a less restricted site than the Travellers', an almost symmetrical arrangement of rooms was possible. Their character, like that of the astylar exterior, and the careful study of kitchen planning to which Barry, rather surprisingly, gave great attention, became one of the models for London club houses of the next three decades.

Other prototypes followed in the 1840's, of which those of the Conservative Club (1844) and the Carlton (begun 1847) were the most significant. Like Arthur's Club, also in James Street, the Conservative was the joint work of Sidney Smirke and George Basevi. Its importance lies more in its scale than anything else, for the planning is much less coherent than Barry's and the exterior, with its vocabulary of rustication, Corinthian order and balustrade make it a rather ordinary late Georgian building.

The remodelling of the Carlton Club house, on the other hand, was very much an architectural event and in this case the commission was won by Smirke in competition with most of the leading club architects of the day – including Barry. The winning design took as its model Sansovino's Venetian Library of St Mark, introducing a few modifications to relate it to Pall Mall, the climate and taste of the English, but generally marking a movement towards a plastic, arcaded style which, with its elaborate moulding and carving, exercised a profound influence on later Victorian commercial architecture.

These clubmen's palaces in Pall Mall and elsewhere are the Early Victorian equivalents of the great houses of the eighteenth century and the last survivors of an epoch in which style was concerned with manners and architectural character was disciplined by a distinctive grammar. A new ruling class with new sources of wealth was moulding a new patriarchal society: its leaders, the kind of men who carried the Reform Bill (and named their club after it), were seldom given the chance to do anything similar in their private houses. Two exceptions, however, are worth quoting; one is Barry's Bridgewater House, and the other, Lewis Vulliamy's attempt to outshine Barry at Dorchester House, Park Lane. The planning of Bridgewater House is almost indistinguishable in principle from that of the Italianate club houses and the large central court is its main feature. Externally, the dominant elements are the windows of the first floor, lighting the principal rooms, their heavy segmental pediments filled with elaborate carving, and the rustication of the ground floor and corners. As in the Travellers' and Reform Clubs, Barry's interior decorations are outstanding, and indicate a growing taste for elaborate surface decoration.

On the more open site of Dorchester House, Vulliamy also used a rusticated ground floor. This was emphasized on the entrance side by a large projecting porch, while on the Park front a dramatic effect was achieved by omitting the centre section of the second floor.

In domestic architecture other signs of restlessness had appeared long before the end of the eighteenth century. The cult of the Gothic, beginning as a harmless affectation with buildings like Walpole's Strawberry Hill, had gathered momentum with Beckford's Fonthill, and during the Regency drew into its wake the cult of the picturesque, the *cottage orné*, Hinduism and chinoiserie. These little essays in sophistication led nowhere. Gothic was not yet a style, but only a decoration; but the change was not far off and was due to work itself out largely in the field of ecclesiastical architecture.

'Commissioners' Gothic'

In 1818, the Church Commissioners allotted a million pounds to the building of 214 new churches; of these 174 were Gothic. During the 1820's the youthful Barry was among the architects of the Gothic school which included not only those whose reputation rested entirely on neo-Medieval churches, but others who, like Barry himself, were versatile in both styles. Of these, one of the most competent was Thomas Rickman, an antiquarian who in 1817 produced *An attempt to Discriminate the Styles of Architecture in England* ..., thereby bringing into usage the classifications Early English, Decorated and Perpendicular. Rickman produced some scholarly churches in Birmingham and other provincial

C

cities and added the new buildings at St John's College, Cambridge (1826–30).

Barry at Westminster

Barry's Gothic work included the King Edward VI School, Birmingham, now destroyed, but his great *tour de force* was his prize-winning design for the new Houses of Parliament following the Great Fire of 1834. The conditions of the competition make interesting study. Yevele's Westminster Hall survived the fire and had to be incorporated in the new scheme, which was, according to the select committee, 'to be either Gothic or Elizabethan'. For a Parliamentary committee so to endorse the Gothic style for Westminster, shows how well established and respectable it had now become. Furthermore, a patriotic note is sounded, even though many contemporary critics questioned whether 'Elizabethan' signified any real architectural style at all.

Barry's design was, as Hitchcock puts it, 'comprehensive and logical'. His building was planned as no building before the Renaissance could have been, for both the organization of internal spaces and the composition of the halls and towers possess a degree of sophistication unknown in English Medieval architecture – or even Elizabethan. Superficially, however, the design resembled a perpendicular palace, and for the detailing of the exterior Barry was indebted to Augustus Welby Northmore Pugin. (Ironically the style in which Pugin worked at Westminster was that which he was later to call 'debased'.) Not least among the many controversies aroused by the competition and its result was the dispute as to the true authorship of the winning design. In fact there is little doubt that the credit belongs principally to Barry: yet the building and the collaboration are both significant. Designed just before Queen Victoria's accession, the Houses of Parliament were not completed until the 1850's. By virtue of its size and the time taken to bring it to fruition, it occupies a central and dominant position in the period under review. Yet it is not a typically Early Victorian building nor even an influential one. It is more properly the last of a group of buildings conceived by detached and non-moralizing architects capable of turning their hands to any style.

What Barry achieved at Westminster he also essayed in the remodelling of Highclere Castle in Hampshire, where a plain Georgian block was converted, between 1840 and 1844, into another neo-Jacobethan palace. Here is picturesqueness without irregularity, the horizontal string-courses combining with the vertical pilasters to give a uniform reticulated exterior. At each corner Barry placed a tower with another in the centre dominating the composition and repeating the fretted and pinnacled silhouette of the main building.

Barry's work at Shrubland Park near Ipswich in the late 1840's is in quite a different category and also shows him at his best as a landscape architect. Shrubland, it is true, has a dominant tower, but it is Italian in character, with an open loggia top and linked to an elaborate Italianate garden. At Cliveden, rebuilt for the Duke of Sutherland in the 1850's, corner towers were included in Barry's first scheme, but gave way to a more economical design, regular, unromantic and combining many of his palazzo details with an Ionic order reminiscent of the early Palladians.

None of Barry's contemporaries possessed his extraordinary coherence as a designer: but coherence had almost ceased to be a virtue and was rapidly being overtaken by the enthusiastic exploitation of Gothic, Tudor and other revivalist styles.

Of Barry's contemporaries in the domestic field, Anthony Salvin was one who achieved a remarkable degree of authenticity in his neo-Jacobethan houses. This is especially true of Harlaxton, an enormous and very complex house near Grantham, whose erection was almost continuous between 1837 and 1860.

Harlaxton has a typical Elizabethan plan, a profusion of gables, bays and chimneys, and detailing of a kind not easily distinguishable from that of the early seventeenth century. Indeed, it has been suggested that this is actually a better Elizabethan house than many built in the reign of Queen Elizabeth I – a comment which raises the whole question of whether any kind of reproduction architecture can ever be satisfactory and the nicer issue of whether it is a virtue in an architect successfully to adapt the architecture of another period to the needs of his own. From this point of view Barry and Pugin may be regarded as successful architects, for their buildings, in spite of their borrowed details, have something to say which could only have been said in the first half of the nineteenth century. This is, indeed, the essence of the Early Victorian period and the reason why architects such as Salvin, whose work is archæologically interesting, cannot be regarded as typical. At Peckforton Castle in Cheshire, for instance, Salvin produced a fake castle which in siting, planning and massing, and every other quality expected of a castle, except that of falling into a state of picturesque decay, must be allowed to stand comparison with the best castles of the fourteenth century. At Scotney Castle, on the other hand, Salvin appears to have been caught between the genuine Elizabethan tradition and the Regency conception of a castle. Since the latter was a branch of the 'picturesque' cult it must therefore be regarded more as an example of survival than of revival and more allied to James Wyatt's work at Belvoir and Windsor and the castellated villas of John Nash.

Much the same can be said of Ramsey Abbey in Huntingdonshire, the work of Salvin's chief competitor in this field, Edward Blore, who enjoyed the double distinction of succeeding Nash at Buckingham Palace and Wyatt at Windsor. Ramsey Abbey is a tall building, three full storeys and a semi-basement, and the effect of height is increased by the strong vertical lines of buttresses and mullions on the face and by the pinnacles, turrets and chimneys which rise above the balustraded roof.

Built at the end of the 1830's, Ramsey Abbey was closely followed by Blore's large house at Worsley, near Manchester, for Lord Francis Egerton. Here again the planning is symmetrical and Elizabethan motifs are used only decoratively. Where the building differs essentially from those designed fifty years earlier to a similar formula is in the coarseness of detailing, the limited sophistication which could now be passed off as picturesque, and a total absence of charm.

What Blore achieved in decorative stonework at Worsley, P.C.Hardwick (son of the Philip Hardwick who was architect to the London and Birmingham Railway and his collaborator in the hotels at Euston and Paddington) attempted in the early 'fifties at Aldermaston Court, near Newbury, in a mixture of red brick and bath stone. This combination of materials, together with diaper patterning in the brickwork, was to become as familiar a feature of Victorian design as the restless outline and untidy profusion of forms for which Aldermaston is also remarkable.

Oddly enough, both these features were handled more successfully by the better church architects, who were, on the whole, inclined to avoid them when they turned their hands to secular building. Such discrimination was as rare as the really successful adaptation, but it is evident in the work of S.S.Teulon, particularly in his bold handling of Tortworth Court in Gloucestershire, which has the same firmness and confidence that make his later churches more than essays in copying. It also possesses the characteristic Victorian virtue of seriousness, which eventually displaced the picturesque, in the employment of towers, gables and turrets; not, as in the work of Salvin and Blore, merely for decoration, but each in order to express some distinctive element in the plan.

A. W. N. Pugin

Far more influential than Teulon, however, though his exact contemporary and also active in both ecclesiastical and domestic fields, was A.W.N.Pugin. Indeed, with the possible exception of Barry, there was not an architect in the whole of this period who exercised such an influence as this remarkable man.

Pugin's share in the new Palace of Westminster was, as we have seen, untypical, and his most important work was between 1835 and 1850. Both didactic and intolerant in his writing, Pugin observed consistently in his buildings the rules he laid down for others. He was the son of a French émigré, Auguste Charles Pugin, an authority and a prodigious publisher of works on Medieval architecture. Pugin was something of a prodigy as a draughtsman and an early convert to Roman Catholicism. Having 'ghosted' for Barry (and probably for Gillespie Graham as well) in the Westminster competition, Pugin published in 1836 *Contrasts or a Parallel between the Architecture of the 14th and 15th centuries and similar buildings of the Present Day.*

This was more than an affirmation of neo-Gothic. Gothic could be appropriate or 'debased' and what Pugin decided was appropriate was the Decorated or Middle Pointed Style. Moreover, he claimed that architecture was better or worse according to the morality and the religion of its creator – thereby ruling out all 'pagan' art, including that of the Georgian period. Nothing could equal his scorn for the frivolities of the Regency; and his adherence to truth, as he conceived it, included fidelity to purpose, place and time.

The arguments in his *True Principles of the Pointed or Christian Architecture* (1841) go further in their execration of 'shams' and anticipate many of the truisms of twentieth-century functionalism. But above all Pugin was a traditionalist and believed that truth was embodied exclusively in English architecture of the fourteenth century.

In a brief working life Pugin designed a large number of churches, including St Mary's, Derby, and St Chad's, Birmingham. At Ramsgate he designed and paid for St Augustine's (1846) and his own house, the Grange. This house, completed in 1843, seems a modest structure when compared with the palatial *tours de force* of the 'thirties and 'forties designed by the recognized architects of great houses. It is certainly one of the least pretentious of Pugin's own works, and although larger than his first house at Salisbury, built in 1835, has none of its eccentricity. Planned round a large hall rising the full height of the building and containing a gallery landing, the Grange owes to the basic form of a medieval house as much as, if not more than, it does to the superficial aspects of style. Externally the house almost achieves a look of crispness, with large areas of unadorned brickwork, simple bays with widely-spaced mullions, sharp gables and broad uncarved barge-

boards. A simple brick tower adjoins the house on the east side.

Something of the same aversion to the purely picturesque may be seen at Bilton Grange, near Rugby, built by Pugin between 1841 and 1846. Here, as at Teulon's Tortworth, a strong sense of composition prevails, and instead of the irregular, almost fortuitous outline of houses whose plans are generated by the process of addition, we see bays and gables used as a series and reflecting the rhythmic pattern of rooms all more or less equal in size. Again, the crisp detailing of stonework is consistent with the firm outline of the timber structure where exposed in the interior and with the unadorned panelling of the main rooms.

At Scarisbrick Hall, near Manchester, Pugin enjoyed the patronage of an eccentric Catholic landowner, Charles Scarisbrick, whose father and grandfather had already commissioned Gothic extensions to an Elizabethan building. Pugin's commission began in 1837 and was unfinished at his death in 1852. Charles Scarisbrick was succeeded by his sister Anne in 1860, and she in turn commissioned Pugin's son, E.W.Pugin, to continue the work. It is therefore not easy to discern the contribution made by the elder Pugin: but it seems certain that he remodelled the west wing, completed the great hall, and added a clock-tower. The younger Pugin added an east wing in the 'sixties and increased the height of the tower so that it is no longer possible to say whether it resembles, as contemporary commentators declared, the tower of Big Ben. Scarisbrick thus achieved the romantic irregularity which so many early Victorians sought, but achieved it by a process very like that of the medieval buildings from which it claimed to draw its inspiration – from piecemeal growth and the attentions of many different owners and builders. Nevertheless, it is the heart of the building, A.W.Pugin's great hall and his richly carved interiors in the west wing, which are chiefly memorable – interiors more reminiscent of Pugin's churches than of the comparatively simple decorations of his other houses. Wall-panelling is used in profusion and is everywhere elaborately carved, painted and gilded, while on the upper walls and ceilings appear canopies and vaults in even brighter colour. In a Pugin church these things were at least an echo of reality: in a house they now strike us as magnificent, but slightly absurd scenery for an imaginary drama.

Just as Pugin's contribution to domestic architecture was coloured by his experience as an ecclesiastical designer, so other church architects of the 'forties and 'fifties bequeathed to the houses of the middle and late Victorian periods a number of novel ideas concerned with the use of materials.

The Tractarian or Oxford Movement in the early 'thirties was followed in Cambridge by the formation of the Camden Society in 1839 – known after 1845 as the Ecclesiological Society. Through its organ *The Ecclesiologist* this body continued to propagate Pugin's ideas and found a willing interpreter in William Butterfield.

William Butterfield

Butterfield was strictly a 'High Victorian'. His early works included a Perpendicular Dissenting Chapel at Bristol (1842), St Saviour's, Coalpitheath (1845) and St Augustine's College, Canterbury (1845–8). His most significant work is All Saints', Margaret Street – a model Ecclesiologists' Church. Designed in 1850, this was far more than a throw-back to English Decorated: it embodied many ideas quite foreign to English architecture, the most novel of which was the principle of 'Constructional Polychromy', which meant the incorporation of decorative courses of coloured brickwork and tiles, a feature which was widely imitated in High Victorian architecture and which gives a great deal of it such a restless appearance. The interior was equally colourful: as well as the novelty of red brickwork, Butterfield used mosaic tiles, red Peterhead granite, alabaster and gilding.

Second only to Butterfield as the darling of the Ecclesiologists was Richard Cromwell Carpenter, a perfectionist and devoted follower of Pugin. Apart from an erratic start in Georgian Tudor at Lonsdale Square, Islington (1838), Carpenter's work, largely on churches, is correct and dull. It includes St Magdalene's, Thurston Square (1849–52), St Paul's, West Street, Brighton (1840–8), All Saints', Hove (1848–52), and a thirteenth-century design for the Anglican Cathedral in Colombo. He also designed St John's College, Hurstpierpoint, built in 1851–3, and the college of Saints Mary and Nicholas at Lancing (1854–5) – finished in 1872 by Slater.

Scottish Baronial

Hardly less influential than the example of the Church was that of the State, and particularly of the Crown. Stimulated by the enthusiasm of Queen Victoria for travelling and living in Scotland, a new phase emerged in country-house design which is well described as Scottish Baronial. When analysed, this style proves to consist of little more than a mixture of the early fourteenth and seventeenth centuries, in which castellated details are juxtaposed with Jacobethan bays and gables while robust battlemented towers are conjoined with sharp pitches and clusters of chimneys: planning is additive and often functional but possesses little sense of modulation.

What commended the Scottish Baronial to the young Victoria and her subjects, however, was its romantic association with the novels of Sir Walter Scott. The archetype, Balmoral – which closely resembled Scott's Abbotsford – was acquired by the Crown in 1848 and extended by William Smith of Aberdeen, who had built the original house for Sir Robert Gordon. Thereafter the style became widely popular for houses of all sizes on both sides of the border.

The foremost specialists in Scottish Baronial were William Burn and David Bryce, who built Fettes College, Edinburgh, in the 'sixties. Before this Burn moved to London, and his largest work is at Fonthill, Wiltshire, where, in the late 'forties, he built a great house for the Marquess of Westminster. Sited auspiciously near to Beckford's Folly, Fonthill House has a romantic silhouette, but is coarse in detailing and dull in composition. It is nevertheless compactly planned (Burn enjoyed a reputation for being a 'convenient' planner), and only the obligation of the style makes the house look more complicated than it really is.

At home in London, the Queen dismissed from her mind the sentimental associations of Scotland

and set about the serious task of proving that the monarchy was respectable. One of her ways of doing this was to alter the face of that scandalous reminder of Regency depravity – Buckingham Palace. Whereas Nash's east front had been a tolerable Georgian, Blore's new elevation managed to look both conventional and vulgar at the same time. The Prince Consort, however, priding himself on his taste, ensured that in the interior of the new south wing added by James Pennethorne in the 'fifties the decorations should be neo-Raphaelite. Set in spandrels or rectangular panels, the fresco figures and cupids shared the walls with mirrors and patterned silks. In this respect too the Royal example was widely copied in homes and rooms very much more modest in scale.

Town houses

Almost every town possessed a neighbourhood which middle-class house building was to convert into a fashionable suburb. Eschewing what they regarded as the 'monotony' of Georgian and Regency street architecture, many developers offered the same plan with a variety of alternative elevations. Nevertheless, these houses were usually well sited and well built with large gardens often linked to the houses by conservatories or flower-rooms.

On a genuine town-planning scale, and highly prized by the London *bourgeoisie*, were the residential developments of districts on the north and south sides of Hyde Park. In Belgravia, as is normal in speculative development, the pace of building was uneven and work begun in the 1820's continued for many years after Queen Victoria's accession. This was essentially late Georgian planning, and the designs which George Basevi produced for the builder-developer Thomas Cubitt bear comparison with the best of Nash. They were followed by less happy examples in Bayswater and other suburbs, houses which, lacking the adaptability to survive the metamorphosis into apartments and boarding-houses, must, where they have not done so already, soon make way for twentieth-century planning.

The interiors of the better town houses retained much of the charm of their eighteenth-century counterparts, from which the basic planning differed only in detail. Certain changes in materials, finishes and equipment, however, were to change fundamentally the traditional idea of how the inside of a gentleman's house should be decorated. Of these, the invention of plate glass was one; and the consequent increase in the size of windows and the omission of glazing bars not only resulted, in the short period before the introduction of very heavy curtaining, in a marked increase in the degree of daylighting, but also changed the character of elevations by introducing large unbroken black rectangles and, of course, affecting the view of the outside world from within.

Equally significant was the introduction of gas for artificial lighting, which became available for most towns by the 1840's. Gas was usually brought to brackets on each side of the chimney-breast and to an ornate brass chandelier in the centre of the ceiling. The quality of light was more uniform and certainly no less pleasant than that of candles, and the equipment itself became a characteristic Victorian accessory.

Whereas rooms in the 1830's had a light rococo flavour combining gilt, rosewood and papier-mâché furniture with muslin and silk draperies, mirrors and light-flowered wallpapers and carpets, the 1840's saw the introduction of heavy materials and darker colours. Velvet and rep replaced the diaphanous curtains, falling in ponderous folds of crimson and dark green. Furniture increased in size and crowded into the centre of rooms, leaving less space to be enjoyed as space. Walls, also, ceased to be significant as walls and became surfaces on which to hang pictures, often so close together that hardly any of the wall itself was visible.

The fireplace remained the focal point of most rooms and marble the most popular material for its surround. Hard shiny and often dark marbles were preferred, and the shelf, in order to accommodate the accumulation of clocks, vases and other ornaments, became deeper. Cast-iron grates also became a standard feature, frequently with brass ornaments and usually restless and contorted in design. This was the sort of object for which industry had created a new kind of taste which the

Victorians, because the evidence of its commercial origin was so carefully disguised, regarded as artistic and which filled the pavilions of the Great Exhibition of 1851.

This remarkable building was regarded by its contemporaries as a novelty: its contents as significant 'designs'. Yet although we now claim to think the building more significant than its contents, reading the Exhibition Catalogues for amusement and tracing the evolution of the modern prefabricated framed building from Paxton's Crystal Palace, there are many, including architects, who have never really accepted the implications of the Industrial Revolution. For this failure to make contact with reality the architects of the Victorian era must take a fair share of the blame.

Public buildings

Almost equal with the spate of Early Victorian church building was that of Town Halls and similar public and semi-public buildings. This remained a sphere into which the Gothic Revival was slow to penetrate, and the best examples of the period are either very literal examples of Classical Greek buildings or ingenious and scholarly variations on the same theme.

Of the literal character, Birmingham Town Hall by J.A.Hansom, built in 1832, is a complete copy of a Corinthian Temple. Dramatically sited on sloping ground, the building stands on a rusticated podium above which fluted columns stand out against a wall, to which successive decades of grime have given an appearance not unlike that of an ancient naos seen in dark Ægean shadow.

More impressive in scale, and still one of the most imaginative designs for a public building in any period, is the even blacker silhouette of St George's Hall, Liverpool. Actually a combination of Hall and Assize Courts, this very Grecian building was the result of a competition held in 1839 and won by Harvey Lonsdale Elmes. The handling of the Corinthian order is confident and strict and there is a marked freedom from affected ornament and a willingness, as in certain French buildings of the same genre, to rely entirely on the powerful rhythm of columns and entablatures.

By contrast there is a restless character to the Fitzwilliam Museum at Cambridge, the work of George Basevi, in which a two-storey building is also faced with a massive Corinthian order. The Fitzwilliam was completed by Charles Robert Cockerell, who also designed the Ashmolean Museum at Oxford (1841–5) of which the incoherent plan is likewise concealed behind an unusual Greek order based on one studied by Cockerell at Bassae.

Cockerell was professorial by disposition and a great admirer of Wren. The son of S.P.Cockerell, with whom he was associated in the surveyorship of the East India Company, he was also the nephew of the nabob for whom Humphrey Repton designed the strange villa at Sezincote. In 1833 he succeeded Soane as Architect to the Bank of England, and introduced there a stricter and more trabeated style. Some of his most scholarly and, at the same time, most attractive work is in the interior of St George's Hall, where he worked after Elmes' tragic death, from 1851 to 1856. Of special charm is Cockerell's decoration to the elliptical hall, where his low relief, delicate cast-iron balconies, and graceful caryatids have all the grace of an early Georgian interior.

James Pennethorne, a late Georgian like Cockerell, who succeeded to Nash's practice, added a wing to Somerset House and designed the former Geological Museum in Piccadilly (1837) which is a derivative of the Doge's Palace in Venice.

The engineers

Sir Gilbert Scott said that it was the function of an architect to decorate structure. Many critics would now say that the structures which were architecturally most successful in the nineteenth century were the ones which the architects did not get their hands on.

Before the end of the eighteenth century, engineers had produced designs of real quality, such as the cast-iron bridge at Coalbrookdale (1779) and the Jones' Malting Building in Shrewsbury. John Rennie and Thomas Telford produced a number of bridges in the first thirty years of the century; Rennie's chief contribution being in London at Waterloo, Vauxhall and Southwark –

all now replaced – while Telford is best known for his road suspension bridge across the Menai Straits, built in 1819–24 and still the longest in the British Isles. Nearby is the Britannia Bridge, built in 1850 by Richard Stephenson and Francis Thompson for the Chester and Holyhead railway, in which tubular wrought iron succeeded the cast-iron technique of constructions.

The designing of bridges and aqueducts was stimulated by the growth firstly of canals and secondly of the railways. 1830 saw the building of the earliest important railway station at Crown Street, Liverpool, followed by the first of the Lime Street complex in 1836 (the work of John Cunningham), both using wooden queenpost trusses on cast-iron columns. Lime Street Station was built in 1846 to the design of Richard Turner, a contracting engineer whose inventiveness and imagination in creating a structure 360 feet long and $153\frac{1}{2}$ feet in span far outran that of the architect William Tite, who designed the brick and stone façade.

A more striking and also more familiar piece of railway architecture is the great doric arch or propylæum at Euston designed by Philip Hardwick. When the London, Midland and Scottish Railway extended its line to central London, Robert Stephenson (son of George Stephenson) designed the large 200-foot shed at Euston with metal trusses and elegantly detailed cast-iron supports. A similar shed and arch terminated the line at Curzon Street, Birmingham.

The Great Western Railway had as their engineer the brilliant I.K.Brunel, designer of the Clifton Suspension Bridge and of numerous stations between Paddington and Bristol. At the latter terminus Temple Mead Station (1839–40) was an essay in Tudor Stylism, using a wooden hammerbeam roof spanning 72 feet. By contrast the work of Lewis Cubitt at the Bricklayers Arms Station off the Old Kent Road (1842–4) and that of Sancton Wood at Cambridge (1844–5) was markedly Italianate. Cubitt was also the designer of the great twin-arched station which the Great Northern built for its London Terminus at King's Cross in 1852.

Among the Early Victorian iron constructions which merit serious consideration as architecture are the covered markets and the great conservatories. As a designer of markets, Charles Fowler was outstanding. He was responsible for Covent Garden and Hungerford Market and also for the interesting lower market at Exeter (1836). Smithfield was built in 1845 to the design of Boulnois, and Billingsgate and the Metropolitan Cattle Market, both in the early 'fifties, by the architect James Bunning and his successor Sir Horace Jones.

James Bunstone Bunning also used cast-iron extensively in the Coal Exchange, Lower Thames Street, London, where the delicate sections of the dome ribs show a real sympathy for a material which was in danger of becoming more widely used merely as a reinforcement to traditional constructions when enlarged to the scale required in Victorian building.

The great conservatories brought together glass and iron and created 'ferrovitreous' construction. Decimus Burton, designer of the Athenæum, was the architect for the conservatory built at Chatsworth (1837–40) for the sixth Duke of Devonshire, but it was the Duke's head gardener – Joseph Paxton – who was really responsible for the daring plan of an iron-framed building measuring 277 feet by 173 feet and roofed entirely with glass. Burton was also the architect for the beautiful conservatory at Kew – in a happy collaboration with Richard Turner, the engineer of the second Lime Street Station at Liverpool. Only the design of its chimney – disguised as an Italian Campanile – reveals the as yet inadequate vocabulary of architects working in these new materials.

The Crystal Palace

By far the most famous 'ferrovitreous' building of the nineteenth century was the Crystal Palace, erected in Hyde Park to house the Great Exhibition of 1851. Paxton, whose design was finally selected, had carried his experiments beyond the great conservatory at Chatsworth with an ingenious lily-house. The Crystal Palace was remarkable in many ways. It was enormous, with a cubic content of thirty-three million cubic feet and contained 900,000 square feet of glass in a three-tiered building crossed by a gigantic dome 'transept' in which several elm-trees were preserved. It was not only a feat of engineering, but one of organization, for the cast-iron structure was entirely prefabricated and the working drawings were begun only nine months before the exhibition opened.

The story of the exhibition itself is well known and its financial success is embodied in the museum buildings of Kensington, whose architecture pays no homage whatever to Paxton's brilliant invention. Modern architects, however, are almost unanimous in expressing their acknowledgement. The Crystal Palace buildings were re-erected with towers at Sydenham in South London in 1854 and perished in a great fire in 1936.

Scott

Of all Victorian architects the best known is probably Sir George Gilbert Scott (1811–78). His personality has coloured our view of Victorian architecture as a whole and tended to obscure the qualities of some of his humbler contemporaries. Most of his important work (although in his own opinion he had no other kind) was done in the High Victorian phase: among Early Victorian architects he takes a place subordinate to that of Butterfield and Carpenter.

Scott's practice was founded on workhouses, of which, in partnership with William Moffat, he designed, in the 'thirties and 'forties, more than fifty. Of his early churches, St Mark's, Swindon (1843–5), received the approval of the Ecclesio-logists, and St Andrew's, Leeds (1844–5), is of a simple Early English character which compares favourably with his later eclecticism.

Scott achieved international celebrity in 1845 by winning the competition for the Nikolaikirche in Hamburg. Since his German clients were Lutherans, his success lost him the support of the Camdenians, but his future was assured. He was a ubiquitous 'restorer' of old buildings, including several major cathedrals, and is famous for two memorials, one of which, the Martyrs' Memorial at Oxford (1841), falls within the Early Victorian period.

Built after 1860, but argued about continuously from 1856 onwards, the Foreign Office in Whitehall was Scott's sole essay in monumental Italian style. This was the subject of a protracted battle between Scott and Palmerston which ended in a rare act of submission by Scott.

If Scott was the High Victorian counterpart of Pugin in practice, John Ruskin (1814–1900) was his counterpart in literature. His main works *Modern Painters* (1843–60), the *Seven Lamps of Architecture* (1849) and the *Stones of Venice* (1851–3), all fall within our period, but it is doubtful if their full effect was felt until much later. Like Pugin, he hated everything Greek or Roman and proposed four styles for universal acceptance: Pisan Romanesque, Florentine Gothic, Venetian Gothic and English Early Decorated. How such suggestions and how his moralizing on Art in general were interpreted by a generation already greedily eclectic is a story which belongs to the years after 1860.

A LIST OF THE CHIEF ARCHITECTS MENTIONED
with their principal works dating from between 1830 and 1860.

BARRY, Sir Charles 1795–1860.

Traveller's Club, Pall Mall	1832	Clumber House, Notts.	1857
Reform Club, Pall Mall	1838–40	Bridgewater House	1847
St Peter's, Brighton	1824–28	Highclere Castle	1842–44
Houses of Parliament	1840	Cliveden House, Bucks	1850
		Shrubland Park, Suffolk	1848

BASEVI, George 1795–1845. Cousin of Disraeli and pupil of Sir J. Soane. Cubitt's architect in Belgrave Square.

Fitzwilliam Museum, Cambridge	1837
Conservative Club (with Sidney Smirke)	1843–44

BLORE, Edward 1789–1879.

Canford Manor, near Wimborne, Dorset	1826–36
Ramsey Abbey, Hunts	1838–39
Worsley Hall near Manchester	1840–45
East front at Buckingham Palace	1847
Architect to Westminster Abbey	

BRYCE, David 1803–76. Partner of Wm Burn.

British Linen Bank, Edinburgh	1850
Fettes College	1860
Numerous Scottish mansions	

BUNNING, James B. 1802–63. Architect to City of London 1843–63.

Billingsgate Market, London	1850
Islington Cattle Market	1852
Holloway Prison	1851–52
Coal Exchange, lower Thames St, London	1849

BURN, William 1789–1870. Specialist in 'Scottish Baronial', pupil of Sir R. Smirke, partner of David Bryce.

Montague House, Whitehall	1860
Beaufort Castle, Inverness	1834
Buchanan House, nr Glasgow	1849
Fonthill, Wilts.	1849

BURTON, Decimus 1800–81.

Athenæum Club, Pall Mall	1827
Hyde Park Screen	1828
Club Chambers, Regent St	1839
Conservatories at Chatsworth	1837–40
(with Paxton)	
and at Kew	1845–47

BUTTERFIELD, Wm. 1814–1900.

St Augustine's College, Canterbury	1845–48
All Saints', Margaret St	1859
Merton College Chapel	1849–50
St Matthias, Stoke Newington	1850
St Thomas, Leeds	1852
Restored Dorchester Abbey	

CARPENTER, R. C. 1812–55.

St Paul's, West St, Brighton	1840–48
All Saints, Hove	1848–52
St Magdelene's, Munster Square, London	1849–52

St John's College, Hurstpierpoint	1851–53
College of SS Mary and Nicholas, Lancing, Sussex	1854–55
Architect to Chichester Cathedral	

COCKERELL, Professor C. R. 1788–1863. Royal Academician 1836. Son of late Georgian architect S. P. Cockerell and assistant to Sir R. Smirke.

Taylorian Museum, Oxford	1841–45
Finished Fitzwilliam Museum Cambridge	1845
Finished St George's Hall, Liverpool	1851–56
Additions to Bank of England after	1833
Westminster Insurance Office, Strand	1833
St David's College, Lampeter	1828
Sun Assurance Offices	1839–42
University Library, Cambridge	1837

ELMES, Harvey Lonsdale 1813–47.

St George's Hall, Liverpool	1836
Collegiate Institution	1843
County Asylum, W. Derby, Liverpool	1840–47

FOWLER, Charles 1791–1867.

Charing Cross Market	
Exeter Town Market	1836

JONES, Owen 1809–74. Author of: *Polychromatic Ornament of Italy*, 1846; *Grammar of Ornament*, 1856.

Superintended Great Exhibition 1851 and Director of its interior decoration.

HANSOM, Jos. A. 1803–1852. Inventor of Hansom cab. Established *The Builder*, 1842.

Birmingham Town Hall	1832
Belvoir St Baptist Chapel, Leicester	1845

HARDWICK, Philip 1792–1870. Architect to London and Birmingham Railway.

Corner House, Belgrave Square	1841
Christchurch, Marylebone	1825
Doric Arch at Euston Station	1835–37
Great Hall at Euston Station	1846–47
Curzon St Terminus, Birmingham	1838
Euston Hotel	1839
Paddington Hotel	1852
Buildings at Lincolns Inn	1843–45

HARDWICK, Philip Charles 1822–92. Son and partner of Philip Hardwick and collaborator in most of his works.

PAXTON, Sir Joseph 1801–65. Gardener to Duke of Devonshire.

Conservatory at Chatsworth (with Decimus Burton)	1837–40
Lily House at Chatsworth	1849–50
Crystal Palace	1851
Mentmore, Bucks (with G. H. Stokes)	1852–54

PENNETHORNE, Sir Jas. 1801–71. Assistant to John Nash and pupil of Pugin the Elder.

W. Wing, Somerset House	1842
Record Office, Chancery Lane	1851
Geological Museum, Piccadilly	1837
Duchy of Cornwall office, Buckingham Gate	1854
Interior at Buckingham Palace	1852–55

PUGIN, Augustus Welby Northmore 1812–52. Author of: *Contrasts*, 1836; *Examples of Gothic Architecture*, 1836; *True Principles of Pointed or Christian Architecture*, 1841; *Apology for the Revival of Christian Architecture*, 1843; *Present state of Ecclesiastical Architecture in England*, 1843; *Glossary of Ecclesiastical ornament and costume*, 1844; *Floriated Ornament*, 1849; *Treatise on Chancel Screens and Rood Lofts*, 1851.

Details for Houses of Parliament	1835–36
St Mary's, Derby	1838–39
St Chad's, Birmingham	1839–41
Oscott College	1837
Killarney Cathedral	1846
St Giles, Cheadle, Staffs	1841–46
Alton Towers	1849
Scarisbrick Hall, Lancs	1837–52
The Grange, Ramsgate	1841–43
Bilton Grange, Rugby	1841–46

RICKMAN, Thomas 1776–1841. Author of: *Attempt to discriminate the styles of Architecture in England*, 1817.

St George's Church, Birmingham	1822

New Court, St John's College, Cambridge and numerous churches in the Midlands

SALVIN, Anthony 1799–1881. Pupil of John Nash.

Harlaxton	1837–60
Scotney Castle	1837
Restored Tower of London and Peterborough Cathedral	

SCOTT, Sir George Gilbert R.A. 1810–77.

Numerous churches and cathedral restorations

SMIRKE, Sir Robert 1780–1867.

British Museum	1823
Post Office, St Martins-le-Grand, London	1825–29
Oxford and Cambridge Club, London (with S. Smirke)	1835–37

SMIRKE, Sidney 1798–1877. Brother of Sir Robert Smirke.

Conservative Club (with G. Basevi)	1843–44
Carlton Club	1847–55
Athenæum Club, Bury	1850
Sorting Office, G.P.O., London	1845

TEULON, S. S. 1812–73

Tortworth Court, Glos.	1849–53
Enbrook, near Folkestone	1853–55
St Stephen's Church, Hampstead	
St Andrew's Church, Stamford St, E.C.	

TITE, Sir Wm. M.P. 1798–1873

Royal Exchange, London	1844
Westminster Bank, London, E.C.	1836
numerous Railway Stations	

VULLIAMY, Lewis 1791–1871

Dorchester House, Park Lane, London	1848–63

DESIGN FOR A NORMAN COTTAGE.

Ground Storey. (A), hall. (B), drawing-room; at the end is an arched recess, having on each side a lobby, one leading into the conservatory (C), and the other into the parlour (D); there is also a window on each side of the fire-place looking into the conservatory, which would have a pleasant and cheerful effect. (E), principal staircase, with water-closet under part, and steps to the offices in the basement story. (F), dining-room, with doorway to back entrance, and staircase to kitchen, for the purpose of serving the dinner quickly. (G), study. (H), bedroom for man-servant, with doorway to back entrance (K), which would be a protection to same in the night-time. (<), areas to admit light to the basement. On the one-pair would be five or six bedrooms and water-closet, and one bedroom in the tower, making in all seven or eight, with the one on the ground storey. In the basement storey are the domestic offices.

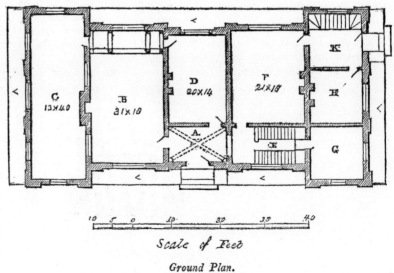

Scale of Feet

Ground Plan.

A cottage design from *The Builder*, December 1843.

Furniture

Furniture

PETER FLOUD

The thirty years from 1830 to 1860 are the most neglected in the whole history of English furniture. There is hardly a book or even an article devoted to early Victorian furniture, and no systematic public or private collections of it. Those few students who venture beyond 1830 usually leap straight on to William Morris and the 1860's, with nothing more than a cursory glance at the Great Exhibition of 1851 to cover the intervening years. Indeed, the total neglect of the period is best epitomized by the fact that of the ten names listed by Matthew Digby Wyatt in 1856 (*Report on the Furniture at the Paris Exhibition of 1855*) as representing the most prominent furniture designers during the previous thirty years, only one – A.W.N.Pugin – is now remembered; three – Bridgens, Whitaker and Dwyer – though entirely forgotten, can still be identified because they published surviving pattern-books, while the remaining six have sunk into total oblivion.

During all other periods since 1700, furniture design has owed much to the inspiration of architects. During the early Victorian period this was not so. With the exception of Pugin, the only architects who seem to have designed furniture were Philip Hardwick and C.J.Richardson. Moreover, even the leading general designers did little in the field of furniture. The two best – Alfred Stevens and Owen Jones – turned to furniture design only at the end of their careers, after 1860, and we have to drop down to secondary figures such as W.B.Scott, L.N.Cottingham any J.K.Collings, before we find any consistent furniture designing.

Documentary evidence

In face of these difficulties, any serious study of the subject must start from an analysis of the surviving *documentary* evidence, and not from an inspection of the increasing quantities of so-called early Victorian furniture now being handled by furniture dealers. This surviving furniture is often quite untypical, and a survey based on it would only perpetuate that process of selective survival which over-emphasizes what is quaint but freakish, at the expense of what is dull but typical.

The available documentary evidence can be listed under seven heads. First, and most valuable of all, are the working records of the leading manufacturers. Unfortunately only one such series – the copious records of Messrs Gillow of Lancaster – appears to have survived intact. In view of the fact that, of all the great early Victorian cabinet-making firms, only two others – Messrs Trollope and Messrs Holland – still survive, and that both have lost all their earlier records, it seems doubtful whether others will come to light. Certainly there can now be little hope of discovering those of long-defunct firms such as Arrowsmith, Banting, Dalziel, Dowbiggin or Wilkinson, whose work was most typical of the period.

Second in importance are illustrated trade catalogues. Very few have so far been traced, and most relate to the single firm of William Smee of Finsbury Pavement. Although their plates are especially valuable as providing irrefutable testimony to actual production, they are almost always undated, and must therefore be used with great circumspection.

Third are the cheaper pattern-books with litho-graphed plates and no text, put together with no pretence of originality by hack designers for the use of firms too small or unenterprising to employ their own designer. They provide a record of the average taste of the times. They are best represented by the many volumes put out by Thomas King for the 1830's, and by Henry Wood for the 1840's and Henry Lawford for the 1850's. Requiring a different interpretation is the fourth category, namely the more expensive volumes, usually with engraved plates and some text, put out by designers with some claim to creative ability – such as Bridgens, Whitaker or Peter Thomson – and consequently including a high proportion of more fanciful 'prestige' designs. Although many of these designs were probably never executed, and although they cannot therefore be taken as a safe guide to general production, they are often useful as illustrating the beginnings of stylistic changes which only later became fashionable.

A fifth source of information is existing furniture which can be dated and attributed by the evidence of surviving accounts or similar records. Further research would no doubt disclose much more of this than the few examples investigated and illustrated for this article. It is perhaps unfortunate that for obvious reasons, some of the most readily available evidence of this kind is provided by furniture associated with the Royal family – as, for example, the library-furniture commissioned for Windsor by William IV, the furniture at Kensington Palace, the furniture designed by Henry Whitaker for Osborne, or the furniture in bedrooms occupied by Queen Victoria during visits to places such as Woburn Abbey or Stoneleigh Abbey. Such furniture is liable to give a distorted picture if used as an index to the dating of stylistic changes, for throughout the early Victorian period (and indeed from the death of George IV onwards) the taste of the Court tended to be some ten years or so behind that of London society generally; apart also from the untypical influence of Prince Albert's German associations.

The sixth category consists of the records of furniture designs registered for copyright purposes with the Patent Office from 1839 onwards. These are meagre for every category except papier-mâché and cast-iron. The last category consists of the copious records and illustrations, both official and unofficial, of the furniture displayed at the various exhibitions of the period, namely at Manchester in 1846, the four Society of Arts exhibitions in London from 1847 to 1850, Birmingham 1849, the Crystal Palace 1851, Dublin and New York 1853, and Paris 1855.

Exhibition furniture

These records have been deliberately placed last because they give an entirely misleading picture of the average production of the times. The illustrated catalogue of the Great Exhibition of 1851, being far more readily accessible than any of the other documentary sources just listed, has too often been used as exclusive evidence of early Victorian taste, without allowance for the fact that the furniture displayed in the Crystal Palace – in common with all the other exhibits – was mainly shown for its novelty and inventiveness. Richard Redgrave, R.A., was certainly not exaggerating when he criticized the whole principle of international exhibitions, and wrote that: 'Each manufacturer is striving his utmost to attain notice and reward ... by an endeavour to catch the consumers by startling novelty or meretricious decoration, leading, in most cases, to an extreme redundancy of ornament. The goods are like the gilded cakes in the booths of our country fairs, no longer for use, but to attract customers.' (*Report on the Present State of Design as Applied to Manufactures*, 1857.)

Where – as with Gillows' – it is possible to compare their exhibits with their everyday production, it is clear that the former were in no way typical of the latter, and the same was no doubt equally true of the other leading firms such as Jackson and Graham, Johnstone and Jeanes, and Snell. Moreover, the exhibition catalogues (especially the illustrations, which were paid for by the exhibitors) give a false impression of the relative importance of the various manufacturers, and in particular greatly exaggerate the real weight of the West End luxury firms such as Morant, John Webb, Levien, and Toms and Luscombe, who

Carved and gilt couch and sofa in the Louis XIV style. Made by W. and C. Wilkinson, under the supervision of Philip Hardwick, for the Court Drawing-room, Goldsmiths' Hall, 1834.

PLATE 21

(A) Carved and padded chair, made by W. and C. Wilkinson, under the supervision of Philip Hardwick, for the Court Dining-room, Goldsmiths' Hall, 1834.

(B) Carved and padded arm-chair, designed by A. W. N. Pugin for Scarisbrick Hall, 1835.

PLATE 22

(A) Side-table, made by W. and C. Wilkinson, under the supervision of Philip Hardwick, for the Court Room, Goldsmiths' Hall, 1834.

(B) Sideboard designed by Henry Whitaker for the Conservative Club (now the Bath Club), 1844.

PLATE 23

Table with inlaid amboyna top, designed by Henry Whitaker for the Conservative Club (now the Bath Club), 1844.

PLATE 24

(A) Original design for carved and painted 'Gothic' sofa for Snelston Hall, Derbyshire, by Lewis Nockalls Cottingham, 1844.

(B) Sofa ('Sociable') with double swivel ends, covered in silk damask woven by Baily and Jackson of Spitalfields. *Stoneleigh Abbey, Warwickshire, c. 1844.*

PLATE 25

(A) Turned 'prie-dieu' chair, with tent-stitch embroidery on wool. *Charlecote Park, Warwickshire, c.* 1845.

(B) 'Elizabethan' chair, with tent-stitch embroidery on wool, *c.* 1845.

PLATE 26

(A) Carved and gilt chair, made by W. and C. Wilkinson, under the supervision of Philip Hardwick, for the Court Drawing-room, Goldsmiths' Hall, 1834.

(B) Carved and inlaid chair, with inset porcelain plaque depicting Queen Victoria. Designed and made by Henry Eyles of Bath for the Great Exhibition, 1851. *Victoria and Albert Museum.*

PLATE 27

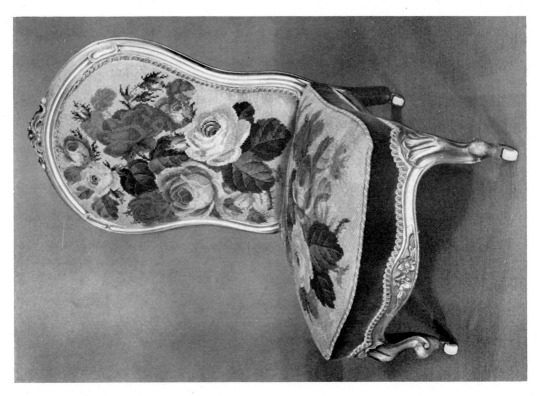

(B) Carved and gilt chair, with back and seat of Berlin wool-work.

(A) 'Elizabethan' fire-screen with panel of Berlin wool-work. c. 1855. *Charlecote Park, Warwickshire, c. 1855.*

PLATE 28

staged elaborate special displays of their wares. Indeed, so distorting are the conclusions usually drawn from these exhibitions, that it is advisable to dismiss the two principal ones before passing to a positive analysis of early Victorian styles.

The first misconception is that early Victorian furniture is fussy and elaborate, and generally covered with carving. This was certainly true of almost all the Crystal Palace exhibits. Few were quite so preposterous as the much-publicized bog-oak examples of Arthur J. Jones and Co. of Dublin, with carving so elaborate that a description of its symbolic significance required several pages, but even respectable firms such as Howard and Sons, and George Trollope and Sons, placed their main emphasis on pieces 'enriched by carved floriated ornament of cunning workmanship', to quote a contemporary account. The same preoccupation is shown by the way in which leading firms such as Snell and Co. and the Coalbrookdale Iron Company, when they wished to improve their standing by some specially-commissioned prestige pieces, turned for designs not to leading architects, as would have been normal in other periods, but to popular sculptors such as Baron Marochetti and John Bell.

This emphasis on decorative carving was no doubt the inevitable result of the competitive ostentation fostered by the spirit of the Exhibition, but it can also be partly explained by the influence of the propaganda and prizes of the Society of Arts in their preparations for the Exhibition, in which the personal enthusiasm of Prince Albert – with his memories of German peasant wood-carving – was a strong ingredient. It cannot, however, be said to have had any influence on the general run of furniture production. Indeed, its only noticeable effect, outside the Exhibition, was to encourage skilful wood-carvers such as W.G. Rogers – often referred to by contemporary commentators as the 'Victorian Grinling Gibbons' – and Thomas Wallis of Louth, and to stimulate noble patronage for the curious school of Warwick wood-carving represented by the firms of William Cookes and James Morris Willcox. Both these firms, and later the firm of William Kendall, who had originally been apprenticed to Willcox, pro-

duced between 1848 and 1860 a considerable quantity of carved furniture in a highly elaborate 'naturalistic' style, in which every article was enriched with carving with a narrative or symbolic significance, executed with the attention to detail of a *trompe l'œil* (Pls. 29–32). Their work is seen at its worst in such over-carved monstrosities as the 'Kenilworth Buffet' (1851) now at Warwick Castle, and at its best in Cookes's Alscot Park buffet (designed by Hugues Protat for the Great Exhibition of 1851 but actually shown at the Manchester Art Treasures Exhibition, 1857, Pl. 29), or Willcox's splendid sideboard (1858) now at Charlecote Park (Pl. 32).

Early Victorian conservatism

The second misconception for which the Great Exhibition catalogues have been mainly responsible is that early Victorian furniture was subject to a constantly shifting succession of stylistic revivals in which it is impossible to discern any consistent thread. A close examination of contemporary pattern-books – and particularly of the Gillow records – shows on the contrary that furniture fashions changed remarkably little between 1835 and 1860, and that the Early Victorian period was in this respect far more conservative than either the Regency or the mid-Victorian. One of the clearest testimonies to this conservatism is the fact that Thomas King's pattern-book *The Modern Style of Cabinet Work Exemplified* (1829) was reissued without alteration in 1862, while the furniture sections of J.C. Loudon's compendious *Encyclopædia of Cottage, Farm, and Villa Architecture* (1833) were incorporated with nothing omitted and very little added in all the later editions (1842, 1846, 1857). By comparison it would be quite impossible to imagine a pattern-book of 1810 being issued unchanged in 1840, or one of 1850 being reissued in 1880.

This Early Victorian conservatism may well have been the direct result of that rise of the *nouveau riche* patron, which is usually held to have upset all traditional standards of taste. Their lack of independent æsthetic standards, and their conformist social aspirations, would seem as likely to have counselled a prudent acceptance of established conventions as to have led these new patrons into any stylistic adventures. Moreover, this tendency would have been reinforced by the fact that, as the demand for furniture increased, so did the proportion that was produced by firms without their own designers, and which were therefore compelled to keep to the repetition of stock patterns with no pretence of originality – a trend which was strengthened by the detailed price-schedules set out in successive editions of the *London Cabinet-Makers' Union Book of Rules* (1811, 1824, 1836), which gave the small employer every incentive to keep to the accepted patterns, rather than to launch out on new designs and thus risk pricing troubles with his workmen.

Before passing to an analysis of the consistent style which subsisted throughout most of the Early Victorian period, we must first glance at the very rapid and radical stylistic changes which were its prelude, over the years 1827 to 1835. Fortunately their documentation is made relatively easy by the survival of a wide variety of pattern-books covering these crucial years. The key to the changes was, of course, the breakdown of that long hegemony of the various styles based on the antique – whether Greek, Roman, Pompeian or Egyptian – which until 1827 had been challenged only by the Gothic – and then in only a very limited field. By 1830, however, they were faced with two new competitors – the revived Louis XIV style, and the revived Elizabethan.

The 'Louis XIV' revival

The reintroduction of Louis XIV furniture and furnishings can be dated precisely to 1827, when Crockford's new club-house was decorated by Philip and Benjamin Dean Wyatt. This was interpreted by the London decorators as authority to abandon the austerities of the 'Modern Grecian', and to revert to the opulent splendours of the *ancien régime*, whether in their baroque or rococo forms. Already by 1828 the change is visible in patterns for mirrors, frames, window cornices and the like, with scrolls and shells replacing the hitherto ubiquitous anthemion. By 1830 it had spread to movable furniture, and particularly to drawing-room chair-backs. Although evidently welcomed by the trade, this change was unanimously condemned by architects and designers who saw it as opening the gates to any hack furniture-maker who could now throw together an assortment of botched-up scrolls, cover them with gilding, and label them 'in the old French style'.

A critical attitude to the new style had already been voiced by George Smith (*Cabinet-Maker's and Upholsterer's Guide, Drawing-Book and Repository*) immediately after the opening of Crockford's Club, with the comment that 'As this mansion is solely appropriated to nightly purposes of pleasure, perhaps such a taste may be in unison with the wasteful transfer of property made in such establishments.' Similar views were presented before the Select Committee on Arts and Manufactures (1835), by witnesses such as J.B.Papworth and C.R.Cockerell, who not only deplored the licence provided to inferior designers by the new style, but also pointed out how what had started as a revival of the baroque splendours of Louis XIV very rapidly degenerated by its own internal momentum into indiscriminate borrowing from the rococo trivialities of Louis XV. Despite this almost universal condemnation by serious architects, however, the spread of these 'old French' styles was very rapid, especially for drawing-rooms and boudoirs. The extent to which the change was limited to these more feminine rooms, while leaving the furnishings of more masculine quarters relatively untouched, is very clearly shown by the suites of furniture supplied in 1833–4 by Messrs. W. and C. Wilkinsons to Goldsmiths' Hall, under the supervision of the architect, Philip Hardwick (Pls. 21–3, 27). It will be seen that, whereas the furniture for the Court Drawing-Room is entirely in the new style, that for the Court Dining-Room and for the Court Room itself shows little variation from the standard patterns of the 1820's. Indeed, for the more traditionalist institutions, these 'Modern Greek' designs remained in vogue for at least ten years longer, as witness the furniture designed by Henry Whitaker for the Conservative Club in 1844 (Pls. 23, 24).

The 'Elizabethan' revival

The Elizabethan revival was, by contrast, a conscious creation of the more sophisticated architects and designers such as C.J.Richardson. It first appears in furniture pattern-books just after 1830, directly inspired no doubt by the plates in T.F. Hunt's *Exemplars of Tudor Architecture and Furniture* (1829–30), closely followed by Henry Shaw's *Specimens of Ancient Furniture* (1832–6). In the early 1830's it was mainly limited to the making up of pseudo-Elizabethan cupboards and coffers out of old fragments, by firms such as Samuel Hanson, and James Nixon (see Loudon's *Encyclopædia* and Georges Fildes' *Elizabethan Furniture* (1844)). After about 1838 it takes its place in all the pattern-books in the form of strapwork carving applied to mirror-frames, sideboard-backs and the like. This Elizabethan revival was supported by the same arguments which were used to condemn the revival of the French styles. It was indisputably British; it was rich without being vulgar; and its coarse vigour did not overtax the somewhat limited finesse of the average British carver. Moreover, its romantic and baronial associations were, of course, entirely in keeping with current literary preoccupations.

By about 1835 both the Louis XIV and the Elizabethan styles had clearly established their right to equal respectability with the Gothic and the 'Grecian', and the long hegemony of the latter had finally ended. The change is summed up by the distinction between two of Thomas King's titles: in 1829 he published *The Modern Style of Cabinet Work Exemplified*, whereas in 1834 his *Designs for Carving and Gilding* bore the subtitle *in a variety of styles*. With four quite different styles legitimate, there was now no obstacle to an even more catholic eclecticism, and during the later 1830's we find an astonishing proliferation of titles, including the *Arabesque*, the *French Renaissance*, the *Cinque-Cento*, and so on. Indeed, the most noticeable feature of the pattern-books of the years 1835 to 1850 – best exemplified by Henry Whitaker's *Practical Cabinet-Maker* (1847) – is the determination that no design should be presented without an attribution to some historic style, and that the greatest possible variety of stylistic titles should be devised for this purpose.

It would be quite wrong, however, to take this eclecticism at its face value, for, oddly enough, it was just when it first became all-embracing – around 1835 – that we can first discern the emergence of a consistent and distinguishable Early Victorian style. We may, in fact, claim that it was only when the rigid classical hegemony had been finally broken, and when designers could at last give form to their personal fantasies in a now un-fettered eclecticism, that the real spirit of the period begins to achieve spontaneous expression in its furniture. Moreover, so strong was the appeal of historicism at this time that even the most individual inventions had to be designated as in some earlier style, and we should not be surprised, therefore, to find designs which bear the unmistakable Early Victorian stamp, and which could not possibly have been produced at any other time, being solemnly described as 'in the purest François Premier taste'. One of the fascinations of Early Victorian furniture is the way in which its original quality is often clearest in just those cases where the designer evidently believed himself to have been most faithfully following historical precedent. This is particularly clearly seen in those frequent cases where the same designer has worked in a different style for each room – Gothic for the hall, Elizabethan for the library, Louis XIV for the drawing-room, and so on – but has nevertheless left a consistent Early Victorian stamp on each in turn.

Emphasis on comfort

It must be admitted that it is easier to refer to this Early Victorian style in general terms than to list its distinguishing characteristics in detail. They can be more readily illustrated than described. Paradoxically, in an age that was so obsessed with problems of stylistic purity, its keynote was the subordination of all stylistic considerations to the over-riding consideration of comfort. In this it contrasts sharply not only with the 1820's (as witness the primacy of stylistic criteria in the designs of Richard Brown, George Smith and the Nicholsons), but equally with the mid-Victorian period, in which – contrary to general belief – comfort once more took second place to various stylistic mannerisms, whether derived from the Middle Ages, from Sheraton or from Japan. A similar contrast also differentiates this early Victorian style from developments in France, and makes it possible to claim it as the first English style which marked a clear-cut divergence from contemporary French trends. It is perhaps no accident, therefore, that one of the earliest recognitions of its emergence, with a clear analysis of its revolutionary emphasis on comfort, should be found in a French discussion of the difference between French and English furniture as demonstrated by the Paris Exhibition of 1834. (Stéphane Flachat, *L'Industrie: Exposition de 1834.*)

Increased use of upholstery

An obvious corollary to this concentration on comfort was the increased use of padding and upholstery of all kinds, and in particular the evolution for the first time of articles of furniture in which the shape is determined much more by the upholstery than by the framework which it covers. It is sometimes suggested that this development can be related to technical advances in spring construction. In fact, however, these had already been made in the first decade of the century, and a more plausible explanation of these Early Victorian changes was the great improvement in cheap worsted covering-materials resulting from the expansion of Yorkshire power-loom weaving during the 1830's. Although these upholstery changes directly affected only chairs, sofas, ottomans and the like, they influenced, by association, the shapes of all furniture, and it is precisely the rounding-off of all corners and the elimination of all angularities and surface irregularities which is the main distinguishing characteristic of the Early Victorian style. All sharp outlines are smoothed down, rectangular frameworks become oval or semi-circular, edges are bevelled, and projecting pediments or finials are removed. At the same time all crispness or spring disappears from members such as table-supports or chair-backs, and is replaced by a uniform, flabby, unadventurous, heavy-handed curve – a curve which almost gives the wood the appearance of having been squeezed from a tube, and which is contrasted not only with the taut and basically rectilinear outlines of the Regency, but equally with the elegant twistings of the 'old French' styles.

Parallel with these developments went a tendency to merge the separate parts of each piece of furniture into a unified, undifferentiated whole. Arms and backs of sofas are joined together in a single enclosing sweep. Front and sides of chiffoniers are likewise embraced in a single enveloping semi-circle. The distinction between pedestal and base in the standard Regency loo-table is obliterated. Moreover, this process was visually accentuated by the virtual elimination of all the many processes by which cabinet-makers have traditionally varied the colour and texture of their surfaces. Inlay, marquetry and boulle-work, and the use of gilding and ormolu, went out of fashion for all normal domestic furniture soon after 1830, and it was not until about 1855 that there was any sign of their revival. The same tendency affected all knobs and handles, which were now usually made of plain wood rather than of metal. Even the use of contrasted woods was frowned on, and the various exotic timbers so favoured during the Regency – such as zebra-wood, satinwood and amboyna – were discarded in favour of plain mahogany, rosewood or walnut, and oak for furniture in the Gothic or Elizabethan taste. It should perhaps be emphasized that this preference for solid unadorned wood did not necessarily involve an increase in weight, for it is often possible to reduce both the size and weight by using solid timber in place of veneered surfaces on a separate core.

When we contrast this use of plain undecorated wood with the metal inlays and zoomorphic carving of the Regency, or with the inset porcelain medallions and embossed leather panels, which were so popular in the 1860's, we can see how wide of the mark is the belief that typical Early Victorian furniture must be over-ornamented and fussy. It may therefore be as well to confirm the point by a quotation from the most perceptive contemporary comment on Early Victorian furniture in general, namely Matthew Digby Wyatt's already mentioned *Report on the Furniture at the Paris Exhibition of 1855*. In his report he laments the conservative habits of the English cabinet-makers, who, for over a generation, had been content with 'good joinery, glueing up, and mitering, smooth, plain, veneering, and clean but not intricate turning', and criticizes them severely for having deliberately turned their backs on more elaborate surface treatments with carving or marquetry.

The use of wood substitutes

Reference should perhaps be made here to the use of wood-substitutes. Perusal of the catalogue of the Great Exhibition, and even more of the catalogues of the four Society of Arts Exhibitions which preceded it, might lead to the conclusion that a great deal of Early Victorian furniture made use of patent materials such as gutta-percha, stamped leather, carton-pierre, Albano's canabic composition, and so on. The evidence of the Gillow records, however, supported by accounts of current trade methods such as the comprehensive report incorporated in Blackie's *Cabinet-Maker's Assistant* (1853), show that, with the exception of papier-mâché, which is in rather a different category, these substitutes never had much currency. Perhaps the only decisive change in materials during this period arose from the universal introduction of Italian marble tops for washstands, and also to some extent for sideboards and chiffoniers, during the 1840's, as a result of price-reductions consequent on the perfection of steam-driven marble-cutting machines in the 1830's. The parallel efforts in the 1840's to popularize British substitutes such as the Derbyshire and Limerick near-marbles, and Magnus' patent painted slate, made no permanent impact, and ambitious projects like the fantastic slate-furniture at Penrhyn Castle must have been quite exceptional.

The use of machinery

A similar false impression results from assuming that the various wood-working machines, especially the patent carving machines of Irving, and of Taylor, Williams and Jordan, as demonstrated at these same exhibitions, were already in regular commercial use during this period and influenced in some way the design of Early Victorian furniture. There is very little evidence to support this view. It is true that Henry Cole, in the guise of *Felix Summerly's Art Manufactures*, attempted, as one would expect, to exploit Jordan's patent, with a fantastic arm-chair called 'The Repose', which incorporated numerous figures designed by J.C. Horsley, the painter. It is also known that C.J. Richardson, the Elizabethan enthusiast, made designs especially for it. Neither the Gillow records nor the Blackie account, however, include any evidence of these mechanical developments. Moreover, the most authoritative contemporary report on the whole subject (a paper by G.L. Molesworth *On the Conversion of Wood by Machinery* to the Institute of Civil Engineers, 17 November 1857) implies that regularly used machinery at that date was limited to circular- and band-saws, and planing and mortising machines, which could have had little influence on design. There is, however, some reason to believe that the increased use of fret-cutting in the 1850's may have been connected with the perfecting of Sandy and Powell's fret-cutting machinery.

Stylistic changes from 1850–60

These generalizations about the 'Early Victorian style', are intended to apply to the whole period from 1835 to 1860. It must be admitted, however, that they require some slight qualifications when applied to new furniture designs produced after 1850. The most marked change thereafter was a tendency away from the completely upholstered chairs and sofas of the 1840's. Shapes remained unchanged, but the wooden framework was now usually visible rather than completely concealed as hitherto, and the incorporation of a little openwork carving, and especially fret-cutting, as just mentioned, became acceptable. Half-padded arms took their place beside the earlier fully-padded sides for easy-chairs. Visible legs were substituted for the solid box-upholstery of ottomans. These changes were not pronounced enough to invalidate the continued vitality of the Early Victorian style down to, and even beyond, 1860, but they anticipated further

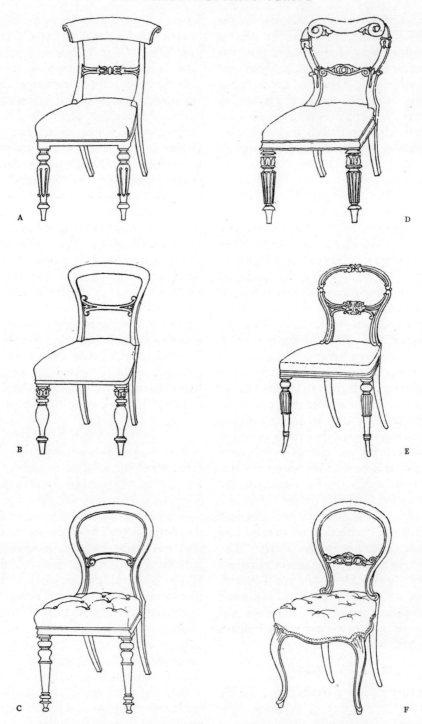

Fig. I. The development of the Balloon back chair. (A), (B) and (C) are typical dining-room chairs, c. 1830, 1835 and 1850 respectively. (D), (E) and (F) are typical drawing-room chairs, c. 1830, 1835 and 1850 respectively.

changes which began to gather momentum in the very last years of our period, and which ultimately affected a radical transformation of English furniture styles in the late 1860's.

All that can be said here is that the basis of this later transformation was a reversal to straight lines in reaction against the Early Victorian curve, and a revival of interest in every type of polychromatic surface-treatment after the long reign of undecorated French polish. Only one facet of this complex transformation was already becoming visible before 1860, namely the revival of Louis XVI styles. This revival was inaugurated at the Paris Exhibition of 1855, and was signalized for English cabinet-makers in particular by a remarkable cabinet exhibited by Jackson and Graham, which gained them a 'Medal of Honour'. This splendid piece – it has unfortunately not proved possible to discover its present whereabouts – broke right away from early Victorian tradition. In the employment of French designers and modellers, in the use of satinwood and tulipwood in place of mahogany and rosewood, in the revival of marquetry and ormolu, and the incorporation of porcelain plaques, it fully anticipated all the characteristics of that elegant, elaborate style – sometimes thought of as a Sheraton revival – usually associated with the work of firms such as Wright and Mansfield or Holland and Sons in the 1860's and 1870's. Indeed, although one or two pattern-books published between 1855 and 1860 already incorporate a few 'Louis XVI designs', and although percipient contemporary commentators such as Richard Redgrave (who curiously called it the 'Gauthier' – though he presumably meant 'Gouthière' – style) noticed the change; its general impact was hardly yet discernible, and the fully-fledged revival of this style can be legitimately placed beyond the limits of the Early Victorian period.

These conclusions about the Early Victorian style in general must now be applied in turn to the main categories of furniture.

Chairs

The Early Victorian period was responsible for two significant contributions to chair design. The first, and most important, was the development of the balloon-back chair. In 1830 this was entirely unknown; by 1860 it had become by far the commonest type both for dining- and drawing-rooms. The stages by which it developed during the intervening years can be traced fairly accurately, but it is very difficult to offer any satisfactory explanation as to why it appeared just when it did. Strangely enough, contemporary writers on furniture seem to have been completely unaware of this basic change, and it has not proved possible to trace even a single contemporary reference to it. All that can be said with confidence is that it was an indigenous English development, not taken over from France.

In 1830 almost all chairs were still of a uniform sub-classical pattern, with a broad horizontal yoke-rail extending well beyond the plain uprights (which merely continued upwards the line of the back legs), a much narrower carved horizontal splat, a padded seat, and straight front legs. In the case of dining-room or parlour chairs, variations of this standard pattern were limited to the carving of the splat and to the slight enrichment of the ends of the yoke-rail with volutes and the like. In the case of drawing-room chairs the basic classical type was being increasingly challenged by the recently revived Louis XIV style, which at the least involved carving the yoke-rail and splat with baroque scrolls, and at the most replacing them by an elaborately carved back entirely made up of contrasting scrolls. In either case the front seat-rail and legs remained straight, and there was as yet no return to the cabriole leg.

The balloon-back seems to have developed from the simultaneous modification after 1830 of both the yoke-rail dining-room type and the scroll-back drawing-room type. By 1835 we find dining-room versions in which the yoke-rail has been rounded-off and made continuous with the uprights, and at the same time a simplified drawing-room chair in which the scroll-carving has been almost eliminated, leaving a plain curved top. The step from these two types to the fully-fledged balloon-back was easily made in the next ten years.

Once established, the balloon-back rapidly

became predominant, until by 1850 almost all trace of the classical yoke-rail had disappeared. It remained the standard pattern until the late 1860's, in a more austere form for the dining-room or library, and with carved enrichments within the basic rounded top for the drawing-room or boudoir. After 1850 cabriole legs usually replaced the earlier straight legs for the drawing-room versions.

Throughout this period bedroom or 'fancy' chairs followed the same changes, but with a lighter build – mahogany being replaced by japanned or stained birch or maple, the padded seat being replaced by cane, and the flimsier legs being strengthened by double side-stretchers.

The second original contribution to chair-design was the tall-backed, short-legged, low-seated, entirely upholstered chair, sometimes called a 'devotional', 'prie-dieu' or 'vesper' chair (Pl. 26A). This typical example of attention to the functional requirements of comfort at the expense of appearance seems to have been derived from the cane-backed Charles II chair, which, owing to a curious and incomprehensible confusion, was thought by the early Elizabethan enthusiasts to be a typical sixteenth-century design. By 1840 it had developed in two different directions. On the one hand, the more ambitious designers, such as Bridgens and Whitaker, elaborated a whole series of tall-backed chairs with turned legs and uprights, and incorporating heavy strapwork carving – a type which was carried into the 1850's by Blackie's already-quoted *Cabinet-Makers' Assistant*. On the other hand, the humbler men such as Henry Wood transformed it into the typical Early Victorian drawing-room chair, covered in Berlin wool-work, and decorated with tassels and fringes. The earliest of these date from about 1835 and they remained in favour until after 1860 (Pl. 26B). The specifically 'devotional' version, as found for example in Henry Lawford's design-books (1855), had a T-shaped tall back with a padded top-rest for use during family prayers.

The only other specifically Early Victorian chair style was the child's chair with straight tall back, tall legs and double-stretchers, called after

Sir Astley Cooper (1768–1841), the anatomist on whose principles it was designed.

Sofas, couches, ottomans and easy-chairs

The Early Victorian emphasis on comfort rather than 'style' can be traced very clearly in the design of sofas, couches and ottomans. In 1830 the standard sofa had a rectangular plan, with straight back, front-rail and ends, all at right-angles to each other. Moreover, although the back might be slightly canted and the ends might curve over, all the horizontal lines were also straight. The only relief to the austere impression was provided by slight carved or inlaid enrichments – usually in the form of the anthemion – to the front-rail and the front surface of the arms, and by the two cylindrical bolster-cushions.

For more opulent interiors this standard neo-classical form had, from 1827 onwards, to meet the competition of the more heavily ornamented revived Louis XIV sofa, which usually took the form of a basically classical shape with the addition of carved and gilt cresting. For more normal domestic use the neo-classic remained in favour until the late 1830's, and was then superseded not by the baroque or rococo scrolls of the French eighteenth century, but by a styleless Early Victorian compromise. This had a straight front rail and plain legs, but a back which was rounded in both elevation and plan and was structurally continuous with the ends or arms. The typical version of the 1840's, as seen in the Smee pattern-books for example, was padded all over, with no wood visible except in the diminutive legs, and variations in design were therefore limited to the outline of the back, which was sometimes humped up in the centre and sometimes at each end.

In the 1850's the basic shape remained unchanged, but there was now a tendency to reintroduce a visible wooden framework to the back and arms, and the single-, twin- or even triple-humped back often incorporated elaborately carved or fretworked open panels. The variant known as the 'sociable', 'conversation sofa', or 'tête-à-tête', with the two ends facing each other on the lines of the French 'causeuse' (Pl. 25B), was popular for a short time during the 1840's,

Sideboard, designed by Hugues Protat and made by William Cookes of Warwick for Alscot Park, Warwickshire, 1853.
Courtesy Mrs Alston-Roberts-West.

PLATE 29

(A) Carved and gilt music-stool in the 'naturalistic style', with seat in Berlin wool-work. *Charlecote Park, Warwickshire, c.* 1855.

(B) Fire-screen designed and carved in the 'naturalistic style', by William Kendall of Warwick. *Stoneleigh Abbey, Warwickshire,* 1858.

PLATE 30

Sideboard designed and carved in the 'naturalistic style', by William Kendall of Warwick.
Stoneleigh Abbey, Warwickshire, 1858.

PLATE 31

Sideboard, designed and carved by James Morris Willcox of Warwick. *Charlecote Park, Warwickshire,* 1858.

PLATE 32

but seems to have already gone out of favour by the mid-1850's. It provided the hack designers with opportunities for some of their most fanciful inventions.

Single-ended couches followed the same changes as sofas, with an emphasis during the 1830's on an entirely plain type with a slightly canted end, designed to support the back while reading. This seems first to have been evolved by Thomas King, but it was immediately taken over by the trade generally as an 'Adelaide' couch.

Ottomans provided a more informal companion to the sofa throughout this period. Up to about 1845 the normal form was extremely simple, consisting merely of a plain free-standing upholstered box with a back and cushions, and with seats either on two or all four sides. By 1850 it had generally become more elaborate, with a visible wooden framework round the upholstery and with short legs in place of the previous box-base. A common pattern had the seat divided into compartments by arms, and sometimes the compartments formed individual segments which could be placed together or separately, as convenient. In the more pretentious examples the central back was surmounted by a *jardinière*.

Easy, or 'lounging' chairs, as they were usually called, tended to follow the same lines of development as sofas, and may therefore conveniently be considered with them. The basic transformation from the rectangular version of the 1830's to the tubby and rounded style of the 1850's can more readily be illustrated than described. For a short time in the early 1850's there was a vogue for a particularly clumsy-looking type in which the back, although separated from the arms, was joined to them by a separate member running from the cresting down to the arm-rest. The only other type deserving mention was the library-chair with the normal back and arms replaced by a heavily padded continuous horizontal semi-circle. This first appears in the 1840's with the semi-circle supported only in the centre, but by 1860 it had been modified so that the padded semi-circle was supported by turned balusters round its whole length, and as such remained a standard type until well into the twentieth century.

Tables

By comparison with other articles of furniture, tables afford little evidence of changes in Early Victorian taste. The standard extending dining-room table, the various types of occasional table, the ingenious rising side-tables operated with pulley and weights on the principle of the sash-window, and even the drawing-room work-table with pouch, altered comparatively little during the thirty years under review. Only the circular loo-table showed significant changes, which took two forms. In the first place, there was a tendency in the 1850's to enrich the top, which from 1830 to 1850 had normally been completely plain, either with a gadrooned moulding or with a scalloped outline. In the second place, the standard 1830 type with a clearly differentiated supporting pedestal – usually pyramidical – resting on a flat triangular block, itself often standing on claw or paw feet, slowly evolved over the next twenty years, until by 1850 it was normal for the three legs to flow directly from the central column in loose and relaxed curves which typify the more spineless qualities of the Early Victorian style. In the 1850's a more elaborate support, with a central column supplemented by three or four thinner ones, was introduced, and is found not only in the designs of men like Peter Thomson and John Dwyer, but even in the cheaper pattern-books. There seems little doubt that this is a case where a design originally evolved as suitable for cast iron, was later taken over and translated into wood.

In considering all Early Victorian tables, it must never be forgotten that, as A.J.Downing put it in 1850, 'they depend for this good effect mainly on the drapery or cover of handsome cloth or stuff usually spread upon their top and concealing all but the lower part of the legs' (*The Architecture of Country Houses*).

Sideboards and chiffoniers

The development of the sideboard during this period gives us the clearest evidence of that tendency to round off all angularities which we have claimed as one of the most typical manifestations of the Early Victorian style. Throughout the whole period the pedestal type of sideboard was the

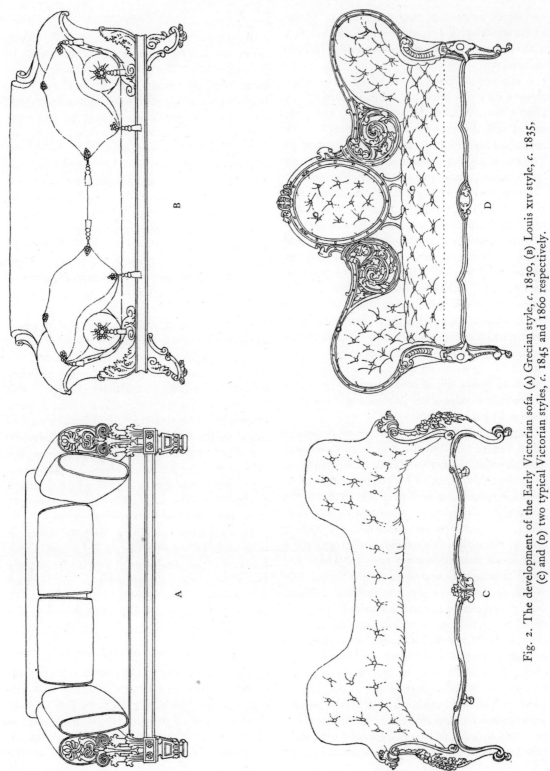

Fig. 2. The development of the Early Victorian sofa. (A) Grecian style, *c.* 1830, (B) Louis XIV style, *c.* 1835, (C) and (D) two typical Victorian styles, *c.* 1845 and 1860 respectively.

standard pattern for normal domestic purposes, with open-legged types rarely used. In 1830 the shape was rigidly rectangular, with a low wooden rectangular backboard. By 1840 backs were being made higher and were beginning to incorporate mirrors, which usually followed the three-fold division of the base, with a larger mirror in the centre, flanked by two smaller ones over the pedestals – still with rectangular outlines. By 1850 backs were higher still, and it became customary to raise the centre mirror above the flanking ones and to give all three semi-circular rather than rectangular crestings. By 1860 it was more common for the whole back to be merged into a single semi-circular mirror. Precisely the same development affected the pedestals, though with a time-lag, and it was not until after 1850 that the change towards a semi-circular elevation for the sideboard was paralleled by a semi-circular plan also, with the outer angles of the pedestals rounded-off.

The same changes can be traced even more clearly in the more modest chiffonier, which was regarded as the appropriate article for a dining-room which was too small or unpretentious for a full-scale sideboard. As an anonymous domestic manual of 1851 (*How to Furnish a House and Make it a Home*), points out, a sideboard with pedestals looks ridiculous if less than about 4 ft. wide, whereas a chiffonier, with its solid front, could reasonably be as small as 3 ft. wide. The standard type in the 1830's had a small shelf projecting from the wooden backboard, and supported on turned balusters or Louis XIV trusses, according to taste. There were usually two cupboards in front, with wire-grille doors backed with pleated silk. More elaborate examples incorporated a set of small bookshelves. As with the sideboards, the wooden backboard was gradually replaced by a mirror-back, the pleated silk was replaced by wooden or glass doors, the plan became semicircular, and curved open shelves were fitted on either side of the central cupboards.

When we turn to the more pretentious designs, either for sideboards or chiffoniers, we find a particularly rich crop of 'Elizabethan' examples. Whereas the first enthusiasm for the revived Louis XIV and XV styles during the years 1827–35 found its most natural expression in upholstered drawing-room furniture, the 'Elizabethan', with its emphasis on heavily carved solid oak, was thought to be especially well adapted to the more manly articles such as sideboards or buffets. The first examples, in the early 1830's, were merely reproductions of original Jacobean pieces. By 1838, however, we find men like Bridgens designing original 'Elizabethan' sideboards covered with carved strapwork for their rich clients (such as James Watt, the then owner of Aston Hall), and even the conservative firm of Gillow produced in 1841 a whole suite of most elaborately carved furniture in the Elizabethan style for the Richmond-Gale-Braddyll family of Conishead Priory. Every pattern-book of the 1840's, such as those of Henry Wood, automatically contained some elaborately carved Elizabethan sideboards, and these were continued into the 1850's also by Peter Thomson and others. The only slight change after 1850 – no doubt stimulated by the Great Exhibition – was for plain strapwork to be enlivened by the incorporation of naturalistic carved ornament usually with a 'literary-functionalist' flavour. In the case of sideboards this required the introduction of dead game, fishing-tackle, grapes and the like, as the appropriate symbols. Apart from the few first-class examples, which have already been referred to in connection with the Warwick school, this trend produced little of merit, for the carving is almost always perfunctory and mechanical.

Miscellaneous furniture

Of the many miscellaneous articles of furniture which made up the typical Victorian home, not much need be said. Certain types which were in regular use up to the 1830's, then virtually disappeared – such as the semi-circular wine-table, the ubiquitous Regency tripod-stand, the commode and (after about 1840) the classical hall-couch. Other types, such as footstools, fire-screens (Pls. 28A, 30B), work-tables and flower-stands, continued in use and faithfully reflected the changes of taste already mentioned for the more important items. Still others, such as

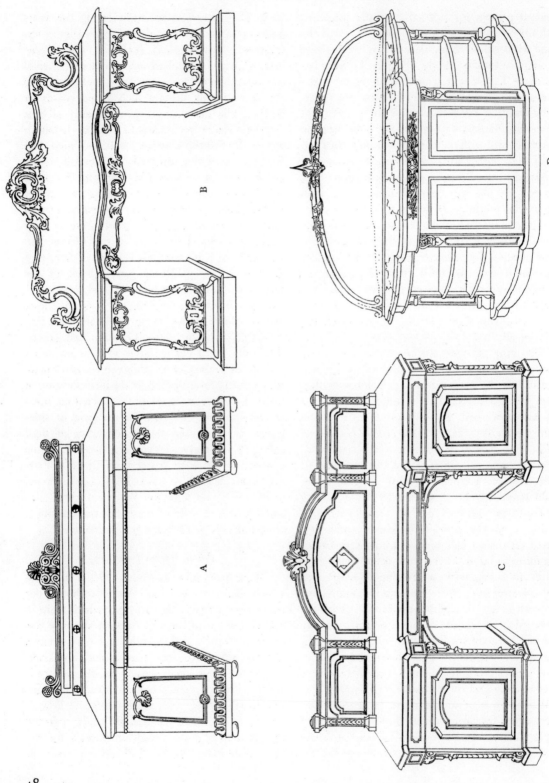

Fig. 3. The development of the Early Victorian sideboard. (A) Grecian style, c. 1830, (B) Louis xiv style, c. 1835, (c) Elizabethan style, c. 1845, and (D) a typical Victorian style, c. 1860.

davenports, table-flap cases, canterburies, music-stools and portfolio-stands, changed little throughout the period.

Almost the only article of furniture which first sprang into regular use during this period was the whatnot. Although known earlier, it only became a standard article after about 1840. The only change worth mentioning is that after about 1855 the earlier free-standing type takes second place to the later corner variety.

Gothic furniture

Gothic furniture requires separate mention, for throughout this period it remained rather isolated from normal furniture fashions. It was rarely regarded as appropriate for rooms other than the hall or library, or exceptionally for panelled rooms in old houses. The production of a whole range of Gothic furniture, such as that designed for Snelston Hall, Derbyshire, by L.N.Cottingham, the antiquarian, in 1844 (Pl. 25A), was quite exceptional. Normally speaking, the term merely implied a superficial tracery-pattern on the back of a hall-seat, or the incorporation of linen-fold panelling into a library settle. For obvious reasons the Elizabethan revival in the 1830's led to a good deal of confusion with the Gothic, and in many pattern-books of the 1840's it would be quite impossible, were it not for the captions, to know which style was intended.

It does not seem that the publication of A.W.N.Pugin's *Gothic Furniture* in 1835, and his many other efforts to propagate a true understanding of Gothic principles, had any marked effect on general furniture production; presumably because his admonitions appeared to be addressed mainly to architects and because the excellent and chaste Gothic furniture (Pl. 22B) which he himself designed for several of his clients was never illustrated. The only sign of his influence was the elaborate Gothic furniture which J.G.Crace – who had previously worked in entirely different styles – began to produce at the end of the 1840's, and which is typified by the well-known bookcase, supposedly to Pugin's own design, exhibited in the Medieval Court of the 1851 Exhibition, and now in the Victoria and Albert Museum, a remarkable range of pieces which he produced for Sir James Watts of Abney Hall near Stockport, in 1847, and an imposing piece which earned him an award at the Paris Exhibition of 1855.

Metal furniture

Metal furniture also requires separate mention. It falls into two categories. The first comprises cast-iron garden-furniture and hall-furniture, such as hat and umbrella stands and flower stands. This was made as a by-product of their normal industrial work by iron foundries such as Coalbrookdale, Shropshire, the Carron Company, Stirlingshire, and various smaller foundries in the area round Birmingham, such as Archibald Kendrick of Walsall, and Thomas Marsh of Dudley. It was already in production before 1830, but had a particular vogue between 1845 and 1855. During this period Coalbrookdale especially made great efforts to produce a full range of indoor cast-iron furniture, including pieces for living-rooms upholstered in damask or velvet. The majority were designed by Charles Crooke, but they also called in outside artists. Judging from contemporary illustrations of examples such as the 'hall stand for hats, cloaks, umbrellas, with looking glass, lamp, letter and brush box, and inkstand all combined', designed 'after a suggestion by Felix Summerly', which won a Gold Isis medal from the Society of Arts in 1849, and the 'deer-hound table' designed by John Bell, the popular sculptor, for the Paris Exhibition of 1855, one may hope that these ludicrous and impractical examples have all long since disappeared. The present-day habit of painting surviving pieces white may help to conceal their inherent ugliness, but at the cost of falsifying their original appearance, for they were normally produced in only three finishes: 'Berlin-black, bronzed, or japanned in imitation of oak'.

The second category consisted of brass furniture, produced by a different section of the Birmingham trade, namely the brass-foundries, who added beds to their traditional output of cornice-poles, fenders and the like. Although brass beds were being manufactured by 1825, they made so little impact at first that as late as 1844 the 'Art Union' reported the French metal furniture shown at the Paris Exhibition of that year as a great novelty. After about 1845, however, there was a spurt in Birmingham production, mainly as a result of Peyton and Harlow's patent (1841) for taper tubing. Their main competitor was R.W. Winfield, who produced some very attractive ornamental brass beds in the late 1840's.

In addition to these two main categories, there was also during this period a certain amount of experimental metal furniture, ranging from Mallet's preposterous chairs made of riveted gas-tubing, sponsored by J.C.Loudon in the 1830's, to elegant and practical pieces in square-section or strip brass.

Papier-mâché furniture

Although it is papier-mâché furniture which most readily comes to mind when the Early Victorian period is in question, it would be quite wrong to suppose that it was as frequently found in the average Early Victorian home as it now is in second-hand shops or in 'period rooms' in museums. The fact that the bulk of papier-mâché furniture can safely be assumed to be early Victorian, that marked pieces are fairly common, and that its pictorial decoration makes it susceptible to classification into various sub-groupings, has contributed to invest it with an exaggerated importance. If allowance is made for the fact that almost all the more attractive examples were made by the single firm of Jennens and Bettridge, and that both they and the other leading firms such as Loveridge, Thomas Farmer, Dean and Benson, and Footherape, Showell and Shenton of Birmingham, and Walton of Wolverhampton, were mainly occupied in making trays and boxes rather than movable furniture as such, it is statistically obvious that the total output of papier-mâché furniture must always have formed a very small fraction of the wood furniture turned out by cabinet-makers in every large town in the country. It is, indeed, symptomatic that none of the half-dozen or so domestic and house-keeping manuals in general circulation before 1860 mention papier-mâché furniture at all.

There is only space here to mention the two main technical developments which influenced the appearance of the furniture. Both are to the credit of Jennens and Bettridge. In 1825 they patented the use of pearl-shell in papier-mâché decoration, and in 1847 of so-called 'gem-inlaying'. Both processes are found applied not only to papier-mâché proper, but also to the stained and painted wooden furniture which is often confused with it.

Coat of Arms of H.M. Queen Victoria from a printer's Specimen Book of 1850.

Painting and Sculpture

SIR DAVID WILKIE. King William IV, 1833. *Wellington Museum, London.*

PLATE 33

(A) SIR GEORGE HAYTER. Princess Augusta, 1837.
Courtesy John Quilter, Esq.

(B) JOHN PARTRIDGE. Sir Charles Eastlake.
c. 1825. *The National Portrait Gallery.*

(C) SIR CHARLES EASTLAKE. Mrs Bellenden
Kerr, 1835. *The Tate Gallery.*

(D) WILLIAM ETTY. James Atkinson, 1832.
Yorkshire Philosophical Society, York.

PLATE 34

(B) SIR EDWIN LANDSEER, Princess Victoire de Nemours, 1839.
Kensington Palace, London.
Reproduced by gracious permission of H.M. The Queen.

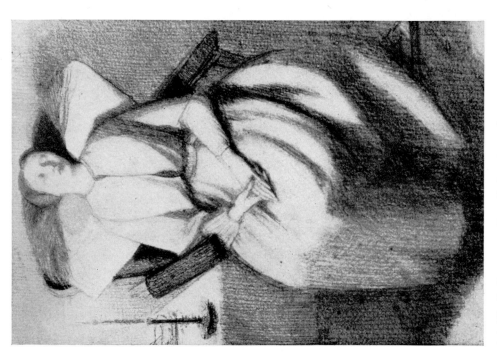

(A) D. G. ROSSETTI. Pencil drawing of Elizabeth Siddal,
c. 1860. Courtesy Sir Kenneth Clark.

PLATE 35

(B) F. X. WINTERHALTER. Harriet, Duchess of Sutherland, 1849. *Courtesy the Duke of Sutherland.*

(A) G. F. WATTS. Augusta, Lady Castletown, 1846. *The Tate Gallery.*

PLATE 36

SIR CHARLES EASTLAKE. Pilgrims arriving in Sight of Rome, 1828. *Woburn Abbey, Courtesy the Duke of Bedford.*

PLATE 37

(A) SIR EDWIN LANDSEER. Van Ambrugh and his Animals, 1839. *Buckingham Palace.*
Reproduced by gracious permission of H.M. The Queen.

(B) DANIEL MACLISE. *Detail from* Death of Nelson, 1865. *House of Lords, London.*

PLATE 38

(A) DAVID SCOTT. Philoctetes left by the Greek Fleet, 1840.
The National Gallery, Scotland.

(B) EDWARD ARMITAGE. Samson 'But the Philistines took him', 1851. *Whereabouts unknown.*

PLATE 39

(A) WILLIAM DYCE. King Joash Shooting the Arrow of Deliverance, 1844.
Kunsthalle, Hamburg.

(B) H. P. BRIGGS. First Conference between the Spaniards and Peruvians, 1531, *c.* 1826.
The Tate Gallery.

PLATE 40

(B) WILLIAM MULREADY. A Dog of Two Minds, 1830.
Walker Art Gallery, Liverpool.

(A) WILLIAM MULREADY. Burchell and Sophia in the Fields, 1847.
Courtesy Lord Northbrook.

PLATE 41

(A) E. M. WARD. Lord Lytton in his Study, 1851.
Courtesy Lady Hermione Cobbold.

(B) AUGUSTUS EGG. Queen Elizabeth discovers that she is no longer Young, 1848.
Whereabouts unknown.

PLATE 42

(A) WILLIAM ETTY. Hero and Leander, 1829.
Courtesy Mrs E. J. Britten.

(B) SIR DAVID WILKIE. The Peep O'Day Boy's Cabin, 1836. *The Tate Gallery.*

PLATE 43

(A) SIR DAVID WILKIE. Study for Mary
Queen of Scots Escaping from Loch
Leven, 1837. *City Art Gallery, Birmingham*

(B) SIR DAVID WILKIE. Mehemet Ali, wash
drawing, 1841. *The Tate Gallery.*

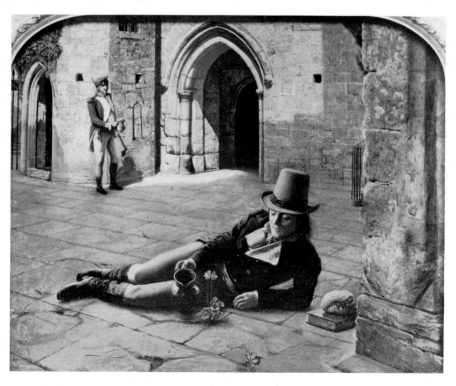

(C) R. B. MARTINEAU. Picciola, 1853. *The Tate Gallery.*

PLATE 44

(A) W. Holman Hunt. Rienzi, 1849. *Courtesy Mrs E. M. Clarke.*

(B) Ford Madox Brown. An English Autumn Afternoon, 1854. *City Art Gallery, Birmingham.*

PLATE 45

(A) D. G. ROSSETTI. Sir Galahad at the Ruined Chapel, 1859.
City Art Gallery, Birmingham.

(B) SIR JOHN MILLAIS. The Disentombment of Queen Matilda, 1849. *The Tate Gallery.*

PLATE 46

(A) JOHN E. CAREW. Henry Wyndham, 1831.
Courtesy John Wyndham, Esq.

(B) WILLIAM BEHNES. Prince George of Cumberland, 1828. *Windsor Castle, by gracious permission of H.M. The Queen.*

(C) THOMAS WOOLNER. Alfred, Lord Tennyson, 1857.
Trinity College, Cambridge.

(D) JOHN GIBSON. Queen Victoria, 1848.
Corporation of Liverpool.

PLATE 47

(A) JOSEPH DURHAM. Waiting his Innings, 1866.
Corporation of London, City of London School.

(B) WILLIAM THEED THE YOUNGER. Narcissus,
c. 1847. *Buckingham Palace. Reproduced by gracious
permission of H.M. The Queen.*

(C) JOHN E. CAREW. Adonis and
the Boar, 1826. *Courtesy John
Wyndham, Esq.*

PLATE 48

Painting and Sculpture

JOHN WOODWARD

Portraiture

King George IV died in 1830, surviving by only a few months the painter who had served him so well as Regent and King. Sir Thomas Lawrence had created not only a splendid visual image of his master, but had brought to a superb and fitting climax the lifelong passion of George IV for surrounding himself with the portraits of the men of action of his day. The journeys undertaken in Europe to paint the portraits of those persons who had helped to bring about the ultimate overthrow of Napoleon, and destined for the Waterloo Chamber at Windsor, had not only added to the reputation of Lawrence himself, but had also brought about an entirely new respect for English Art. Although the influence of Lawrence continued to be noticeable for some years, taste was changing towards a more solid and domestic type of portraiture, more consistent with the changing style of costume and the return to a more domestic way of life. The sparkle, 'chic', and soulful sensitivity of Lawrence's men and women were alien to the Victorian drawing-room, bearing as they did something of the lightness of behaviour of their times.

The new King, William IV, turned wisely to Sir David Wilkie for his first official likeness, and the result was one of the most imposing, but neglected, portraits produced by an artist in the nineteenth century (Pl. 33). Wilkie's earliest portraits, such as the *Mr Morrison and Miss Bethune* 1805), were painted very much in the Raeburn tradition of solidarity and truth of character, but

they lacked subtlety. His fellow Scotsman Andrew Geddes in his early *Self-portrait*, or in the portraits of his mother, is far more arresting and sympathetic. Wilkie, however, found his true *métier* in small cabinet portraits which were among his greatest achievements, and which come as a welcome relief among the acres of canvas used for vapid and stiff full-lengths which the less-gifted fashionable painters have left us. These small paintings vary from crowded conversation pieces such as the *Neave Family* of 1810 to his undoubted masterpiece of *The Duke of York* (1823, National Portrait Gallery). His only competitor in this genre is perhaps Geddes, who painted the exquisite small portrait of Wilkie himself leaning on a chair. By 1830 Wilkie had abandoned these small-scale portraits and embarked on the grand full lengths inspired by his continental travels. They were thought to be Spanish, but were, in fact, much more in the style of Lawrence worked with the palette of Rembrandt and with reminiscences of the swirl and dash of Rubens. Unfortunately, many of these have been eaten away by bitumen, but those that remain – *George IV* (Apsley House), *Duke of Sussex* (Buckingham Palace), and *The Earl of Kellie* (Cupar Town Hall, Fifeshire) – are extremely impressive in colour and pose and with a solidarity of stance and cast of countenance that is reminiscent of the full-length figures in Holbein's Whitehall fresco. The full-length of William IV is the most remarkable achievement of Wilkie as a portrait painter. He has chosen to represent the Sailor King in the uniform of the Grenadier Guards using his

E

'Rembrandt–Rubens' manner with strong lighting contrasts and thick creamy paint. The painting of the cock's feathers of the hat is in itself a fine passage of still-life. It is hard now to understand why one critic found it 'stiff and starched as any drill Sergeant, glittering with varnish'. It is stark, and curiously still, in comparison with the sumptuous, restless, Coronation portrait of George iv by Lawrence, but it matches it in dignity, never allowing the pale face of the old King to be swamped by the scarlet of his uniform. Sir Martin Archer Shee, who succeeded Lawrence as President of the Royal Academy, was a far better man of affairs than he was portrait painter; and his work is consistent but seldom inspiring, and never reached the efficiency and breadth of his successor, Sir Francis Grant.

Younger painters, trained abroad and influenced more by continental Academic portraits than by Lawrence, dominated the early years of Queen Victoria's reign, and she herself had no doubts, as she confided to her diary, that George Hayter was the best portrait painter living. Hayter had gone to Italy to study when a very young man, and had produced while there some sensitive drawings of his family and of Italian life, as well as harbouring ambitions to be a history painter. On his return to England he quickly built up a lucrative practice, but his matrimonial troubles, although known and condoned by the Queen, kept him outside the Royal Academy. He was never a very gifted painter, alternating between lyrical but rather insubstantial full-length portraits and rather sombre and solemn half-lengths. None the less, he rose far higher than could reasonably be expected in his State portrait of Queen Victoria, seated crowned and holding the sceptre (National Portrait Gallery), a portrait so well known that its merits are sometimes overlooked and which is perhaps the most endearing State portrait of an English monarch that we have. Youth, dignity and ease are all suggested, and it blazes out, with its powerful colouring, among the portraits of black-coated statesmen who surround it in the Portrait Gallery. The extent of Hayter's achievement can be seen in the abysmal failures of Wilkie and Archer Shee to rise to the occasion in

their own portraits of the Queen. It is not without significance that the Queen commissioned a portrait of Lord Melbourne from Hayter, as she so strongly disliked the 'daub' by Lawrence. Melbourne himself, so the Queen records in her diary, had no doubt that C.R.Leslie was the best portrait painter of the day. In the 'forties Hayter, after a railway accident and a disagreement with the Prince Consort, gradually began to fall from favour, and as his star waned, royal patronage fell on F.X.Winterhalter, a painter of charm, from the Black Forest, whose earliest work in England is attractive but somewhat spoiled by some coarse painting; but he left a series of paintings without which our understanding of the Queen, her family and her Court would be considerably less than it is. Winterhalter worked at all the principal European capitals, and it is to his credit that all his sitters so completely belong to their own country. There is no attempt to place a Tuileries Second Empire gloss over Buckingham Palace or the Hofburg. His grandest English portraits are those of *The Duchess of Sutherland* (Pl. 36B), and *The Duke of Beaufort* (Badminton, Gloucestershire). Hayter had spent much of his time in the composition of vast group assemblages which are, despite their overwhelming mass portraiture, extremely able. The first of these, *The Trial of Queen Caroline* (1823, National Portrait Gallery), contained 186 portraits, and his last, *The House of Commons* (1833, National Portrait Gallery), had 375 portraits. This labour, seemingly of love, made enormous demands on his time and energy, but the portrait sketch-heads made for these finished works are among his best work, free in handling and clear in colouring (Pl. 34A). There was a demand for such assembly pieces during the whole century, and many of the commissions came from the Queen. C.R.Leslie, John Phillip, E.M.Ward, and W.P.Frith were all employed in this way; but although their standard was high, none of them excelled Hayter. The style was to deteriorate into what may be called 'Guildhall Processional'.

The taste of the Court reflected that of the nation as a whole; and there were painters, such as John Lucas, J.C.Horsley and Sir John Watson

Gordon, who could be relied on to give a solid performance and to produce portraits to be added to the family gallery or adorn public institutions. John Partridge, who had studied in Italy, was, perhaps, rather more talented, and had a gift for finding a correct and uncommon pose for his sitter and also experimented with the horizontal half-length, as in the portrait of Lord Aberdeen (National Portrait Gallery), which allowed him to paint more of the sitter's surroundings. An album of sketches of artists working in Italy in 1825 has recently been purchased by the Portrait Gallery and includes a portrait of *Charles Lock Eastlake* (Pl. 34B).

Some of the most pleasing portraits were those emanating from painters whose main work was not primarily concerned with portraiture. Sir Edwin Landseer must be considered first both for his charming conversation pieces, with or without animals, and for his single figure portraits. Queen Victoria made constant use of his brush for depicting herself, her Consort, the royal children, and the royal pets. When the painter died, she recorded in her diary that she had 'thirty-nine oil paintings of his, sixteen chalk drawings (framed), two frescoes, and many sketches'. These works include the well-known conversation piece with dead game, which depicts the Queen, Prince and their eldest child in a room at Windsor, while visible through the window is the old Duchess of Kent being propelled through the gardens in her bath chair; the sketch for this is at Kensington Palace. That the painter had a nice sense of humour is evident from the small portrait of *Princess Victoire de Nemours*, the Queen's Coburg cousin, where the juxtaposition of the lady's hair and the dog's ears cannot be entirely accidental (Pl. 35B). A perfect gift for the painter was *Van Ambrugh and his Animals*, which allowed him one human and a great variety of animal life (Pl. 38A). The collection of family portraits belonging to the Duke of Abercorn and the unfinished *John Gibson* (Royal Academy) show him at his best as a straightforward recorder of the human face. Sir Charles Eastlake painted a few portraits, and among these, one, of great charm and brilliance of colour, of Mrs Bellenden Kerr as an Italian Contadina (Pl. 34C); but as Lady Eastlake remarked: 'These "fancy portraits" as they were called were greatly admired, and would have filled his hands with this class of occupation, had he not pertinaciously refused to devote himself to portraiture'. William Etty also produced several portraits of his family and friends of great strength of perception, an example being *James Atkinson* (Pl. 34D). Daniel Maclise rose to dramatic heights in at least two portraits, *Macready as Werner* (Victoria and Albert Museum) and *Lord Lytton* (Knebworth). John Linnell painted on a smaller scale some portraits of extreme delicacy, which are sometimes marred by a rather woolly application of paint; but his portrait drawings of Blake (Fitzwilliam Museum, Cambridge) are masterpieces. George Richmond was a competent craftsman, but his more delicate painting and drawing (often in silver-point) tend to be over-weighted, in any assessment of his work, by his full-size competent, historically important, but deadly dull drawings of heads done in black chalk heightened with white. His self-portraits in the Birmingham Art Gallery and the Uffizi seem to have been influenced by Raphael and the German Nazarene painters. One of the most splendid portrait drawings of the period is the *Self-portrait* by Samuel Palmer (Ashmolean Museum, Oxford), where the painter has boldly projected his features and managed to convey the short-sightedness of his natural vision.

Those artists who formed or are connected with the Pre-Raphaelite Brotherhood between 1848 and 1862 all painted remarkable portraits, but thereafter their taste and skill deteriorated in a marked fashion, degenerating into either extreme affectation or into the realms of 'pot-boiling'. J.E. Millais is the most obvious case in point if one compares the sparkling jewel-like portraits of *James Wyatt and his Grand-daughter* (1849) and its companion, or the stern authority of *Ruskin at Glenfinlas* (1854) with the weakly painted acade-mical likenesses of his later years. D.G.Rossetti left a touching and perpetual record of Elizabeth Siddal in the hundreds of delicate studies he made of her during their life together (Pl. 35A). Her death in 1862 – a date which makes such a convenient dividing line in the study of the Brotherhood's work – caused the features of Jane Morris and professional models to dominate his later work, which is on a larger and coarser scale. Holman Hunt also in his youthful self-portraits and in his *Canon Jenkins* (Jesus College, Oxford) showed an intimacy and spontaneity which later left him entirely, though his Portrait of *Wentworth Monk* (Ottawa) has a direct and rather alarming impact. Madox Brown painted few portraits but his *Self-portrait*, which so exactly mirrors his character as it is known to us, and his studies of his wife Emma make one regret that he did not turn his talents in this direction more often. One of the most hauntingly romantic portraits of this period is that of *Swinburne* by William Bell Scott (Balliol College, Oxford), where the small red-haired poet is posed against a part of the Northumbrian coast.

Lord Leighton in 1853 painted oval companion portraits of himself and his sister, Mrs Sutherland Orr, which clearly mirror his continental training and his knowledge of the Nazarenes in Germany. G.F.Watts, whose main work lies outside the boundary of 1860, painted some of his best portraiture when he was in Florence as the guest of Lord Holland in the 'forties and in his first years at Little Holland House. These include the studies of *Lady Holland* (Buckingham Palace and Compton), the full lengths of *Augusta, Lady Castletown* (1846, Tate Gallery) (Pl. 36A), an immature but ambitious attempt at grand portraiture, and the *Sir Anthony Panizzi* and *Princess Lieven* (both in the collection of the Earl of Ilchester). One of his most remarkable portraits dates from 1862, of *Lady Margaret Beaumont and her Daughter*, a work redolent of the era and strangely 'Gothick' in its pose and treatment.

The portrait painter had a constant patronage through the early nineteenth century not only from the Court and the aristocracy but also from the middle classes, whose wealth and social standing were being steadily consolidated. Many portraits were painted as deliberate bait for the visitors to the Royal Academy, and there was a steady flow of orders from civic authorities, institutions and colleges for the likenesses of their distinguished members and alumni. The sombre and solid worth of the majority of these likenesses is intensified by the dark clothes of the men, usually posed against dark backgrounds, and later by the fashion for wearing a beard, which was no less of a handicap to a painter than the wig had been to those of the later seventeenth century. Occasionally a painter could enliven his dark palette by a glittering fob or watch-chain. With women and with children it was easier to achieve a gayer colour scheme and a lighter background, but first the spaniel-ear arrangement of ringlets followed by the very severe arrangement of the hair smoothly across the head made the painter's task a heavy one. This severity of dress and hairdressing for both men and women has had a corresponding effect on the judgement of posterity on portraits painted between 1830 and 1860.

Historical painting

Thackeray had some wise remarks to make on the state of historical painting in England when, under the name of Michelangelo Titmarsh, in 1842 he wrote of the painters:

'They wisely, I think, avoid those great historical "parades" which cover so much space in the Louvre. A young man has sometimes a fit of what is called "historical painting"; comes out with a great canvas, disposed in the regular six-feet heroical order; and having probably half ruined himself in the painting of his piece, which nobody (let us be thankful for it!) buys, curses the decayed state of taste in the country, and falls to portrait-painting, or takes small natural subjects, in which the world can sympathise, and with which he is best able to grapple.'

In the following year he said much the same thing:

'They do not aim at such great subjects as heretofore, or at subjects which the world is pleased to call great, viz., tales from Hume or Gibbon or royal personages under various circumstances of battle, murder, and sudden death. Lemprière too is justly neglected, and Milton has quite given place to *Gil Blas* and *The Vicar of Wakefield*. The heroic, and peace be with it! has been deposed; and our artists, in place, cultivate the pathetic and the familiar.'

Certainly the old historical themes were dying out and the proud titles such as *Edward the Con-*

fessor Spoiling his Mother or *Scenes from the Life of Elizabeth Woodville*, which figure so frequently in the earlier catalogues of the Royal Academy, were no longer tempting painters. Vanishing too were the heroic allegorical subjects summed up again by Thackeray as *Britannia, Guarded by Religion and Neptune, Welcoming General Tomkins in the Temple of Glory*. The majority of visitors to the Royal Academy were intelligent and well-read families, who indeed spent a good deal of their quiet domestic evenings reading aloud to each other from history and from fiction. They therefore studied critically the attempts of painters to bring to life the people and scenes familiar to them from the written word. It was not a coincidence that the *Vicar of Wakefield* found so many painters eager to render the ever-popular episodes.

History painting during the period 1830–60 can roughly be divided into five main groups.

1. *The Grand Style*. This had fewer devotees than in the previous fifty years, but the teaching and inspiration of Reynolds lingered on in a few minds; and the irrepressible Benjamin Robert Haydon was always at hand to preach the cause of grand art and to cover acres of canvas, inspired by those 'perpetual urgings to future greatness' with what must be admitted were rather arid results. His most engaging works are the *Cassandra* and *Venus and Anchises* (S.A.Oliver Esq.), which have recently reappeared. It could be argued that Haydon has done a great disservice to the study of history paintings by being such an essential and key figure in its structure. We know so much of his hopes and failures and 'the hum of mighty workings' from his own writings that in assessing first the tragedy and then his disappointing canvases there is a tendency to ignore all the other painters who were working in the same vein.

The decoration of the New Palace of Westminster, which arose after the disastrous fire of 1834, led to grandiose schemes which were to engage many painters between 1841 and 1863. There were those who admired the frescoes of the German painter Peter Von Cornelius, but rather deplored the system of the 'master mind' and pupils which it entailed. Eastlake urged that the frescoes of Raphael should be followed rather than

German Christian art. Lady Eastlake, his remarkable and intelligent consort, had found Cornelius' work extremely boring: 'He is the great gun of German Art, and a mere pop-gun in reality: covers miles of cartoon with what are called grand historical compositions, and which consist of an endless repetition of ill-drawn figures of the largest size and the smallest interest.' Prince Albert was made President of a commission to study the scheme for decoration, and Eastlake was the secretary. A competition was announced for cartoon drawings illustrating subjects from British History, or from the works of Spenser, Shakespeare or Milton. Haydon, to whom the whole idea was so dear, failed to gain one of the premiums. The final decorations are disappointing, but the work of William Dyce, A.C.Cope and Daniel Maclise merits more attention than it is usually allotted. The two major works of this scheme are the great frescoes by Daniel Maclise in the Royal Gallery, *The Death of Nelson* (detail, Pl. 38B) and *The Meeting of Wellington and Blücher*. Time and central heating have blackened these works, but the scenes of carnage which surround his central groups are indicative of his ability to draw and compose. The end of the commission saw the end of the desire for a national school of history painting, and the new generation of painters moved out of the Medieval or Early Christian world into the sumptuous marble surroundings of Greece and Rome as conjured up from the brushes of Lord Leighton, Sir Lawrence Alma Tadema and Albert Moore.

One or two painters of the Grand Style deserve a passing reference, and in particular David Scott, from Edinburgh, who worked on a gigantic scale and studied the Old Masters. Unlike Haydon, he travelled abroad and assimilated something of Delacroix and Géricault from France, as can be seen in his *Philoctetes Left on the Island of Lemnos* (Pl. 39A) and the German Nazarene style in his *Vintager*. On a smaller scale he painted one of the best Victorian history pictures, *The Traitors' Gate*. All of these are in the National Gallery of Scotland in Edinburgh.

Another neglected but historically important figure is Edward Armitage, a student under Paul

Delaroche in Paris, and who was the winner of one of the Premiums for the Palace of Westminster decoration. After visiting Rome he began to exhibit battle-scenes and history pieces. But it is his Biblical subjects, many admittedly painted after 1860, which are his chief monument. Rather statuesque in quality, but filled with glowing rich colour, they make an imposing impact on the spectator. The best of these are *Samson, But the Philistines Took Him* (1851, whereabouts unknown) (Pl. 39B) and *Esther's Banquet* (R.A. Diploma work, 1865). Paul Falconer Poole was another ambitious composer of historical groups, but at times he almost caricatures the style and shows all the dangers that lay in wait for a painter of mediocre talents. His *Solomon Eagle* is an excellent example of history getting out of hand and verging on the ridiculous. *The Visitation of Syon Nunnery* is a better venture in this vein, but his best work is probably *The Death of Cordelia* (Victoria and Albert Museum).

2. *The Medieval Style.* This term is only a very general one to cover the Early Victorian interest in the period of English history stretching from Harold to the death of Edward III. It is sometimes called *style troubadour*. This same interest can be seen in the vast tournament which was held in the grounds of the Earl of Eglington's castle in Ayrshire in 1839, a magnificent spectacle, somewhat spoilt by rain, and there are commemorative portraits by Francis Grant and Edwin Landseer of participants wearing armour. Later, a Court fancy-dress ball was held at Buckingham Palace with the Queen as Queen Philippa and Prince Albert as Edward III, and Landseer painted a double portrait to commemorate this (Buckingham Palace). Eastlake made several sorties, from his beloved Italy, into this period of history, and one of his most remarkable achievements is a painting full of his knowledge of the Venetian School, *The Champion* (Birmingham), which shows a knight wearing armour and a helmet having a favour tied to his arm by a lady who might have been painted by Paris Bordone. Maclise was also a successful exponent of a style which was to reach its climax in Landseer's *Chevy Chase* (Birmingham) and *Scene in the Olden Time at*

Bolton Abbey. Henry Perronet Briggs is remembered now mainly as a portrait painter, but his historical works should give him a more solid position if such works as *First Conference between the Spaniards and Peruvians* (Tate, Pl. 40B) and *The Challenge of Rodomont to Ruggiero* (Birmingham) are taken into consideration. This medieval style has dug deeply into the visual impressions of history not only because of the engravings which appeared in innumerable nineteenth- or early twentieth-century history books, but also for the influence it has had on the stage and on film companies.

3. *Biblical.* Apart from essays of Haydon, Maclise and Armitage, and, later in the century, Solomon J. Solomon, in grand Biblical painting, a new attitude was apparent. Wilkie, on the eve of his journey to the Holy Land, explained to his nephew his enthusiasm for the immense advantage he might derive from painting upon holy land, on the very ground on which the event he was to embody had actually occurred. One of his last works was a small painting of *Christ before Pilate*, and it may well be indicative of the work he would have done if he had lived longer. This doctrine of geographical accuracy was taken to its furthest point by Holman Hunt. William Dyce, inspired both by Raphael and the German Nazarene painters, produced his small Biblical works, which are beautiful in form and colour and strike an ideal middle course between sentiment and cold purity as in *Joash drawing the Bow* (Hamburg, Pl. 40A). His style was to change under Pre-Raphaelite influence. The indignant outcry of Charles Dickens against Millais' *Carpenter's Shop* shows how even an intelligent mind could react to a change in accepted fashions. It is not perhaps surprising that the Pre-Raphaelites should have found their main patrons among the new rich manufacturers from industrial cities, whose minds were less encumbered by knowledge of earlier styles and fashions in painting.

4. *Literary and Historical.* The eighteenth-century habit of depicting scenes from literature in a markedly theatrical manner, and with the characters wearing clothes reminiscent more of the prop. basket than of the period of history por-

trayed, dissolved into two streams. The influence of Charles Robert Leslie is very apparent in both trends. One of these was pure illustration born of the painter's imagination and inspired by his readings. Illustrations to novels and plays were increasingly popular during this period and reflect the current trends in domestic reading and family playgoing. Shakespeare was still popular, but the other authors so much favoured by the earlier generation gave way to Cervantes, Molière, Sterne and Addison. The greatest favourites were the ever-popular *Vicar of Wakefield* and, more strangely, *Gil Blas*. Thackeray became so tired of scenes from the last two that he threatened never to notice any of them again. However, his good resolution was shattered when he saw and greatly admired William Mulready's two scenes from Goldsmith in the Academies of 1844 and 1847. *The Whistonian Controversy* and *Burchell and Sophia in the Fields* (Pl. 41A) (both in the collection of Lord Northbrook), two of his best works, fine in colour and capturing the spirit of the novel. *Choosing the Wedding Gown* (Victoria and Albert Museum, London), a scene from the same book, is an equally charming and affectionate rendering. Leslie's *Autolycus* (1836, Bethnal Green Museum, London), is one of the best of all nineteenth-century attempts to illustrate Shakespeare on a modest scale. The pictures in this stream, although by the very nature of things somewhat dated, have none the less a timeless quality that best serves an author or a reader at the hands of an illustrator.

The next group to be noticed were more theatrical, or perhaps it would be clearer to describe them as charades taking place in the painter's studio. The men and women are clearly models dressed up and have the marked self-conscious air of dancers at a fancy-dress ball. W.P.Frith was a bad offender in this respect, and even the quality of his painting will not efface this conclusion. Towards the end of his long life this feeling of dressing-up became more marked and was the parent of academy period pieces which one associates with children in mob caps and Marcus Stone and E.A.Abbey. E.M.Ward is never at ease in the world of the French Revolution,

which he loved to depict, and one can never feel the tragedy of the *Family in the Temple*; but infinitely preferable is his portrait of *Lord Lytton* (Knebworth, Pl. 42A). Augustus Egg, however, in *Queen Elizabeth Discovers that She is no longer Young* (Pl. 42B), has achieved a more timeless and truly historical illustration.

5. *Academic*. The main exponent of academic historical painting was William Etty. He was born in York in 1787, and was to remain devoted to his native city for the whole of his life. His painting life was built around the life-class of the Royal Academy, where he devoted himself to 'God's most glorious work, Woman'. A visit to Italy instilled into him a love of Venetian colouring, and his subsequent work was to unite this rich colouring to academic forms. His grand compositions were to reflect overmuch the conscious posing of his models and, therefore, to rob them of spontaneity. His appeal was more to the senses than to the intellect. But his work is far more romantic than coldly classical and his paint is juicy, glowing and fluent. His greatest works are his *Judgement of Paris* (Port Sunlight, Cheshire), *Pandora* (Leeds) and *Judith* (Edinburgh); but one of his most memorable canvases is the *Hero and Leander* (Mrs E.J.Britten) (Pl. 43A), which is both romantic and dramatic and yet academically posed. His many male and female nude studies, often left unfinished and then tidied up by lesser hands, have flooded the dealers in recent times and caused his reputation to be engulfed. His landscape and still-life painting has been neglected and his portraiture has only recently been re-valued. In a work such as *The Repentant Prodigal's Return to his Father* (Ashmolean Museum, Oxford), which relies on no academic nudes, we can appreciate his gift for straightforward narrative in the simplest terms, and his rich handling of paint. Etty must always remain an isolated figure, and yet in his knowledge and application he remains essentially an artist of his own time.

Genre Painting

The painting of scenes from English everyday life did not really become popular until the early years of the nineteenth century. This new demand was probably inspired by Dutch cabinet pictures of the seventeenth century which were being collected by certain discerning connoisseurs led by the Regent. In 1812, Edward Bird painted *Choristers Rehearsing*, which was bought by the Regent; a companion was commissioned but never finished. Bird, in fact, preferred painting scenes from Shakespeare and from history. The most important English genre artist, David Wilkie, was born in the manse at Cults, Fife, in 1785. His earliest work was influenced by engravings after Teniers and Ostade. *Pitlessie Fair*, painted when he was only nineteen, is an astonishingly able composition, but the colour range shows clearly that he knew Teniers only through the engraver. In London, where he settled in 1804, he quickly established his reputation and found patrons eager to buy or commission his scenes from Scottish peasant life. His treatment was free from the rustic sweetness and 'Petit Trianon-like' make-believe of the previous century; but they are filled with anecdote and humour, bordering sometimes on caricature, to make them completely palatable. They were never to startle or dismay in the way that Courbet was to startle Paris when he painted the inhabitants of Ornans. Courbet depicted his peasants in a strictly realistic way, without subsidiary anecdote, and on a scale usually associated with history painting. George IV purchased Wilkie's *Penny Wedding* and *Blind Man's Buff* for the royal collection, and he was the first artist of his generation to be hung in the National Gallery. His early works are tightly painted, and the amount of thought that went into their composition can be gauged from the innumerable pen-and-chalk drawings and oil studies which he did as preliminary workings. Wilkie, in fact, almost equals Rubens in the amount of preparatory work that went towards the finished composition. His style broadened after a visit to Spain and Italy, and still found favour with George IV who purchased several examples. It was held in his lifetime, and by many today, that his style deteriorated. Thackeray, as he surveyed Wilkie's later work, sighed for the earlier genre and found his looser brush work, muddier colour and Rembrandtesque lighting a sad tumble from the incident-packed

earlier canvases. His middle and later works are in fact, very fine, and one of them, *Peep O' Day Boy's Cabin* (1836, Tate Gallery) (Pl. 43B) has some claims to be his masterpiece. His last rich colourful sketches and drawings were not seen by the public and critics until the posthumous sale of his works a year after his death and burial at sea, in 1841. His wash drawings (Pl. 44A) have deservedly come to be much sought after and revalued today.

William Mulready, an Irishman, worked at first in a style directed by Wilkie's earlier phase. He was, in fact, to change his method of painting several times, but always, after some initial stumbling, to master it. He worked on a small scale with no further ambition than to depict a scene with sympathy and clarity. His scenes from contemporary life had no social message and are painted with a glowing sense of colour and with perfect underlying drawing. His soundness as an academic draughtsman gives a greater solidarity to his work and raises him above his imitators. He was not only the perfect illustrator to Goldsmith (Pl. 41A), but could render in *The Sonnet* (Victoria and Albert Museum) all the tenderness and embarrassment of young love, as well as the expectation and shyness of reading and showing a self-revelatory poem. He was also fond of depicting the joys and squabbles of children as in *A dog of two minds* (Liverpool, Pl. 41B). Redgrave found violence and a lack of social consciousness in his work and complained that his peasants were too refined. To some extent this point of view is perhaps true and is indicative of his own uneasy temperament, but his pictures give, today, the same pleasure that they gave to his contemporaries. Apart from his anecdotal work, his *Interior of an English Cottage*, purchased by George IV, remains one of his most hauntingly lovely pictures, with its still serenity and soft pink light.

Thomas Webster was another faithful recorder of village life, and his *Village Choir* (Victoria and Albert Museum) or *The Playground* (Christopher Loyd) continue to remain popular favourites. B.R.Haydon in *Punch* or *Chairing the Member* moved from the grand style into London Life. Edwin Landseer painted shepherds in their natural surroundings in the Highlands as well as royal sporting occasions. His animals often hovered on the wrong side of sentimentality, but were lovingly and beautifully rendered. Richard Redgrave was far more direct in his appeal to sentiment, finding his heroines among mournful widows and depressed governesses. Augustus Leopold Egg was to become the friend and patron of the early Pre-Raphaelites, and his own style altered under their impact. In his new style he painted *The Travelling Companions* (Birmingham), two young ladies in their carriage passing the Mentone coast oblivious of the scenery and his dramatic *Past and Present* (Tate), a commentary in three canvases on the sadness of children when their parents fail to keep sacred the marriage vow. R.B.Martineau also pursued a similar subject in *The Last Day in the Old Home* (Tate), but his more pleasing works are *Picciola* (Tate, Pl. 44c) and *Kit's Writing Lesson* (Tate). The sincerity and skill of these works were almost buried by the social documentaries and moralizing sermons exhibited by many of their brother artists in the annual Academy.

William Collins, the father of Wilkie and Charles Alston, is of an earlier generation, but his peaceful scenes of country and seashore are a happy blend of genre and landscape and are some of the most pleasant and unassuming works of their time.

One artist has enjoyed an almost continual popularity for his popular scenes from Victorian life. W.P.Frith has left in his *Autobiography* a vivid account of his life's work from his early days and fame to the end of his long life, when he had somewhat outlived his earlier esteem with the critics. *Ramsgate Sands* (Buckingham Palace); *Derby Day* (Tate); and *The Railway Station* (Royal Holloway College, London) are always assured of an affectionate place in any anthology of Victorian painting. Nor must this sentiment for his work make one blind to his ability to compose and paint.

The Pre-Raphaelite painters and Ford Madox Brown were all fascinated by scenes from contemporary life. Rossetti dragged himself from his Arthurian and Dante studies to work on the moral picture *Found* (Bancroft Foundation, Wilmington, Delaware, U.S.A.), which was partly based on a poem by William Bell Scott. Holman Hunt went even further in preaching his moral in *The Awakening Conscience* (Sir Colin Anderson, London); but the great masterpiece in this vein to be produced by any member of the brotherhood is *The Blind Girl* (City Art Gallery, Birmingham), by J.E.Millais, a touching and yet unsentimental rendering of two tired figures seated in a landscape bathed in the light of a rainbow.

The Pre-Raphaelites

The term Pre-Raphaelite has been used, for far too long, as a convenient label attached to an untidy parcel of artists, flourishing between 1848 and 1880, many of whom had, in fact, nothing in common and whose painting sprang from different roots. The appellation Pre-Raphaelite should, in fact, belong only to the original Brotherhood, and not to Morris and Burne-Jones and their followers. The original Brotherhood was formed in 1848 and consisted of W.Holman Hunt, J.E. Millais, D.G.Rossetti, Thomas Woolner, F.G. Stephens, James Collinson and W.M.Rossetti. In 1850 their literary organ *The Germ* ceased to be produced and the Brotherhood was fast dissolving and by 1852 was extinct. 'So now,' as D.G.Rossetti wrote, 'the whole Round Table is dissolved.' The limited aims of these seven men have been stretched far further than the facts warrant, and the secret letters P.R.B., which occur on only three of their paintings, have, once revealed, been taken into the bosom of art history and used in a way that would have amazed them in later life; they all, with the exception of Hunt, believed that it was only a boyish enthusiasm. The original members of 1848 looked with disfavour at the annual exhibitions of the Royal Academy and in fact at all the damage that had been done to art since the time of Raphael. They floundered into a vague idea of early Christian art which was crystalized when they found a book of indifferent engravings by Lasinio, after the mural paintings in the Campo Santo at Pisa. These were Pre-Raphael, and so the name was born. The inevitable sad aftermath of the Brotherhood, men of such varied temperaments and ambitions, has been recorded by W.M.Rossetti:

'It is a sad and indeed a humiliating reflection that, after the early days of *camaraderie* and of genuine brotherliness had run their course, followed by a less brief period of amity and goodwill, keen antipathies severed the quondam P.R.B.s ... Woolner became hostile to Hunt, Dante Rossetti and Millais. Hunt became hostile to Woolner and Stephens, and in a minor degree to Dante Rossetti. Stephens became hostile to Hunt. Dante Rossetti became hostile to Woolner and in a minor degree to Hunt and Millais. Millais, being an enormously successful man while others were only commonly successful, did not perhaps become strictly hostile to anyone; he kept aloof however, from Dante Rossetti and I infer from Woolner.'

J.E. Millais was almost an infant prodigy. At sixteen he painted *Pizarro Seizing the Inca of Peru*, a remarkable performance perhaps influenced by Henry Perronet Briggs' *First Conference between the Spaniards and Peruvians*, 1826. (Pl. 40B). His early paintings and his masterly angular drawings are truly 'Pre-Raphael' (Pl. 46B) in spirit and touched with the lyrical beauty of Keats and Tennyson, his favourite poets, and their names conjure up the glowing jewel-like medieval world of his imagination – *Lorenzo and Isabella*; *Mariana*; *Ophelia*; and *The Return of the Dove to the Ark*. The furore caused by *The Carpenter's Shop* died down and was followed by his election to the Royal Academy in 1853. His marriage to Mrs Ruskin, and perhaps the new-found cares of family life, caused him to follow the amazing fluency of his brush and to become an over prolific painter of subject pieces and portraits. Sadder still was the extinction of his earlier gifts of poetry and imagination, which gave way, after 1857, to some unforgivable sentiment, and the voice of Keats was muffled by Tupper. Not all his later painting is bad; his technical ability never left him. He is reported to have said to Lady Constance Leslie, as he left, in tears, the retrospective exhibition of his work in 1886, 'In looking at my earliest pictures I have been overcome with chagrin that I so far failed in my maturity to fulfil the forecast of my youth.'

William Holman Hunt pursued to the end of his life what he believed to be the original aims of the Brotherhood. Like Millais, he studied nature closely, accepting and depicting everything seen, selecting and rejecting nothing, and firmly believing in the hard toil of obtaining verisimilitude of fact. His early work is ambitious and his composition and grouping in *Rienzi* (Pl. 45A) and *The Converted British Family* is remarkably effective. His imagination was on a higher level than any other member of the Brotherhood, but his work was overladen by the very painstaking method he chose to adopt, and the lyrical moments which he achieved in *The Hireling Shepherd* were soon swamped by his exact reportage from the Holy Land. He saw colour 'without eyelids', and the resulting harshness detracts from his merit as a painter. In addition, the woollen garments worn by his figures have the quality and appearance of having been knitted from wire mesh and detract from his ability to paint the human face.

Dante Gabriel Rossetti was both painter and poet, and his enthusiasm soon overcame his early stumblings. To both Hunt and Millais, overawed by his infectious but suspicious temperament, he must have seemed only an amateur. He was deeply read in Dante and the Arthurian legends; and in the beauty of his future wife, Elizabeth Siddal, he found his ideal Beatrice and Guenevere. The glowing colours of his watercolours found many admirers, including Ruskin, though the latter failed to mould the character of his protegé in the way he would have liked. *Dante Drawing an Angel*, *Leah and Rachel* and *Sir Galahad* are among the finest of these works, far surpassing the *Girlhood of the Virgin Mary* or *Ecce Ancilla Domini*, which were his first major works before he met Miss Siddal. The many studies of his wife are among his best drawings; 'Drawers and drawers of lovely Guggums,' as Madox Brown observed. The long illness of Elizabeth Siddal, which ended in her death in 1862, witnessed a change in Rossetti's style, and the face and dark hair of Jane Morris came to dominate his work. His later style was coarser, and the early medieval vision was buried under the large-scale portraits of his favourite models, who were labelled with exotic-sounding names.

Of the rest of the Pre-Raphaelite Brotherhood little need be said; Collinson and Stephens painted only a few pictures; Woolner was a sculptor and

W.M.Rossetti never painted, but was to be the faithful friend and chronicler of the whole movement.

Two other painters were on the fringe of the movement, Walter Deverell who died young, and Arthur Hughes (Fig. 1). Hughes was one of the most delightful artists, and his early work is full of a poetic beauty which was to leave him towards the close of his long life. His early lyrical works are never too obvious in sentiment or lacking in craftsmanship. How nearly he bordered disaster is apparent in his titles, *Home from Sea*, *The Tryst*, and *April Love*; but his triumphant handling of his subject matter gives him an assured place in the group.

Ford Madox Brown was never a Pre-Raphaelite, thought often classed as one. His training had been in Belgium, and his work reflects the current continental theories closely: his *Chaucer* is a very German picture. Much emphasis has been laid on the influence of German painters, such as Cornelius and Overbeck, on the Brotherhood, but their aims, apart from a sort of cousinly resemblance, are not really apparent except in Brown. Brown was the lifelong friend of Rossetti, but to the end of his days he refrained from identifying himself with any section of the art world. His greatest contribution lies perhaps in his landscape painting (Pl. 45B), which is redolent of his great clarity of vision; though it is sometimes marred by violent use of colour. His scenes from everyday life and from history are well drawn and composed, but rather spoiled by the toothy grimaces of his figures. Brown's influence was negligible, but, none the less, he remains the most considerable figure of the period.

The sight of Millais' *Return of the Dove to the Ark* in an Oxford shop caused two Oxford undergraduates, Edward Burne-Jones and William Morris, to devote the rest of their lives to art. Burne-Jones was influenced in his early work by Rossetti, whom he admired as an artist and loved as a man, but his roots were entirely different from the Pre-Raphaelites and sprang from his visit to Italy and his admiration for Botticelli and Mantegna. His pale, elongated and wide-eyed beauties have often, mistakenly, been held up as the ideal Pre-Raphaelite type. Subtle as a draughtsman, it was his misfortune to drive his talents towards compositions which were far too large in scale to house his imagination comfortably. His subject-matter was set in a timeless age and he was content, unlike the Brotherhood, to tell a story as a story-book picture and not as a projection of probability. His attainments lie outside the period and his influence was to continue for many years.

Landscape

The landscapes shown each year at the Royal Academy were dominated by those of the veteran J.M.W. Turner until he ceased to exhibit in 1850. His later works clearly demonstrate, year by year, his attempts to render light at the expense of form. Such famous works as *The Fighting Téméraire*, *Rain, Steam and Speed*, and the interiors at *Petworth* were done at this time. John Constable died suddenly in 1837, and the rising generation could not be thought the equal of two such undoubted masters. The Early Victorians demanded landscapes, with or without figures and animals, which had a straightforward rendering of nature and the elements and the simple rustic life for the adornment of their rooms. The atmospheric effects of Constable or the frenzy of light in a Turner were not nearly so comprehensible as the mediocre landscapes of Augustus Callcott. Callcott was knighted in 1837, and it is not at all easy now to understand his popularity or reputation. His wife, Maria Graham, better known as the author of *Little Arthur's History of England*, was an important influence on young artists whom she asked to her home and whose careers she encouraged. Thomas Creswick and F.R.Lee were other popular but commonplace artists. So many painters added to the vast output of landscape painting during these thirty years that it is impossible to chronicle their work. Reference must, however, be made to the Romantic vision of Francis Danby as well as to his depiction of the sea in both its gentle calm and its rock-grazing fierceness. His *Upas Tree* (Victoria and Albert Museum) is a sad wreck but *Disappointed Love* in the same collection will serve as an example of his vein of romantic sensibility. In *The Sixth Seal* (Dublin) he essayed a John Martin-like biblical explosion, the full effect of which is now obscured by grime. E.W.Cooke painted the calm of a shore liberally strewn with lobster-pots, and T. Sidney Cooper was to spend the ninety-nine years of his life recording the placid existence of cows in the English landscape. Cooper's 'Cowscapes', as they are so often termed, have been too easily despised. He is vastly superior to the hoard of Highland-cattle painters who arose to decorate the English dining-room. Painters not always associated with landscape also made their considerable contribution. Landseer, the painter of domestic and wild animals, also produced some exquisite landscapes; and Eastlake varied his rather bookish historical style with views of the monuments of his much-loved Rome (Pl. 37). Richard Redgrave also occasionally left his over-sentimentalized interior scenes to paint the landscape outside. This he did feelingly as in *Valleys Thick with Corn* (Birmingham), though his hand lacked the necessary breadth of touch.

Certain painters travelled extensively abroad. James Holland found his inspiration by the canals of Venice, where he painted with a richly loaded palette, making an interesting comparison with the effervescent effects of Turner. W.J.Muller varied his style between passable attempts in the manner of Constable and reportage of life in the Near East. A composition with a Bedouin encampment, an oasis and a palm-tree was almost certain of an immediate sale.

The Romantic artists of the previous twenty years outlived the poetry of their early work. John Linnell lived until 1882, and his work is less spontaneous, but seldom dull. His son-in-law, Samuel Palmer, died a year earlier, and although he is rightly most esteemed for the work he did under deep inspiration and religious intensity of feeling at Shoreham in the 'twenties and 'thirties, his later work in both Italy and England shows a grasp of medium which should not be undervalued. His water-colours done in Rome are especially skilful and mirror the feelings of English artists for the monuments and people of the eternal city, the mecca of so many artists. His illustrations to Milton are over-hot in colour, with a pre-

ponderance of purple, and far the least pleasing of his work.

The importance of landscape in the work of the Pre-Raphaelites is discussed under that heading, but it can be stressed that Madox Brown is probably the best landscape painter of the period, even if the intensity of his colour is at first inspection rather too rich and raw. *Walton-on-the-Naze* (Birmingham), *The Hayfield* (S.J.Gillum, Esq.) and above all *An English Autumn Afternoon* (Pl. 45B) are remarkable achievements. They show all the necessary 'truth to nature', and because there is no breaking down into irritating and scientific detail they preserve the largeness of a sympathetic and loving vision. John Brett is the exact opposite, following slavishly the teachings of Ruskin and demonstrating a painstaking understanding of the underlying geology. William Dyce in *Pegwell Bay* (Tate) also shows an acute feeling for landscape but with a shade too much precision of touch at the expense of atmospheric effect. Madox Brown wrote of his *An English Afternoon* 'a literal transcript of the scenery round London, as looked at from Hampstead. The smoke is seen rising halfway above the fantastic shaped, small distant Armule, which accompany particularly fine weather. The upper portion of the sky would be blue, as seen reflected in the youth's hat, the grey mist of Autumn only rising a certain height. The Time is 3 p.m., when late in October the shadows already lie long, and the sun's rays (coming from behind us in this work) are preternaturally glowing, as in rivalry of the foliage. The figures are peculiarly English – they are hardly lovers – mere boy and girl neighbours and friends.'

If it is hard to list the landscape painters it is certainly harder to enumerate the countless artists who found a ready market for their water-colours. There was a demand for framed water-colours, with their gilt surrounds, to decorate the walls of houses great and small. The older generation had tended to keep water-colours with drawings and prints in portfolios. Now they were full-dress exhibits, and it could be argued that the decline in the English Water-colour School can be measured from the time the painter began to think more in terms of framed exhibition-pieces, and less in terms of a more intimate vision. The greatest, and perhaps the least understood in his lifetime, was J.S.Cotman, who felt deeply all that he saw in the silhouette of buildings and trees and the freshness of the landscape. David Cox was an uneven painter varying between a clogging heaviness of colour and sentiment and light brilliance which recalls the French eighteenth century. Redgrave said of him that 'the sparkle and shimmer of foliage and weedage, in the fitful breeze that rolls away the clouds from the watery sun, when the shower and the sunshine chase each other over the land, have never been given with greater truth than by David Cox'. The high standard of watercolour painting was not only to be found in the acknowledged masters but also in many amateur hands whose names have long since evaporated. Drawing masters, like the hero of *The Woman in White*, passed on their gifts to many a young lady or gentleman they were called upon to teach.

Travellers abroad

During the first thirty years of the nineteenth century many English artists made the pilgrimage to Rome, and several stayed there for long periods. They painted scenes from peasant life, sketched in the Campagna, and searched for models on the Spanish Steps. Several published letters and memoirs testify to their life there. Eastlake, indeed, seems to have been inspired to paint *The Spartan Isadas* (Chatsworth) after a rather similar incident had happened in a fire at Joseph Severn's house, but his best works are taken from the life around him. *Pilgrims in First Sight of Rome* (Woburn, Pl. 37) and *Peasant Woman Fainting from the Bite of a Snake* (Victoria and Albert Museum) are two of his most attractive canvases, which mirror the life he and his fellow artists sought and which inspired their subject-matter. Thomas Unwins is now a neglected and forgotten artist, but his *A Neapolitan Boy Decorating the Head of his Inamorata* and *An Italian Mother Teaching her Child the Tarantella*, both in the Victoria and Albert Museum, testify to his gaiety and sense of colour. Severn, forgetting Keats for a moment, produced a hauntingly romantic *Shelley*

in Rome (Keats–Shelley House, Rome). The inspiration they found in Rome was to be taken up by American artists, who were also drawn there and formed a similar colony. Later in the century Spain and the Near East was to draw John Frederick Lewis. Wilkie records in his letters his meeting with this artist, who had been absent from England so long. His works glow with a richer colour than those of any other artist, and today tend to be difficult to hang in other company for that reason. In fact, he achieved and recorded much more than Holman Hunt on the same territory. *The Doubtful Coin* (Birmingham) and *The Siesta* (Tate) are two excellent examples of his virtuosity. John Phillip, a Scotsman, spent most of his days in Spain, but his work is more *mouvmente* and fussy in grouping. His scenes are more studied from a picturesque angle of the ceremonies he witnessed, while Lewis preferred anecdotal reportage.

Sculpture

Four sculptors were to continue their craftsmanship into the period 1830–60 – years, in fact, which saw some of their finest works. Sir Francis Chantrey died in 1841 and his masterpiece *Mrs Jordan* (Earl of Munster) was completed ten years earlier, and his delicate bust of *Robert Southey* (National Portrait Gallery, London) dates from 1831. William Behnes lived until 1864, his busts and statues sometimes showing the delicacy of his earlier years, but at others demonstrating the dangers of over-productivity in a rather insensitive lumpiness. His bust of *Prince George of Cumberland* (Windsor, Pl. 47B) shows his skill with children. Samuel Joseph's two finest statues date from 1833 and 1842 respectively, namely his *William Wilberforce* (Westminster Abbey) and *David Wilkie* (Tate). A recent acquisition by the Victoria and Albert Museum is his bust of *George IV* (1831), a swagger piece which is almost a Lawrence done over in marble. John Gibson continued to be the doyen of English artists in Rome until 1866. His American pupil Harriet Hosmer described him as 'A God in his Studio but Heaven help him out of it.' His inability to cope with everyday life caused a railway porter in Italy to inquire if he was a foreigner. 'No,' replied Gibson, 'I am not a foreigner, I am a sculptor.' Twice he returned to England to make statues of Queen Victoria (Pl. 47D), the earlier of which he 'tinted' in the same way as his *Venus*. His great *Hunter and his Dog* dates from 1843.

The new generation produced no men as remarkable as these, though there was a continual demand for memorials, statues, busts and decorative works. The plethora of commissions seems almost to have deadened ingenuity, and the weight of white marble left in the churches and houses of England was to cause the best work to be unjustly neglected in a too-sweeping condemnation of the bulk.

E.H.Bailey was both a decorative and monumental sculptor. His work is uneven, but at its best comes close in quality to Chantrey. He made the statue of Nelson in Trafalgar Square. An excellent example of his wall monuments is that to the *Earl of Pomfret* (1830, Easton Neston). Joseph Durham trained under Bailey, and executed some worthy work, and is best known for his statue of the Prince Consort in front of the Albert Hall. *Waiting his Innings* (City of London School, Pl. 48A) is a charming rendering of youth, free of the sentiment that was soon to overwhelm nearly all sculpture of children, and his accuracy of detail ensures that even the studs in the boots are carefully sculpted. Resurrected for exhibition in Holland Park in 1957, it showed a surprising solidarity and perfection. On the other side of the Albert Hall towers the Albert Memorial, and John Foley was responsible for the statue of the *Prince Consort*, which was finished after his death, and which falls below his statue of *Charles Barry* in the Houses of Parliament. Much of his work is of the historical fancy-dress variety and fails to be convincing. A posthumous statue looks far more of an artificial fabrication than most painted historical scenes, and it would be a great boon to the world if worthy Societies would not attempt to commemorate the famous but long-dead by commissioning posthumous monuments and persuading deans to erect them. It may make good the neglect of an earlier age, but is seldom an ornament or a pleasure. The decoration of the new Houses of Parliament with statues of famous fighters for liberty, for two of which Foley is responsible, was a dismal error. His statues of *Outram* and *Hardinge* are in Calcutta. Patrick Macdowell is best known for his *Flora* (Royal Academy), and although his brother artist, Henry Weekes (Fig. 2), considered that he 'makes his appeal to our best and noblest feelings', this claim appears to be excessive. Weekes himself produced one of the best memorial busts of the period, *Robert Southey* (Westminster Abbey).

William Theed the younger was another pupil of Bailey, but who increased his knowledge of the neo-classical School by studying under Thorwalsden and Gibson. The influence of this School can be seen in his *Narcissus* (Buckingham Palace, Pl. 48B). He later left the neo-classical School and his *Queen Victoria and Prince Albert* in Anglo-Saxon costume, now in the Frogmore Mausoleum, Windsor, is one of his most startling works in this new manner. Richard Wyatt also studied in Rome, under Canova and Thorwalsden, and, like Gibson, settled there. He achieved fame late, but his *Glysera* and *Penelope* were both purchased by the Queen. Of the latter, the Hon. Georgiana Lidell wrote: 'Such a beautiful statue arrived here yesterday from Rome, a full length statue of Penelope by Wyatt, standing in a pensive attitude, with one hand on her heart and the other holding a crook, with a fine dog looking up in her face, the drapery is exceedingly graceful, and the expression of her beautiful countenance very lovely but sad. The Queen is much pleased with it and it is considered Wyatt's *chef d'œuvre*.'

John Lough was a controversial figure in his lifetime, either praised or execrated to excess by sections of the Press. His work could certainly be ludicrous and fussily flamboyant at times. *Milo* (Blagdon) is a fine work of great power and now shown magnificently in a setting by Lutyens, and his finest monument is that to *Bishop Middleton* (St Paul's Cathedral, London,) the first Protestant Bishop of India, blessing two members of his great diocese. This, although somewhat cumbersome, has strength and proves the sculptural possibilities of lawn sleeves. John Edward Carew was befriended by the Earl of Egremont up to the latter's death in 1837. Unfortunately, he made a consummate fool of himself in trying to extract money from the Earl's executors. He was a sculptor of originality and charm as can be seen by his *Adonis and the Boar* (1826, Petworth, Sussex, Pl. 48c) and the bust of *Henry Wyndham* (1831, Petworth, Pl. 47A).

The tastes for neo-classic and Renaissance ran side by side and never really resolved itself during this period. Royal taste turned towards Baron Marochetti and Jacob Boehme, worthy but pedestrian men. The one talent to span the time between the older generation and the appearance of Alfred Stevens was that of Thomas Woolner, an original member of the Pre-Raphaelite brotherhood. In 1852 he set sail to make his fortune in the Australian gold-fields. When this failed to be the lucrative adventure he had supposed, he returned to England and sculpture. His work rightly still enjoys a considerable reputation, and his busts, on their characteristic socles, are always rewarding to study. *Tennyson* (Trinity College, Cambridge, Pl. 47c); *Newman* (Keble College, Oxford) and *Gladstone* (Ashmolean) on his splendid pedestal, ornamented with bas-reliefs from the *Iliad*, are perhaps his deepest character studies. His monuments are less pleasing. The minor Pre-Raphaelite Sculptor Alexander Munro made the charming fountain in Berkeley Square, and among his other work is the bust of his wife (Mrs Munro, Oxford) which has a fresh spontaneity rare at this time.

Fig. 1. An illustration by Arthur Hughes from *Enoch Arden* by Alfred Tennyson. Published by Edward Moxon, London, 1866.

Fig. 2. Weekes' Sleeping Child and Dog. *Illustrated Catalogue of the Great Exhibition*, Vol. II.
(*formerly coll. Sir Archibald Weigall*)

(A) Teapot (height 6¾ in.), Britannia metal, *c.* 1830. Maker's mark of James Dixon and Son, Sheffield, and a cream jug (height 3¾ in.), Britannia metal, *c.* 1840. Maker's mark of Joseph Wolstenholme, Sheffield. *Sheffield City Museum.*

(B) Teapot (height 6⅜ in.), silver, London, 1833–4. Maker's mark E. F. (Edward Feline?). *Victoria and Albert Museum.*

PLATE 49

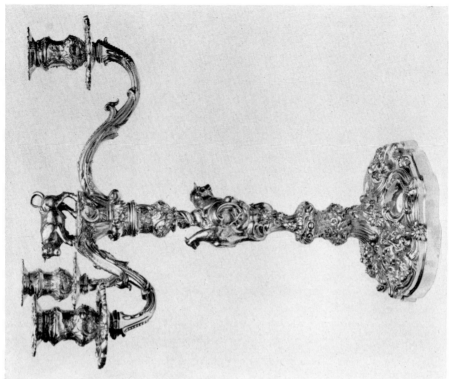

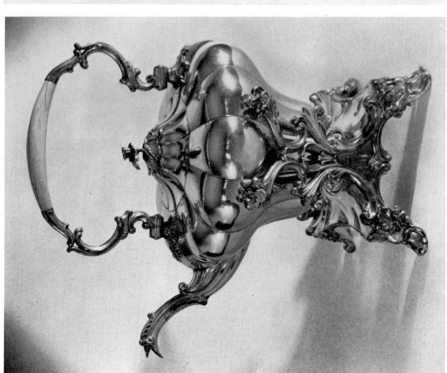

(A) Kettle and Stand (height 16 in.), Sheffield plate, *c.* 1838. Maker's mark of Henry Wilkinson and Co. *Sheffield City Museum.*

(B) Candelabrum (height $17\frac{1}{2}$ in.), silver, London, 1839–40. Maker's mark of Richard Sibley.

PLATE 50

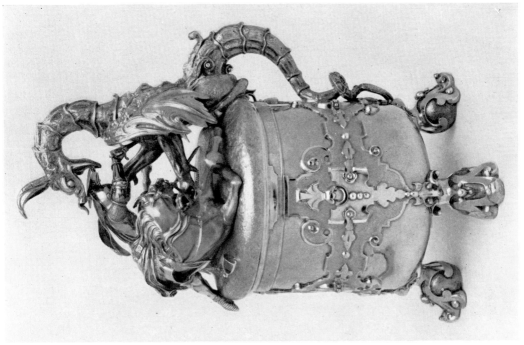

(B) Tankard (height 18½ in.), silver, parcel-gilt, London, 1846–7. Maker's mark of Robert Garrard. Inscribed on base: R & S GARRARD PANTON STREET LONDON.

(A) Wine cooler (height 13½ in.), silver, London, 1844–5. Maker's mark of Benjamin Smith.

PLATE 51

Tea and Coffee set (heights: sugar basin 5 in., jug 6 in., coffee pot 11 in., teapot $8\frac{1}{4}$ in.), silver, London, 1848–9. Maker's mark of Edward Barnard and Sons. Part of a service in the Tudor style presented to William Chadwick, Esq., the chairman of the Richmond Railway, in February 1849.
Courtesy Lady Lenanton.

PLATE 52

(A) Mug (height 4 in.), silver, parcel-gilt, London, 1834–5. Maker's mark of Paul Storr. Inscribed: STORR AND MORTIMER NO. 356. *Victoria and Albert Museum.*

(B) Christening mug (height 4 in.), silver; designed by Richard Redgrave for the Summerly Art Manufactures, *c.* 1849. Exhibited by S. H. and D. Gass at the Great Exhibition, 1851. Reissued later by H. Emmanuel, London, 1865–6. *Victoria and Albert Museum.*

(C) Teapot (height 7½ in.), Britannia metal, electro-plated, *c.* 1850. Maker's mark of James Dixon and Sons, Sheffield. *Private Collection.*

PLATE 53

(A) Teapot (height 7¾ in.), silver, designed by A. W. N. Pugin *c.* 1848, Birmingham, 1861–2. Maker's mark of John Hardman and Co. Exhibited by Hardmans at the International Exhibition, London, 1862. *Victoria and Albert Museum.*

(B) Cake basket (diameter 10¾ in.), silver, Sheffield, 1853–4. Maker's mark of Henry Wilkinson and Co. *Private Collection.*

PLATE 54

(A) Jug (height 12½ in.), silver, parcel-gilt, designed by Pierre-Emile Jeannest *c.* 1853. Exhibited by Elkington and Co. at the Universal Exhibition, Paris, 1855. Reissued later by Elkingtons, Birmingham, 1884–5

(B) Tray (length 18 in.), nickel silver electro-plated, designed by Alfred Stevens, 1856. Maker's mark of Thomas Bradbury and Sons, Sheffield. *Victoria and Albert Museum.*

PLATE 55

Group (height 26 in.), silver, London, 1854–5. Maker's mark of J. S. Hunt (Hunt and Roskell). One of a pair commissioned by the Goldsmiths' Company to illustrate the business duties and the benevolence of the Company. Exhibited at the International Exhibition of 1862. *The Worshipful Company of Goldsmiths*

PLATE 56

Silver and Silver Plate

F

Silver and Silver Plate

SHIRLEY BURY

A great epoch in English silversmithing came to an end with the death of George IV in 1830. A few months afterwards, advancing age caused John Bridge, the senior partner of Rundell, Bridge and Company, the royal goldsmiths, to give up personal attendance on George's successor, William IV. The association between George IV and John Bridge, which began even before the Regency, was responsible for the revival or development of many styles as well as the accepted neo-classicism of the day; some of the most remarkable additions to the Royal Collections were made at this period. Royal patronage had also largely contributed, directly or indirectly, to the enormous wealth of Rundells, whose premises at Ludgate Hill were the resort of the world of fashion.

William IV showed little concern for plate, although he might perhaps have been induced to develop an interest if John Bridge had not retired. Bridge died in 1834, and the decline of the firm, which had begun in the late 1820's, continued steadily, partly as a result of bad management by the remaining partners. Rundells no longer went to the expense of commissioning designs from fashionable academicians, for in past years they had suffered badly from cheap pirated copies of work on which they had spent a great deal of money. Nevertheless, one member of the firm retained his interest in the patronage of artists. John Gawler Bridge, the nephew of John Bridge, gave two prizes for silver designs by students of the Government School of Design in 1841. Rundells were disbanded in 1843 and their

stock sold, but their effect on the organization of the trade was lasting. Most of the important work of the early Victorian era was carried out by large firms with extensive workshops in the tradition of Rundells, while the small family concerns often failed to survive.

Two firms competed for predominance in the 1840's. One, R. and S. Garrard and Company, the royal goldsmiths, were eighteenth century in origin, while the other, Hunt and Roskell, were the successors of Storr and Mortimer, the firm founded by Paul Storr after he relinquished the direction of Rundells' Dean Street workshops in 1819. These two firms, and other well-known London establishments such as that of Edward Barnard and Sons, had large workshops, although they also sold work by provincial makers. The Birmingham firm of Elkingtons appointed a London manager soon after 1840, and one of his first duties was to sell their productions to London firms with retail premises, while from 1843 onwards Hunt and Roskell purchased small batches of silver designed by Pugin from the makers, Hardmans of Birmingham.

Although London retained her importance as a centre for fashionable silverware during the thirty years under consideration, most of the major technical innovations belong to the provinces. The only contribution to which London silversmiths could lay claim was the revival of embossed work in silver. During the Regency period ornamental detail was generally cast, and this method of working continued well into the 1840's. An embossed silver table ornament shown by Benjamin Smith at the Society of Arts exhibition of 1847 was considered unusual enough to warrant a detailed catalogue note explaining the process of manufacture.

At the outset of the period manufacturers in Sheffield were still mainly concerned with the production of articles in Sheffield plate, although many makers also offered a small selection of their designs in silver. Sheffield plate had long since ceased to be made in Sheffield alone, and the term was used merely to describe goods made of copper plated with silver by fusion. With a few outstanding exceptions, however, the most important firms were to be found in Sheffield. A manuscript account of the industry, compiled between 1820 and 1832 by R.M.Hirst,[1] who was associated with the Sheffield plating trade, is an invaluable source of information about contemporary methods of production. Hirst begins with a description of the process of preparing the plated metal. Ingots of copper, slightly alloyed with brass, formed the basis, and to these sheets of silver were fused, generally on two sides of each ingot. After the fusing had been effected in a furnace, the ingots were sent to the rolling mills, where they were gradually rolled into the required thickness for working. Hirst makes no mention of a new foundation material, 'German silver' (now known as nickel-silver), consisting of copper, zinc and nickel, which had by that time reached Sheffield. As its name implies, it came to England from Germany. Samuel Roberts, Junior, of the firm of Roberts, Smith and Company, took out a patent in 1830 (No. 5963) for the introduction of a 'layer of German silver between the silver and copper (or copper and brass) usually constituting plated metal. By this means [he submitted], whenever the silver is partially or wholly worn off the defect will scarcely be perceptible'. This alloy was at first too brittle for general use, but its composition was varied by later experimentation and by 1845, then sometimes known as 'Argentine silver', it had largely replaced copper as the foundation metal for plate.

The manufacture of articles from the prepared plate remained much the same as in the earlier part of the century, with one important departure from tradition. This was the general use of spinning for the shaping of articles. Small pieces, such as candlestick nozzles, were sometimes spun on a foot-operated lathe in the late eighteenth century, but it was not until about 1820 that steam-powered machinery made it possible for larger articles to be spun. Hirst explains how the flat metal was forced round the wooden 'chuck', or form, while being revolved at high speed, so that it gradually took the exact form of the chuck itself. Teapots, cream jugs and shallow wares were frequently produced by the process of spinning, as were also plain feet, spouts and covers. Very large pieces (Hirst instances tea-urns and ice-pails) had still to be cut out in parts, which were soldered together, the achievement of the shape being 'partially assisted' by the use of mallet and stakes.

Spinning was also used in the manufacture of articles from 'Britannia metal', a soft and easily worked mixture of tin, antimony and copper, which since the late eighteenth century had been used as a cheap alternative to Sheffield plate. The principal makers included Joseph Wolstenholme and James Dixon and Sons, both of Sheffield (Pl. 49A).

There were few Birmingham manufactories in 1830 which were comparable to the Sheffield firms. Matthew Boulton's factory, then known as the Soho Plate Company and administered by his son, Matthew Robinson Boulton, was still producing reputable work, although its days of real distinction were over. Second to Soho was the firm started in 1793 by Edward (later Sir Edward) Thomason, who had trained with Boulton. Both these manufactories included in their production domestic articles in silver and Sheffield plate. In general, however, Birmingham silversmiths and platers were concerned with the 'toy' trade (i.e. the manufacture of buttons, rings, beads for necklaces, and other very small objects exempted from licence and hall-marking). Some toy-makers produced their wares in Sheffield plate, others, although increasingly few, used the old system of close plating, which was suitable only for small

[1] R.M.Hirst: *A Short Account of the Founders of the Silver and Plated Establishments in Sheffield.* Bradbury Records, No. 299, Sheffield City Library.

articles. The object to be plated was dipped first into sal ammoniac, which acted as a flux, and then into melted tin, after which a shaped foil of silver was placed on top and made to adhere by the application of a soldering iron.

In 1840 the situation in Birmingham was radically altered by the introduction of electro-plating. The successful application of this process to commercial production was made by George Richards Elkington and his cousin, Henry Elkington, who took out the decisive patent in March 1840 (No. 8447). The two Elkingtons had been experimenting with the possibilities of electro-plating for some years, both separately and together, and G.R.Elkington, in collaboration with O.W.Barratt, had obtained a patent in 1838 for a process involving what was in fact, to judge from the specification, a primitive form of single-cell battery.

All the early attempts at electro-plating stemmed from Alessandro Volta's invention of an electric battery in 1799/1800. Volta's electric cell consisted essentially of two plates of different metals connected by an electrolytic solution, by means of which a sustained current could be produced. From 1801 to 1804 various experiments were made by William Hyde Wollaston, William Cruikshank, W.Hisinger and J.J.Berzelius on the decomposition of chlorides and other salts by the action of electricity, establishing the fact that metal was freed from the solutions and deposited on the negative pole. Brugnatelli was probably the first to achieve a practical piece of electro-gilding. In 1805 he coated two silver medals with gold by the action of electricity. The process, however, continued imperfect for some years; the metallic coating often failed to adhere through oxidation, and the electrical action was erratic.

Michael Faraday made an intensive study of electrolytic phenomena from 1821 onwards, basing his experiments on the work of Wollaston, Davy, H.C.Oersted, Ampère and others. His discoveries relating to electro-magnetism were later used by J.S.Woolrich of Birmingham, who in August 1842 obtained a patent for the first plating dynamo (No. 9431). It is recorded that in 1845, when the British Association met in Birmingham, Faraday visited the workshops of Thomas Prime, where he was delighted to see the machine in action.

Between 1830 and 1840 there was a renewed spate of experimentation in electro-deposition; J.F.Daniell devised his constant voltage battery in 1836, and this became the standard equipment for research. A number of people, including M.H. Jacobi of St Petersburg, Thomas Spencer of Liverpool, and C.J.Jordan of London, were engaged in investigating a curious phenomenon noted in the *Philosophical Magazine* of 1836 by W. de la Rue, who described how the metal deposited on the negative pole of a battery 'has the counterpart of every scratch of the plate on which it was deposited'. In 1839, within a few months of each other, Jacobi, Spencer and Jordan announced similar findings, which had apparently been made quite independently of each other. In September of that year Spencer delivered a lecture to the Liverpool Polytechnic Society, in which he explained how he had made copies of medals by electro-deposition, using a wax preparation to enable him to separate the medals from the copper deposited on them. The process was later called electrotyping. None of the people concerned attempted to patent their discoveries, which were afterwards used by Elkingtons.

The patent specification submitted by Elkingtons incorporated an improved electrolyte which ensured continuous action by the battery and a firm deposit of metal. The credit for this is usually given to John Wright, a surgeon, who had made a series of successful experiments after coming across a passage in Scheele's *Chemical Essays*, where the solubility of the cyanides of gold and silver in cyanide of potassium is mentioned. Wright sold his discovery to G.R.Elkington, who undertook to pay him royalties for every ounce of gold or silver deposited. The surgeon's right to the discovery was disputed at the time; it was suggested that he owed less to Scheele than he did to Dr Sherman (or Shearman) of Rotherham, whose pupil he had been.

In 1840 the Elkingtons were established in their newly completed premises in Newhall Street, Birmingham, and there followed a period of rapid expansion. In 1842 they were joined by Josiah Mason, and the firm became known as Elkington, Mason and Company. Their employees were encouraged to suggest improvements in manufacture and were rewarded accordingly. Alexander Parkes, one of the firm's most expert metallurgists, invented a process for making electrotypes from non-metallic moulds, which he patented on behalf of Elkingtons in March 1841 (No. 8905). William Millward, another employee, evolved a method of producing bright deposits of metal that needed little burnishing, which he similarly patented in March 1847 (No. 11,632). It was also the firm's policy to buy up all other relevant patents, perhaps partly because their 1840 patent was being continually challenged as being vague and indefinite. Woolrich's patent for his plating dynamo was acquired in 1845, Thomas Prime undertaking shortly afterwards to operate the machines on Elkingtons' behalf.

In 1845 trade opposition to the process, which at first was intense, had begun to give way. The first licence to manufacture electro-plate was granted by Elkingtons to J. Dismore of Liverpool in about 1844. The next was acquired shortly afterwards by John Harrison of Sheffield, who sent one of his employees to Elkingtons to study the process. By 1855 there was hardly a manufacturer of plated goods in England who had not at least partly gone over to electro-plating, although it was still some years before Sheffield plate ceased to be made in small quantities.

The methods of manufacture employed in the electro-plating process were almost the complete reverse of those used for Sheffield plate, and often resulted in a loss of precision and clarity in the final appearance of the articles. This was due to the fact that articles were finished and cleaned before plating. Most works were cast, and the time, money and labour which were expended on the original model were fully justified by the innumerable casts that could be made from it. The design could therefore include modelled figures, relief work and chasing, techniques which were particularly suited to the French artists and craftsmen recruited for the firm by Henry Elkington. The casts were made from sand moulds taken from

the model, and were usually of German silver. The simpler objects were made in one piece, and the more complicated or ornate in a number of separate parts. Another form of decoration, often used for mass-produced goods, was the simulation of engraved work by etching, which was first practised in the early 1840's. Spinning seems not to have been used in the new manufacturing process until the late 1840's, when it became possible to electro-plate Britannia metal and other soft alloys.

The electrotype technique was normally used for copying examples of metalwork, usually pieces of historic interest. In about 1844 the process invented by Alexander Parkes for the production of electrotypes from non-metallic moulds was considerably improved by the introduction of unvulcanized rubber. This was used to make moulds from the works to be reproduced. The procedure then varied, but it was basically as follows: wax, mixed with a conductible material, was poured into the moulds, which were sufficiently elastic to be removed when it had set; the metal was then deposited on the wax. Parkes' method was also employed in the production of facsimiles of natural objects such as plants and flowers, and even small animals, which were coated with a conductible material and then immersed in a plating bath.

These innovations undoubtedly influenced the stylistic development of Victorian silversmithing, and in addition were the means of abolishing the gap that had previously existed between the design of silver and of plated articles. It became a frequent practice to produce articles in both silver and electro-plate. An example of this is the wine-cooler, dated 1844, by Benjamin Smith (Pl. 51 A). Smith, who was a relation, presumably the son, of the Regency silversmith of the same name, had a business arrangement with Elkingtons that lasted from 1839 until his retirement ten years later. The same wine-cooler appears in an Elkingtons' catalogue of electro-plated articles issued in 1847.

Despite the anxious discussion of æsthetic questions that continued throughout the early Victorian era, styles were somewhat slow to evolve. Manufacturers always made a prestige showing at exhibitions, yet this did not preclude

74

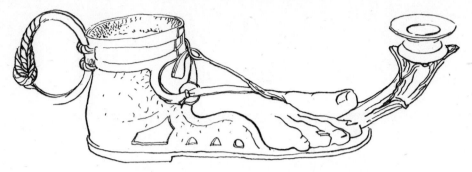

Fig. 1. Taperstick manufactured by Elkingtons. The design was supplied by
Benjamin Schlick and registered in October 1844.

the display of works which were in fact several years old. A vase and shield executed by Antoine Vechte was shown by Hunt and Roskell at the Great Exhibition, at the Paris Exhibition of 1855, and again in London in 1862, gaining high praise from the Juries on all three occasions. The vase (Fig. 7) actually dates from 1847, and the shield, begun in about 1850, was finally completed in 1855. These were admittedly virtuoso pieces, but more modest work also enjoyed a lasting vogue. The teapot made by John Hardman and Company from a design by A.W.N.Pugin (Pl. 54A) was made in 1861 and shown in the 1862 exhibition, but the existence of the original annotated drawing proves that it was designed well before Pugin's death in 1852, and that a prototype had been executed in about 1848.

The classic style of the Regency continued in a modified form throughout the 1830's and 1840's. Its adulteration with naturalistic ornament had begun in the 1820's, and the process was accelerated during the following decade. After 1840 it survived only as a very minor tradition. A few firms, such as that of Sir Edward Thomason, which was taken over in 1835 by G.R.Collis, continued to devote part of their output to straightforward reissues or copies of Regency pieces until quite late in the period, even including them in exhibition displays. Until his retirement in 1839, the great Regency silversmith, Paul Storr, still occasionally worked in the classic manner (Pl.

53A). Versions of classic designs remained among the staple productions of manufacturers in London and the provinces, but the recognizable Regency motifs of acanthus, vine leaves, masks and gadrooned ornament became markedly less conventional and symmetrical in character. It is possible to plot from the pattern-books of the 1830's the development of such details as the insertion of star-shaped flowers and posies into acanthus leaves and the progressive unfurling and irregular placing of the leaves themselves, resulting in a blurred and often unbalanced shape.

Soon after 1840 a style of more definitely antiquarian character began to emerge. This again stemmed from the Regency period, for Paul Storr and other silversmiths had occasionally made direct copies of Roman metalwork. A bronze reproduction of the Warwick vase, carried out in 1820 by Sir Edward Thomason, remained one of the show-pieces of G.R.Collis and Company, and is mentioned as late as 1855 in a guide to Birmingham. Elkingtons, however, were able to cater for public demand on a wide scale with their electrotype facsimiles of antique pieces. In 1844 they engaged for this purpose the Chevalier Benjamin Schlick, a Danish architect who had access to many European collections of Greek, Roman and Etruscan antiquities, both public and private. Schlick was responsible for making the moulds, and he also made good any deficiencies in the original, rearranging the parts if he felt it to be

75

Fig. 2. Tureen in the Greek manner manufactured by
Dixons. Shown at the Great Exhibition 1851.

necessary. The taperstick (Fig. 1) is an early example of his work for the firm. A group of his pieces was shown at the Birmingham Exhibition of 1849, and again at the Great Exhibition. He ended his connection with Elkingtons in about 1849 and was replaced by Dr Emil Braun, of Rome.

Elkingtons, and other manufacturers, also adapted Greek and Roman forms to domestic articles. A cream ewer, 'copied from the antique', was shown by J.Dismore of Liverpool at the Manchester Exhibition of 1845–6, and similar pieces were included in the display of several firms at the Great Exhibition. The current interest in the antique was possibly responsible for the appearance of a specifically early Victorian shape for jugs and coffee-pots, characterized by a tall, thin neck, high lip and rounded, flat-based body which is reminiscent of the Portland Vase. This shape emerged in about 1849 and was widespread at the time of the Great Exhibition. It is perhaps significant that copies of the Portland Vase were made in the 1840's by a number of silversmiths, including Dismore and Hunt and Roskell.

From about 1846 onwards there was a concurrent use of classic motifs in a much freer, in-spirational sense, and by 1850 this had become canalized in the Greek style. James Dixon and Sons included a 'plain but truly elegant' Grecian dish and tureen in the firm's contribution to the Great Exhibition. The shapes of these pieces were simple and controlled, owing more to the Adam period than to the Regency; the ornament was confined to bands of engraved key pattern, with beaded and gadrooned borders (Fig. 2). Throughout the 1850's many similar designs were patented by manufacturers under the Copyright of Designs Act of 1839. Some were rather more exuberantly ornamented than the early Dixon pieces, others were directly derived from Greek vase shapes, but they were usually distinguished by a common discipline of shape and decoration. The principal patentees of work in this manner (in addition to Dixons) were Edward Barnard and Sons, Elkingtons; and Henry Wilkinson and Company, Thomas Bradbury and Sons, and John Harrison, all of Sheffield. Towards the end of the decade the Greek style had become of major importance.

The Victorian rococo manner is characterized by a heavy use of naturalistic motifs. Until late in the 1840's the rococo was generally known as the

'Louis XIV' style, a term which led to a good deal of contemporary confusion on the part of designers and manufacturers, and often resulted in an admixture of the baroque and rococo. J.B.Papworth, the architect, giving evidence to the Select Committee on Arts and Manufactures in 1835, said that the style was not properly that of Louis XIV, but was 'the debased manner of the reign of his successor, in which grotesque varieties are substituted for design'. The style was never popular with the intelligentsia, but fifteen years after Papworth had condemned it, the *Journal of Design* had still regretfully to remind manufacturers that 'the detail of the age of Louis XV we would rather forget than perpetuate'.

In 1830 rococo shapes were widely used for small domestic articles in both silver and Sheffield plate. Teapots, cream jugs and so on, were often made in the rather flattened spherical or oval form, lobed like a cantaloupe melon, which was popular in the previous decade. Pear-shaped bodies, inverted and otherwise, were also produced at this time, although they became much more general in the late 1830's. The lobed ornament, known as 'melon pattern', was frequently used in the decoration of these pear-shaped articles (Pl. 50A), although this was not invariable, as is shown by the teapot illustrated (Pl. 49B). The decoration of this piece with scenes of debauch, and with four shell feet terminating in the busts of pirates, seems somewhat inappropriate to its function, but genre subjects of this kind appear intermittently on silver and plate throughout the period, and a similar teapot was shown at the 1862 Exhibition. A more common ornamental device was a stylized posy of flowers and leaves, used in conjunction with rococo scrolls and shells.

The larger pieces were usually more ambitious, in that the scroll and shell ornament was combined with a profusion of foliage and flowers, and with animals and figures, free-standing or in high relief. All these elements of design appear in *Knight's Vases and Ornaments*, one of a series of pattern-books issued by this publisher. The 'Vases' was published in January 1833; the list of subscribers includes many well-known firms in London and the provinces, such as Storr and Mor-

timer, Benjamin Smith and Dixons. An analysis of the plates shows a marked preponderance of rococo motifs, not only in the original designs for Racing and other presentation cups, but in the decoration of objects based on historic examples, which are frequently perverted into a more fashionable form. The floral decoration, though plentiful, remains fairly conventional, consisting either of acanthus arranged in an asymmetrical fashion, or of scattered bunches of roses or other flowers. The candelabrum illustrated (Pl. 50B) is typical of the elaborate rococo ornament of the 1830's, although the choice of animals appears to indicate that it might have been specially made for presentation to someone with agricultural interests.

The rococo tradition was continued throughout the 1840's. Spherical and pear-shaped tea- and coffee-pots, both plain and melon-patterned, were predominant, although the pear shape was now sometimes modified by wide facets round the neck of the body. The first innovation, which seems to date from about 1845, was the introduction of a multiple-footed body whose shape can best be

Fig. 3. Teapot from a tea and coffee set modelled on the pitcher plant, manufactured by Dixons. The design was registered in April 1851 and the set shown at the Great Exhibition.

compared to eighteenth-century rococo tea-caddies. The new shape was perhaps evolved from the early practice of casting electro-plated goods (Pl. 53c). Flowers and foliage, either in high relief or chased, as in the 1830's, were still often used in decoration, and occasionally showed signs of having been taken more directly from nature. Handles and feet were frequently entwined with foliage, or were themselves made in the form of plants. In addition, chinoiserie, arabesque, Gothic, Elizabethan (or Tudor: see Pl. 52), and seventeenth-century motifs were used, sometimes in combination with rustic elements. From about 1846 numerous pieces were made which were almost entirely covered with foliated or floral ornament, although the standard rococo shapes were still discernible. In 1850 Dixons patented an electroplated tea set in which the body and feet were overlaid with a simple leaf form. The *Journal of Design* for that year complimented the firm on the 'appropriate design'. Rococo pieces were still produced in some quantity in the following decade. Several manufacturers, including Broadhead and Atkin, Roberts and Hall, and Hawkesworth and Eyre, showed work in this manner at the Great Exhibition. There were few stylistic changes after this date. The cake basket illustrated (Pl. 54B), is an adaptation of a design registered by Henry Wilkinson and Company in 1849; the form is identical, but vine leaves have been substituted for the original ears of corn. The multiple-footed shape appears to have largely died out in the early 1850's, and to have been replaced by an upright oval form, often widening at the base.

The design of some small pieces, and of many of the larger articles produced in the 1840's, was so strongly affected by contemporary interest in naturalism that they must be regarded primarily as belonging to the naturalistic style, although a certain affinity with rococo is still often evident. The formative influences (apart from the character of Victorian rococo itself) which led to the development of naturalism in silversmithing are difficult to assess. One was probably the invention of the electrotype and its application to natural objects, another was contemporary French metalwork design, some examples of which were purchased from the Paris Exposition of 1844 by the Director of the Government School of Design at Somerset House. These, together with work in other media, were circulated round the principal manufacturing towns in England. Nevertheless, it is unlikely that this touring exhibition had as marked an effect on English manufacturers as their employment of French artists and craftsmen and their long-standing practice of purchasing designs from the Continent. From 1845 onwards, for the benefit of manufacturers, the *Art Union* published a series of illustrations of French pottery and metalwork, which included, together with examples of work in the Renaissance style, pieces such as a metal boudoir candlestick shaped as a leaf, with the candle-holder and handle in the form of a flower and stalk. English manufacturers took up this particular design with enthusiasm, and two rival versions of it, one of which was patented by the firm concerned, were the subject of the first case relating to infringement of the Copyright of Designs Act. The same principle was applied to other articles. Benjamin Smith showed thistle and convolvulus cups, made in the shapes of the plants, at the Manchester Exhibition of 1845–6.

It can be argued that this development is implicit in Knight's designs of 1833, in which figures, animals and natural objects are used with obviously allusive purpose on a fairly recognizable foundation of rococo or, more rarely, classical shapes. A pair of Dianas form the handles of one of his cups, the body of which is covered with huntsmen and dogs, partly in high relief, and partly, it appears from the design, free-standing, while foxes spring from acanthus leaves round the base. The classical vase shape has been treated in a similar way by Benjamin Smith in the wine-cooler, dated 1844, which is illustrated (Pl. 51A). The handles, stem and base are completely rustic, while the lip has dissolved under pressure of vine and foam ornament.

The most striking manifestation of the style was in Testimonial or Presentation plate, a category which includes Racing plate, decorative centrepieces, and table services whose primary function was adornment. Dickens described a typical set of such plate in *Our Mutual Friend*, in which 'a caravan of camels take charge of the fruit and flowers and candles, and kneel down to be loaded with the salt'. Broadly speaking, there were two kinds of naturalistic Presentation plate. One, which was the first to emerge, was concerned mainly with the sculptural and allegorical, and the figures rarely had to serve a structural purpose, while the other, which dates from about 1845, aimed at the closest possible reproduction of forms in nature, which were used as both structure and decoration.

The demand for sculptural plate gave manufacturers their greatest incentive to employ artists and modellers of repute. Edmund Cotterill, the sculptor, was already working for R. & S.Garrard in 1840. He produced the group of St George and the Dragon on the Garrards tankard illustrated (Pl. 51B) which was the Ascot Queen's Vase for 1844. Hunt and Roskell's modeller, Alfred Brown, was responsible for one of the most ambitious suites of sculptural plate of the 1840's, the Ellenborough Testimonial, which included a grand centrepiece, a pair of table ornaments and candelabra, and four ice pails (one of which is illustrated: Fig. 4). Most of the major firms had permanent designers, but in addition, following the Regency tradition, frequently commissioned work from independent artists such as Daniel Maclise, R.A., and Sir George Hayter, R.A.

In 1850 the *Journal of Design* made some severe criticisms of the sculptural treatment of silver, which were taken up and amplified by Richard Redgrave, R.A., in his report on design at the Great Exhibition. After remarking that the worst features of the naturalistic style were particularly apparent in silver and plate, he went on to deplore the 'imitations of textures, chain and plate mail' characteristic of the style, asking further what in these pieces 'could justify the employment of the precious metals, and what ought to be the more precious labours of artists?' Redgrave regretted that, on the evidence of the exhibits, the English were more culpable in this respect than any other nation. There were in fact few prominent manufacturers in this country who failed to show work of this kind at the Great Ex-

Fig. 4. Ice pail formed as lotus leaves and other plants, with figures of Indians grouped round. Part of the service of plate manufactured in 1848 by Hunt and Roskell for presentation to Lord Ellenborough by 'his friends and admirers in India'. Shown at the Great Exhibition, 1851.

hibition. In some of these Presentation pieces an architectural construction was used on which the figures were placed, but in others the groups were commingled arbitrarily with scroll ornament or with natural forms. Five years later, Redgrave, reporting on the design of British manufactures at the Paris Exhibition of 1855, found a marked improvement in the taste of English silver and plate, which he attributed in part to the influence of the French artists and craftsmen working in this country. The group illustrated (Pl. 56) was completed in 1854, and bears out Redgrave's comments regarding the higher standard of design in the 1850's. The ornament, although still lavish, has been kept subordinate to the finely modelled figures. This piece is one of a pair which were commissioned by the Goldsmiths' Company from Hunt and Roskell to illustrate respectively the business duties and the benevolence of the Company. They were shown at the 1862 Exhibition.

The fashion for Presentation plate made in direct imitation of natural forms reached its climax at the Great Exhibition, where a good deal of attention was aroused by the 'silver dessert service, of new design' modelled from water-plants in Kew Gardens and shown by S.H. and D.Gass, of London. The Exhibition catalogue gives an exact botanical description of each plant represented. Dixons exhibited a tray shaped as a leaf of the Victoria Regia lily, acknowledging their debt to Joseph Paxton, who had supplied the original leaf for copying, and a tea and coffee set modelled on the pitcher plant (Fig. 3). After the Great Exhibition the style lost favour to a certain extent, and was more generally found in electroplate than in silver.

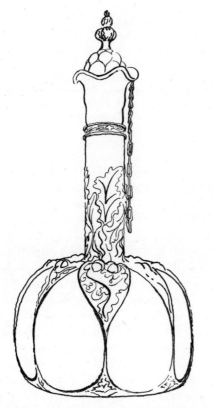

Fig. 5. Gothic wine flagon manufactured by Lambert and Rawlings. Shown at the Great Exhibition.
Victoria and Albert Museum

One of the earliest intellectual reactions against the extravagancies of the rococo and naturalistic styles was led by Henry Cole, who later became a member of the executive committee of the Great Exhibition. Using the pseudonym 'Felix Summerly', he submitted an earthenware tea set, made to his design by Mintons, to the first competition for Arts and Manufactures organized by the Society of Arts, and was awarded a silver medal. This was in 1846. His success encouraged him in his conviction that 'an alliance between fine art and manufactures would promote public taste', and in the following year he issued the first notice of the formation of 'Summerly's Art Manufactures'. The preliminary announcement stated that a number of well-known artists had agreed to design 'familiar articles in everyday use' for execution by the 'most eminent British manufacturers'. As far as works in metal are concerned, these manufacturers included Benjamin Smith (from 1848, B. and H.Smith), Hunt and Roskell, S.H. and D.Gass, Dixons, and Broadhead and Atkin. The organization lasted for about three years; Cole abandoned the project in 1850 because of his preoccupation with the Great Exhibition.

The whole scheme was based on the assumption, widely held at the time, that painters and sculptors, usually without knowledge of manufacturing processes, were the most suitable persons to design for the industrial arts, and that, moreover, these designs could equally well be rendered in several completely different media. The milk-jug from Cole's own prize-winning tea set was executed in porcelain and glass, and also in silver by Hunt and Roskell. The designs themselves were sometimes liable to suffer from an over-literal interpretation of the Summerly principle that decoration should consist of 'appropriate' motifs drawn from nature and relating to the use of the article. This led to a repetition of some of the faults of the naturalistic style and a consequent lessening of functional qualities. The *Journal of Design* pointed out this weakness in Richard Redgrave's 'Guardian Angel' christening mug (Pl. 53B) in 1850. The *Journal* approved of the 'perfect propriety' of the ornament, but found it disproportionate to the whole, and suggested that the rim would be better raised and widened so that the cup could be drunk from more easily.

There was widespread and bitter contemporary criticism of the Summerly Art Manufactures, which arose partly as a result of the generous showing afforded them at the second and fourth annual exhibitions of British Manufactures held at the Society of Arts in 1848 and 1850. Their influence, however, was probably greater than was suspected at the time by many indignant designers and manufacturers not in the scheme.

The Gothic style was primarily a religious manifestation during this period. Its chief protagonist was Augustus Welby Northmore Pugin, the architect, who as a boy of fifteen was briefly employed by Rundell, Bridge and Rundell to design church plate in the Gothic manner. He never lost his interest in silver, and continued designing on his own account. In 1836, by then a convinced Catholic, he published a collection of his drawings, begun in 1833, as *Designs for Gold and Silversmiths*. He met John Hardman the younger, a fellow Catholic, in the course of his architectural duties in 1837 and within a year had a business arrangement with him for the production of ecclesiastical metalwork. Hardman advertised in 1840 that he was now producing metalwork exclusively from Pugin's designs or from 'ancient examples' under Pugin's supervision. Hardman's early difficulties in finding suitable workmen for the enterprise were frequently referred to by contemporary writers; one of his particular problems was the recruitment of enamellers, for from about 1842 onwards much of the work was designed for enamelled decoration.

Although the greater part of the firm's production was devoted to ecclesiastical metalwork, a certain number of domestic pieces were also made. Pugin's house at Ramsgate was furnished with a silver service made for him by Hardmans, and examples of domestic silver and brassware were included in the firm's display at the Birmingham Exhibition of 1849, at the Great Exhibition and at the 1862 Exhibition. After his death in 1852 Hardmans continued to work from Pugin's designs. The teapot illustrated (Pl. 54A) is an example of such posthumous production. Pugin was

Fig. 6. Kettle from a Gothic tea and coffee set manufactured by Elkingtons. The design was registered in April 1851 and the set shown at the Great Exhibition.

of course unable to find Gothic models for such latter-day inventions as teapots, and he had to be content with the use of decorative detail. For other domestic pieces he was usually able to adapt a medieval form. The popularity of his designs led to a good deal of imitation by other manufacturers specializing in ecclesiastical metalwork. The closest rival to the Hardman firm was that of Francis Skidmore, who began making metalwork in the same manner in about 1847.

The use of Gothic motifs, or, more rarely, Gothic forms for domestic wares occurs on a minor scale throughout the period, although rarely inspired, even during the 1840's, by Pugin's antiquarian interests. Dixons had a few Gothic tea-sets among their stock styles from 1846 onwards, but the medievalism was confined to the ornament, for the shapes were rococo. Lambert and Rawlings of London contributed a remarkable pair of silver and gilt Gothic wine-flagons, each twenty-four inches high and holding twelve quarts, to the Great Exhibition (Fig. 5), while other manufacturers, including T.Wilkinson and Company and William Gough and Company, both of Birmingham, showed small electro-plated articles, such as cruet frames and butter coolers, which were pierced with perpendicular tracery. Elkingtons exhibited a Gothic tea and coffee set (Fig. 6), whose designer had obviously shared Pugin's difficulty in finding suitable shapes, and had solved the problem by using architectural features. In the 1850's several manufacturers, including John Harrison, registered a number of designs for articles with engraved Gothic decoration.

There were styles other than the Gothic which presented difficulties in the adaptation of decoration to nineteenth-century domestic silver and plate. The compromises involved often make it impossible to distinguish clearly between styles. The Victorians found it equally difficult, particularly where work in the manner of the fifteenth, sixteenth and seventeenth centuries was concerned, for here the problem was intensified by an uncertain historical knowledge. The *Art-Journal* of 1850 used the term 'Renaissance' to describe a sugar basket by Broadhead and Atkin decorated with Gothic tracery, and this mistake was not uncommon. In the 1851 exhibition Garrards showed ewers and cups variously listed as in the style of the sixteenth century and in the style of Cellini; C.F.Hancock and J.V.Morel, both of London, contributed respectively a tea set and a casket in the Florentine style, while many manufacturers included work in the cinquecento, Venetian and Italian styles. Many of these works, to judge from surviving illustrations, are very similar.

Only one sixteenth-century style, the Elizabethan, sometimes called the Tudor style, is consistently different from the rest. Its characteristic features are bold strapwork and scrolling cartouches which, in common with other styles of the period, were as frequently applied to rococo

and other shapes as to sixteenth-century forms (Pl. 52). The style was already popular by about 1840. From 1843 onwards some dozens of designs for Elizabethan soup tureens, candelabra and so on were registered by manufacturers, including Henry Wilkinson, who appears to have made a speciality of the style. Garrards often used it as an ornamental background to their Presentation pieces, as on the tankard illustrated (Pl. 51B). In 1851 a florid version of the Elizabethan manner was employed in the decoration of one of Elkingtons' special display pieces, the Vase representing the triumph of Science and the Industrial Arts at the Great Exhibition, while a number of other firms, including Gass, Henry Wilkinson, John Harrison and William Gough, showed more modest interpretations of it for domestic use. In the four years that intervened between the Great Exhibition and the Paris Exhibition of 1855 the style lost favour, and few new designs were produced after the latter date.

The term 'Cellini style' appears to refer, in particular, to the ewers of sixteenth- or early seventeenth-century form decorated with embossed or engraved figure groups. These were nearly always exhibition pieces made for prestige purposes. Antoine Vechte, the greatest exponent of this style, was probably in part responsible for the adoption of a form of ewer which was a much closer approximation of the true Renaissance shape than the pyriform version of the 1830's. Several firms, including Martin, Baskett and Martin of Cheltenham, showed ewers of this kind at the Great Exhibition. A curious variant on the pyriform ewer was the elongated jug or coffee-pot shape, with narrow curving body, which first made its appearance in the late 1840's and which was fairly widespread by 1851. Joseph Angell, of London, showed a coffee-pot of this shape at the Great Exhibition.

The Renaissance style, in the accepted sense, was current throughout the period, although it was not of major importance until the 1840's. Much of the work in this manner was executed from French designs or by French artists and craftsmen employed in this country. After the

1848 Revolution the number of French people in England was considerably augmented by the arrival of silversmiths who had lost their patrons, and Vechte and Paul-Emile Jeannest apparently came at this time. Vechte almost immediately started working for Hunt and Roskell, for whom he had already carried out a number of commissions while still in France. Jeannest spent some two years in London, contributing regularly during this time to the *Art-Journal*'s series of 'Original Designs for Manufactures'. Jeannest's designs were frequently illustrated with the qualification that their 'essentially French' character was not entirely suited to British taste. He nevertheless made few modifications to his style when he began working for Elkingtons, as is shown by the jug illustrated (Pl. 55A), whose design is very characteristic of his work. The decoration of acanthus foliage and cherubs is based on the work of the French seventeenth-century engraver, Jean le Pautre. The jug was shown at the Paris Exhibition of 1855 and again at the Crystal Palace in 1856. Another French immigrant was J.V.Morel, who entered his mark at Goldsmiths' Hall in 1849. The *Art-Journal* published an article on his work in 1850, commenting that it represented a compromise between the Renaissance and Louis XIV styles. His silver, which was usually richly jewelled and enamelled, appears to have had a great effect on other makers. Before Morel's arrival in this country, enamelled decoration was largely confined to work in the Gothic style. In the 1851 exhibition Morel's own display was closely rivalled by that of Joseph Angell, who showed pieces in gold and silver-gilt, heavily engraved and enamelled.

One of the great English designers in the Renaissance manner was Alfred Stevens, who had studied at the Academy in Florence for eight years, and whose designs were always based on the sculpture and architecture of that city. In 1851 he went to Sheffield to design grates and stoves for Henry Hoole and Company, and while working there he made a series of drawings and models for a set of so-called 'hunting knives', which were specially executed by George Wostenholme and Son for the Great Exhibition. After his return to London in 1852 he continued to design silver, sending up models to Sheffield from time to time. One of his pieces, a tray made by Thomas Bradbury and Sons is illustrated (Pl. 55B). Stevens was one of the few English artists to have a thorough working knowledge of manufacturing processes, and his instructions for the execution of the tray, contained in a letter to Joseph Bradbury, are still in existence. The tray was patented by the firm in October 1856, and produced in a number of sizes in both silver and electro-plate. It is, unfortunately, the only remaining example of Stevens' designs for these makers, although he is known to have supplied them with a number of models, including a dessert stand and an epergne, between 1856 and 1859.

The arabesque style, which late in the 1830's represented work in the style of the painted and stucco decoration carried out by the studio of Raphael in the Villa Madama, was completely changed in character by the time of the Great Exhibition. One of Elkingtons' exhibits was a tea and coffee service, listed in the catalogue as in the arabesque style. Its engraved decoration is, however, reminiscent of the Alhambresque manner which was popularized by the publication between 1842 and 1845 of Owen Jones' work on the Alhambra. There were numerous other styles of Eastern character, including the Turkish, the Persian and the Egyptian. Of these, by far the most defined was the Egyptian, whose ornamental motifs were invariably distinctive. This style was another inheritance from the Regency, although its only manifestation during the 1830's and early 1840's seems to have been in the use of the lotus leaf as decoration. In 1849 S.H. and D.Gass included an Egyptian centre-piece in their display at the Society of Arts exhibition, while Hunt and Roskell showed a large work in the same style, the testimonial to Sir Moses Montefiore, which was executed from the design of Sir George Hayter. Henry Wilkinson, and Hawkesworth and Eyre of Sheffield, showed small domestic articles decorated in the Egyptian style in the Great Exhibition, and later in the 1850's Wilkinson attempted direct reproductions of Egyptian pieces. In general, however, the Oriental affinities were vague.

Fig. 7. A vase by Antoine Vechte of Hunt and Roskell.
Inscribed: ANTOINE VECHTE FECIT 1847.
The Worshipful Company of Goldsmiths.

(A) Two examples of white stoneware made by the firm of Charles Meigh, Hanley. The jug is dated 1842; the mug was the subject of a Society of Arts award in 1847. Heights 6¼ in. and 7¼ in. *Victoria and Albert Museum.*

(B) Blue-printed dish with a fanciful view of Venice, made by Copelands, *c.* 1840. Length 18⅞ in. *Victoria and Albert Museum.*

PLATE 57

(A) Coalport vase of porcelain, painted and with applied flower-work; *c.* 1830. Height 11 in. *Victoria and Albert Museum.*

(B) Parian porcelain vase with applied flower-work on a drab coloured ground, made by Mintons, *c.* 1854. Height 13⅝ in. *Victoria and Albert Museum.*

PLATE 58

(A) Two of Copelands' parian porcelain statuettes. *Left*, 'Innocence' dated 1847 after an original by J. H. Foley; *right*, 'Musidora' dated 1857 after William Theed junior. Heights 16⅜ in. and 16¼ in. *Victoria and Albert Museum* and *W. T. Copeland and Sons.*

(B) Staffordshire flat-back figure of Dick Turpin, *c.* 1850. Height 11½ in. *Victoria and Albert Museum.*

PLATE 59

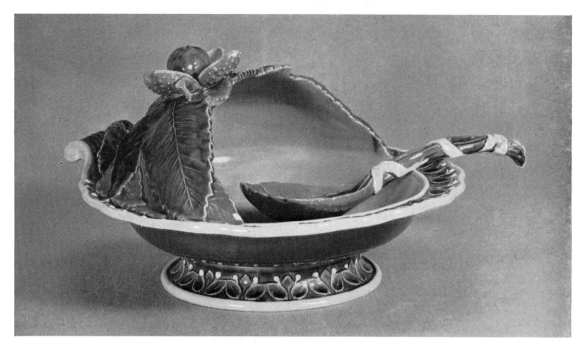

(A) 'Majolica' chestnut dish with spoon, made by Mintons, *c.* 1855. Diam. 9⅞ in. *Victoria and Albert Museum.*

(B) Part of an earthenware tea service designed by Henry Cole and made by Mintons. The service gained a Society of Arts award in 1846. Height of teapot 6 in. *Victoria and Albert Museum.*

PLATE 60

(A) 'Limoges ware', made by Kerr and Binns (from 1862 the Worcester Royal Porcelain Company) with white enamel painting by Thomas Bott. Cup and saucer dated 1859; plate dated 1867, with a pattern originally used on this ware in the middle 'fifties. Diameter of plate 10⅜ in. *Victoria and Albert Museum* and *Worcester Royal Porcelain Company.*

(B) Porcelain standing dish with parian figures representing 'Bottom and the Tinker', from the Shakespeare service shown by Kerr and Binns, Worcester, at the Dublin Exhibition, 1853. Height 15¾ in. *Worcester Royal Porcelain Company.*

PLATE 61

(A) Painted water-carafe, designed by Richard Redgrave for Henry Cole's 'Summerly's Art Manufactures' and made by J. F. Christy, Lambeth, *c.* 1847. Height 10¼ in. *Victoria and Albert Museum.*

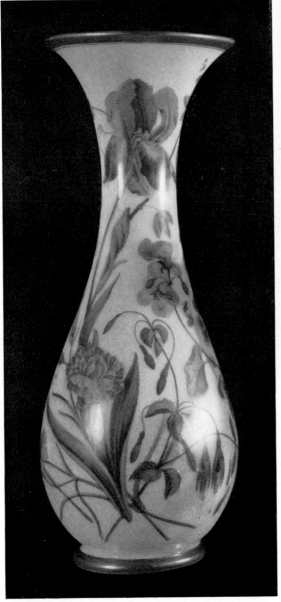

(B) Painted opal vase, made by W. H., B. and J. Richardson, Stourbridge, *c.* 1851. Height 17⅜ in. *Borough of Stourbridge Glass Collection.*

PLATE 62

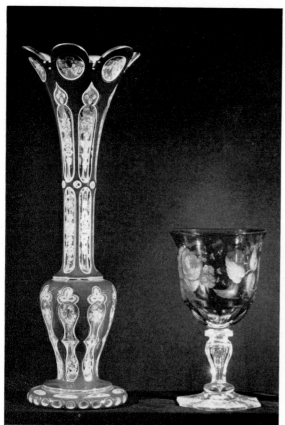

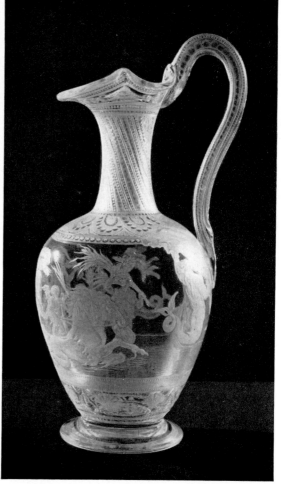

(A) A cased-glass vase with painted decoration, about 1848; and a goblet with cased bowl and with engraving designed by W. J. Muckley, said to have been shown in the 1851 Exhibition. Both made by W. H., B. and J. Richardson. Heights 16 in. and 7¾ in. *Borough of Stourbridge Glass Collection.*

(B) Engraved jug, shown at the 1851 Exhibition by J. G. Green, London. Height 13¼ in. *Victoria and Albert Museum.*

PLATE 63

(A) Comport, dish and decanter of cut crystal, made by W. H., B. and J. Richardson and said to have been shown at the 1851 Exhibition. Heights $5\frac{3}{8}$ in., $2\frac{1}{8}$ in. and $14\frac{3}{4}$ in. *Borough of Stourbridge Glass Collection (comport) and Mrs. E. Worrall.*

(B) Engraved wine glasses, with plain stem and with colour-threaded and convoluted stem, made by George Bacchus and Sons, Birmingham, about the early fifties. Heights $4\frac{1}{2}$ in. and 5 in. *Victoria and Albert Museum.*

PLATE 64

Pottery, Porcelain and Glass

G

Fig. 1. Glassware by George Bacchus & Sons at the Birmingham Exhibition 1849.
Journal of Design and Manufactures (11, 8).

Pottery, Porcelain and Glass

HUGH WAKEFIELD

POTTERY AND PORCELAIN

Among the multiplicity of wares which poured from the British potteries during the three decades 1830–60 a broad distinction can be made between those of a popular nature which tended to persist in traditional forms and those of a more sophisticated appeal which readily reflected the complexities of contemporary fashions. The conservatism of the popular wares can be seen especially in the slipware of the country potteries, the 'mocha' and other more industrialized slipwares, the saltglazed stoneware, the lustre ware and the 'ironstone china' with derived oriental patterns. Such wares continued into or through the Early Victorian period, but their manufacture was mainly associated with styles which had been defined and popularized at an earlier date.

Printed and painted earthenwares

The transfer-printed earthenware, which was at the height of its popularity in the years around 1830, showed largely the same conservatism in an established popular style. A great part of its manufacture was designed for export, and through the 'thirties and 'forties it was made by almost every factory of importance in Staffordshire, and by several elsewhere. The use of fanciful scenes, and of actual scenes in this country, in America and elsewhere, continued as central motifs in the printed patterns. In the border decorations rococo foliage and scrollwork tended to become increasingly common, and this is particularly noticeable in the printed ware from Copelands (the Spode factory, known as 'Copeland and Garrett' from 1833 to 1847, and then 'W.T.Copeland, late Spode') (Pl. 57B). From Wedgwoods came some excellent over-all floral patterns.

Blue remained the most popular colour for underglaze transfer-printing; but from the mid-'twenties other colours were frequently used, and in the 'thirties and 'forties these included black and varying shades of red, green, yellow, brown and purple. The more expensive method of overglaze printing, by transfer from gelatine 'bats' instead o paper, was used where fine detail was required; and this proved especially useful for the delineation of the multitudinous girders of the 1851 Crystal Palace on souvenir ware of that year. Multi-coloured underglaze printing appeared in the later 'forties. Some particularly successful work of this nature was produced by Jesse Austin for the firm of F. and R.Pratt of Fenton. Colour-printing was much used by this firm for the decoration of jar lids, and it was used also on table-wares such as those which were shown at the 1851 Exhibition and which earned the firm a prize medal. The colour-printed tablewares were made chiefly for export to America, where they were still being sold in the 'nineties.

Painted decoration on earthenware tended increasingly to follow the styles of porcelain painting; and this was particularly true of painting on the new hard earthenwares which were being developed as imitations of porcelain. Some notable work, although largely in a porcelain style of painting, was being carried out during the 'thirties and 'forties, and later, by William Fifield junior on the cream-coloured ware of Rings of

Bristol. At Wedgwoods bold over-all patterns were produced in a more appropriately earthenware style, which are reminiscent of the same firm's printed floral patterns; and the earlier Wedgwood mode of painting in opaque colours on a black ground was taken up in the harshly coloured productions of the Lowesby pottery in Leicestershire about 1835.

Pottery figures

Pottery figures were made in great quantities during the period, and like most of the popular wares their styles show relatively slight changes from those which were in vogue earlier in the century. It is noticeable, however, that pottery figures tended increasingly to diverge in style and subject-matter from those made in porcelain (which will be described later). Made mostly by back-street potters in the Staffordshire pottery towns, the early Victorian pottery figures were destined for the most unsophisticated market and show to a surprising degree the simple vigour and ingenuousness of a 'peasant' art. Among the work of this nature produced in the years around 1830 two main types are prominent. One is that of John Walton and his followers, whose figure groups are mainly characterized by the use of 'bocage' backgrounds of trees or foliage. John Walton's own work seems to belong most typically to the 'twenties. Of his followers working in the following decade or so the best known is Ralph Salt who used lustre decoration as well as enamel colours. The second prominent type of figure-work is one which is thought to be associated with Obadiah Sherratt. It is characterized by a curious table base with bracket feet on which are placed groups depicting bullbaiting or else crudely humorous scenes. Much of this work is probably of the 'twenties, but that it continued at least into the middle 'thirties is shown by the use of the new word 'teetotal' in the title of a group illustrating the advantages of sobriety.[1] A later development was the 'flat-back' type of figures, which were mostly left white with a sparing decoration in colours and gilding (Pl. 59 B). These developed

around the middle of the century and achieved great popularity in the 'fifties. Among the makers of these figures in Staffordshire the firm with which they have been mainly associated is that of Sampson Smith of Longton, which continued over a long period to make wares of this nature including pottery dogs for mantelpiece decoration. Flat-backs and other sorts of simple coloured figures were also made in Scotland at Prestonpans and elsewhere.

Other manifestations of Early Victorian work in a broad-based popular spirit were the small models of buildings, such as cottages and churches, and the spirit flasks formed into the shapes of human figures. Many of the model buildings were decorated with roughened patches of vegetation, which also appear on certain dog figures as patches of fur; such work is often described as 'Rockingham', although most of it was probably made in Staffordshire.[2] The spirit flasks shaped into amusing or topical figures were intended for use in inns. They were greatly in vogue in the years around the passing of the Reform Act of 1832 with representations of the leading political figures of the time. In saltglazed stoneware they were made with other fancy wares by the firm of Bournes of Denby, by several small potteries in the Chesterfield district, and by firms in London, including Doultons of Lambeth. Elsewhere similar flasks were made also in earthenware covered with a brown so-called 'Rockingham' glaze.

Fashionable wares

The wares described so far have been mainly popular wares, and most of them were made in styles which were comparatively long-lived. In contrast, the styles of the more fashionable wares are seen in this period to multiply rapidly and to affect different ceramic materials in differing degrees, so that the general pattern of stylistic changes becomes one of great complexity. The ceramic arts were closely affected by the new spirit of self-consciousness which was characteristic of the Victorian approach to the decorative

[1] R.G.Haggar, *Apollo*, L., 1949, p. 146.

[2] W. B. Honey, *English Pottery and Porcelain*, 1947, p. 231.

arts and was expressed by the appearance of the Government Schools of Design in the late 'thirties and 'forties, by the beginning of circulating collections about 1844 from which the Victoria and Albert Museum was to develop, by the appearance of magazines such as the *Art-Union* and the *Journal of Design and Manufactures*, and, in 1851, by the first of the great international exhibitions. Perhaps the extreme instance of this new self-consciousness was Henry Cole's project of 'Summerly's Art Manufactures', which was being worked out in 1847 and 1848. Inspired by his success in winning a Society of Arts award for a simple well-designed tea service made by Mintons (Pl. 60B), he tried the experiment of commissioning designs for useful objects, including pottery and glass, from well-known painters and sculptors, such as Richard Redgrave, H.J.Townsend and John Bell. That such an experiment was made, and was received with initial enthusiasm, is of greater significance than that the artists themselves were unable to rise to the occasion.

The Revived Rococo

In 1830, and during the following decade, the most significant style in English porcelain was that of the Revived Rococo. It had come as a reaction against the formal heavily-gilded French Empire style of the early years of the century and by the 'thirties was at the height of its development. It was scarcely a directly imitative style in the sense of copying precise examples of eighteenth-century porcelain. In effect it used motifs from the general resources of the eighteenth-century rococo style as a medium for expressing a sense of freedom and of a certain extravagant prettiness. Into this category came much of the more pretentious work of the Rockingham factory at Swinton, Yorkshire (which was closed in 1842). It appeared in the work of the Derby factory (closed in 1848) and of the Davenport factory at Longport; but probably the most significant work in this style was that carried out at the factory of John Rose at Coalport (often referred to at the time, and today, as 'Coalbrookdale') (Pl. 58A).

Besides the use of scrollwork and the tendency towards asymmetrical forms which are implied by the title 'rococo', the revived rococo made an extensive and characteristic use of applied flower-work. The great care and skill which was lavished on irregular groupings of flowers on the bodies of vessels, and on elaborate bouquets perched on lids, was in accordance with the Early Victorian respect for naturalism and greatly exceeded in botanical accuracy their eighteenth-century prototypes. In the 'forties the revived rococo style as such was on the wane, but the use of applied flowers continued, and the appearance of the new parian porcelain body in the later 'forties, with its marble-like qualities, led several manufacturers to use applied flower-work in the new body, unpainted and virtually unglazed. At the firm of Pountneys in Bristol Edward Raby was a notable specialist in applied flower-work who turned to parian in this way. The firm of Samuel Alcock of Burslem produced similar work; and at the 1851 Exhibition parian pieces with applied flower-work were shown by T. and R.Boote and T., J. and J. Mayer, both of Burslem. Such work in parian was clearly impractical for normal purposes, if only because of the difficulty of cleaning it, and comparatively little is heard of applied flower-work after the early 'fifties.

Relief decoration

One of the most characteristic products of the 'forties and early 'fifties was a group of wares with cast relief decoration. These were mainly jugs, but sometimes included also mugs and other similar objects. Many of the earlier examples of the jugs stand upon clearly differentiated feet; but in general they have loose sagging bodies with the weight well towards the base and wide upward-curving lips. The looseness of form was often accentuated by the great depth of the relief decoration, and this is in contrast to the comparatively shallow relief of Castleford and other earlier analogous wares. A number of different materials were used, varying from a putty-coloured earthenware to brown saltglazed stoneware and parian porcelain, but most frequently and characteristically the material was some form of hard vitreous white ware which can usually be described as a fine stoneware. Sometimes the jugs were coloured throughout or were painted; sometimes, as in the case of many of those produced by the Samuel Alcock factory, the ground was coloured, leaving the relief decoration in white, or vice versa, to give somewhat the effect of jasper ware. On some of the jugs, particularly in the early 'forties, the decoration was in the Gothic taste, as on examples made by W. Ridgway and Son of Hanley in 1840 and Charles Meigh of Shelton, Hanley, in 1842 (Pl. 57A). Bacchanalian themes were popular, as in an example with which Charles Meigh won in 1847 a medal offered by the Society of Arts for a relief-ornamented mug (Pl. 57A). Others were of genre subjects, such as the jug depicting a boy bird's-nesting shown by T., J. and J. Mayer in the 1851 exhibition, or subjects of contemporary commemorative interest, such as the 'Distin' jug made by Samuel Alcock and by Cork and Edge of Burslem depicting a family of saxhorn players who had given popular concerts in the Potteries.

Probably the most significant relief decorations, however, were the running plant patterns, consisting of long sprays or branches of a plant disposed about the surface of a vessel and originating usually from a rusticated handle. The use of these patterns was an expression of the same feeling for asymmetrical looseness and for naturalism as had inspired the revived rococo shapes and the use of applied flowers in porcelain; but with the important difference that whereas the applied flower decoration on elaborate revived rococo shapes tended to take the form of local embellishment, the running plant patterns were conceived in relation to the whole area to be decorated. A contemporary parallel to this treatment of plant patterns, and perhaps a source of inspiration, was the relief decoration on some of the French 'Beauvais' stoneware, which was shown at the Paris Exhibition of 1844 and was publicized by the *Art-Union* of that year. The free and highly naturalistic early-Victorian style of running plant patterns seems to have developed about the middle 'forties, when it can be seen for instance in the 1846 *Art-Union* in illustrations of the work of the firm of John Ridgway of Cauldon Place, Shelton (Fig. 2). Besides the stoneware jugs and similar wares, it is noteworthy that this style appears also in relief decorated silverware and in engraved glassware. In parian porcelain the running patterns were used, particularly by Mintons, as cast relief decoration on a variety of objects, including even cups and saucers. It is interesting to notice that in the early 'fifties Mintons were also rendering these loose over-all patterns in applied flower-work on parian vases (Pl. 58B); and the style even appeared in jasper ware among Wedgwoods' collection at the Paris exhibition of 1855.

A similar, and more extreme, expression of the Early Victorian passion for naturalism was the use of plant forms for the whole shape of ceramic objects. The whole form and surface of a vase, for instance, might be shaped to represent the leaves of a lily-of-the-valley plant with the flowers protruding from the sides. Such conceptions were by no means new in ceramic history; but the mid-nineteenth-century versions were not normally designed in an imitative spirit, and together with the running plant patterns the plant forms can be regarded as an original expression of the æsthetic ideas of the period. This again was a style which ceramics shared with work in silver and other media. In the years around 1849–51 a great deal of interesting and often beautiful work of this nature was produced in parian porcelain and other materials by such firms as Copelands, Mintons, Samuel Alcock and G. Grainger of Worcester.

'Majolica'

Plant forms and heavy relief plant motifs of various sorts were also found to be appropriate in the Victorian version of 'majolica', which was produced by Mintons just in time for the 1851 Exhibition. In the 1856 *Art-Journal* (the successor of the *Art-Union*) the Minton majolica is described as 'one of the most successful revivals of modern pottery'. It is said that Herbert Minton was inspired by green-glazed flower-pots which he had seen in Rouen in 1849; and the durable coloured-glaze ware which resulted was mainly developed by Léon Arnoux, a young French potter who was later to be art director of the factory. The ware was regarded at the time as an imitation of Italian 'majolica', and in consequence the term (spelled with a 'j') came to be attached to this type of pottery which has little connection with the true tin-glazed and painted 'maiolica' of art history. Sometimes the Victorian majolica was painted, but usually the term was used merely to imply earthenware with coloured glaze or glazes. The heavy majolica, particularly with green glazes, was much used in forms incorporating large leaf shapes, as in the instance of a chestnut dish by Mintons (Pl 60A); and this fashion led Wedgwoods to revive their own eighteenth-century use of green glaze in the production of dishes covered entirely with large-scale naturalistic foliage in relief. Majolica in this sense became the common medium for the innumerable Victorian jardinières with plant-form or other decoration in bold relief, which were made in Staffordshire potteries throughout the rest of the century and beyond.

Sèvres imitations

Alongside these stylistic developments in the free use of rococo motifs and natural forms, much imitative work was being carried out in porcelain in the manner of the eighteenth-century wares of Sèvres, Dresden and Chelsea. Of these the work in the manner of Sèvres was by far the most important and became one of the strongest elements in the later porcelain tradition of this country. Victorian imitations of this sort differed from the 'revived rococo' in so far as the makers were serving an informed taste for the originals, and considerable efforts were therefore made to reproduce the original styles as exactly as possible. Admiration for Sèvres porcelain and the imitation of it had been virtually continuous in this country since the eighteenth century. In the 1830's much work in a distinctively Sèvres style was being carried out at Derby. During the 'forties it became the most fashionable style for the better class of porcelain at nearly all the leading factories, including particularly Roses of Coalport, Copelands and Mintons. The Coalport factory was the one which, under the influence of W.F.Rose from 1841, devoted the greatest amount of attention to the exact reproduction of the eighteenth-century Sèvres colours and decorations. In this the firm was also guided and encouraged by the important London

Fig. 2. Jug with painted relief decoration from the firm of John Ridgway, Shelton, about 1845. *Art-Union* (1846, 318).

dealers, Daniell and Co., whose name often appears on the wares. Great efforts were made to match the coloured grounds of the old Sèvres, and the Coalport versions of such grounds as 'bleu de roi', 'rose Pompadour' (mistakenly known at the time as 'rose du Barry') and turquoise were regarded as triumphs of imitation. Some of the imitations made at Coalport, and elsewhere, were so exact as to include old Sèvres marks: a refinement which can scarcely have been carried out without any intention to defraud.

Porcelain painting

Porcelain painting naturally tended to follow the porcelain styles. It is noteworthy, however, that neither the revived rococo nor the Sèvres style offered such wide opportunities to the porcelain painter as had the French Empire style of the early years of the century, and it is perhaps for this reason that porcelain painting tended to become less interesting and less important during the early Victorian period. The revived rococo was largely concerned with surface modelling and with raised decoration, and only grudgingly accorded the flat areas which are required for composed 'pictures' on porcelain objects. The Sèvres imitations were limiting to the porcelain painter to the extent that they implied the reproduction of a Sèvres manner of painting. By the 'thirties the lush naturalism, which had characterized the flower painting of the early part of the century, had given way in the work of some of the painters to a harder, more mannered and sharply coloured style. Flower painting of this sort, often against a dark ground, is associated particularly with the younger Steeles, the brothers Edwin and Horatio, who had been working at Derby and also, in the case of Edwin, at the Rockingham factory.[3] Similar work is also found from Coalport and from the factories in Staffordshire. The work of the 'forties and 'fifties in the Sèvres style led to carefully placed and over-precious painting, such as the flowers and trophies of William Cook of Coalport. Some interesting bird painting was also produced at Coalport in the eighteenth-century Chelsea manner. One of the more outstanding figure painters was Thomas Kirkby, whose finely painted amorini appeared on some of Mintons' porcelain at the 1851 Exhibition. Much of this artist's later work was carried out on the Minton majolica. Another accomplished figure painter was Thomas Bott of Worcester who became widely known in the later 'fifties and 'sixties for his white enamel painting on the 'Limoges ware' of Kerr and Binns (the Worcester firm which succeeded to the Chamberlain factory in 1852 and was known as the Worcester Royal Porcelain Company from 1862) (Pl. 61A).

Classical and other influences

The mid-century Sèvres imitations in porcelain represented in some degree a bridge between rococo and classical sources of inspiration. The

[3] W.B.Honey, *Old English Porcelain*, 1948, p. 129.

Victorian interest in classical work was not, however, derived from this source. To some extent the direct imitation of classical shape and decoration seems to have continued since the days of the first Josiah Wedgwood; but the greatly increased interest in this sort of work in the 'forties has something of the appearance of an intellectually-inspired movement which had little in common with the general æsthetic outlook of the period. In the mid-'forties writers in the *Art-Union* were repeatedly stressing the importance of Greek inspiration, which in the idiom of the time was described as 'Etruscan' or 'Etrurian'. In the years around 1845 Copelands were producing a quantity of wares in direct imitation of Greek shapes and decorations, and were extending these ideas to such utilitarian objects as ewers and basins. In this phase the high-handled Greek 'oenochoe' jug shape was especially favoured (Fig. 3). During the late 'forties L. L. Dillwyn's Swansea factory was producing its 'Etruscan ware'; and Wedgwoods were reviving their eighteenth-century designs in jasper ware and black basaltes. In the same period, and in the 'fifties, the London firm of Thomas Battam made a speciality of imitative Greek wares, and at the 1851 Exhibition their display took the form of an artificial grotto meant to represent an 'Etruscan tomb' overspilling with appropriate pottery.

Another aspect of the revival of classical ideas can be seen in the widespread fashion in the 'fifties for work in terracotta; that is, in highly-fired unglazed earthenware. Attention had been drawn to French work in this medium at the Paris Exhibition of 1849. The material was considered to be particularly suited to garden ornaments, and at the 1851 Exhibition an amount of large work of this nature, mostly in classical shapes and with classical architectural detail, was shown by firms such as J. and M.P.Bell of Glasgow, Ferguson and Miller, also of Glasgow, and Blanchard of Lambeth.

Classical shapes and classical decorative motifs became part of the general repertoire of ceramic ideas; but so far as directly imitative work was concerned the main influence of classical ideas was naturally on decorative earthenware or stoneware rather than on porcelain. In the 'fifties this museum-inspired interest tended to shift from classical Greek work to that of the Renaissance, and particularly of the French Renaissance. During the years following the 1851 Exhibition Mintons were producing their 'Palissy ware', which was allied to their majolica of the same period and included pieces made in direct imitation of the work of the French sixteenth-century potter and his followers with high-relief decoration covered by coloured glazes. The elaborately inlaid Saint-Porchaire ware, normally known to the Victorians as 'Henri Deux', was another French sixteenth-century source of inspiration for imitative work. The 'Limoges ware' of Kerr and Binns, which attracted much attention at the Paris Exhibition of 1855, had little but a vague technical similarity with the Limoges enamels, but much of the distinctive white enamel painting was based on Renaissance arabesques and figure-work (Pl. 61A). It is noteworthy that versions of Palissy, Henri Deux and Limoges wares can all be found among the work of French factories of the period. Part of this French influence was undoubtedly due to the number of French artists who were employed in Staffordshire, and particularly by Mintons, during the 'fifties. Besides the art director Léon Arnoux, Mintons employed a series of French sculptors primarily in modelling for majolica and parian work. During the 'fifties Emile Jeannest, Albert Carrier de Belleuse and Hugues Protat were employed in succession, and all of them were also instructors at the newly founded Potteries' Schools of Design.

Two other sources of inspiration need to be mentioned – the Gothic and the Moorish – which in the early Victorian context were largely architectural in origin. The use of Gothic patterns on stoneware jugs in the early 'forties has already been noted. In the middle 'forties Copelands were producing porcelain in a 'pierced Gothic' pattern; and in the later part of the decade A.W.N.Pugin, the chief protagonist of the Gothic style, designed decorations for Mintons which were printed and painted on a number of tablewares in the Minton 'New Stone' body and in porcelain, some of which were shown at the 1851 Exhibition. The Moorish decorations were used less frequently, but in a

similar manner to the Gothic. They were most often known as 'Alhambresque' and were derived from published illustrations of the stucco work in the Alhambra at Granada. They appear, for instance, on a jug and a flower-pot by Ridgway and Abington of Hanley which were illustrated in the *Art-Union* in 1845 and 1846: and at the Paris Exhibition of 1855 Copelands' chief exhibit was a three-feet-high Alhambresque vase which was said to be the largest vessel ever made of parian.

After the many imitative and derivative styles which have been mentioned, it is as well to point out that one of the most obvious sources of ceramic ideas, the pottery of the Far East, was largely ignored during this period. It was the period of reaction against the 'Japan' patterns which had been prevalent earlier in the century and which in

Fig. 3. A classical jug by Copelands, from the Manchester Exhibition of 1845–6. *Art-Union* (1846, 32).

93

early Victorian times were only being produced at a low level of fashion. In a review of the work of the John Ridgway factory in the 1846 *Art-Union* a solitary vase in the 'Chinese' style evokes the acid comment that it is 'not of a class we desire to see multiplied'. The Victorian revival of Far Eastern styles lay well beyond 1860. It should also be pointed out that whilst the modern eye is immediately struck by the elements of plagiarism in Victorian pottery and porcelain, it is rare to find that imitation has been so exact as not to leave scope for the expression of a contemporary Early Victorian spirit. Bemused as they were by the many examples of earlier work which were brought before their eyes, the early Victorian potters did nevertheless often combine these elements to produce work of original quality. Besides the free use of rococo and plant motifs, a number of distinctive styles emerged which were associated with particular factories. An example which has not so far been mentioned is the highly personal style of pierced porcelain made by Chamberlains of Worcester which attracted considerable interest in the years between 1846 and 1851 (Fig. 4). In general, the most publicized pieces tended to be the most imitative. Even around the middle of the century, when the Sèvres influence was at its strongest, Sèvres motifs appeared among the everyday table-services as only one element among a vast range of patterns most of which were in their interpretation entirely characteristic of their own period.

Fig. 4. Stemmed bowl of pierced porcelain, made by Chamberlains of Worcester in the later 'forties. *Journal of Design and Manufactures* (II, 95).

Porcelain figures

The earthenware figures of the time have already been described as wares of a 'peasant' quality. Porcelain figures were naturally more susceptible to fashion, and during this period came to diverge markedly from the earthenware figures not only in style but also in the nature of their conception. Some of the new porcelain figures of the years around the 'thirties, as seen particularly in the work of the Derby and Rockingham factories, were characterized by the use of strong contrasting colours applied flatly over large areas. The Derby biscuit figures were no longer made, apparently for technical reasons connected with the

factory's organization of firings. A quantity of new porcelain figures, both glazed and painted and in biscuit, were being made at Mintons in the later 'thirties and in the 'forties, and some at least of these were in eighteenth-century costume.

A notable change of attitude towards porcelain figure-work came with the introduction of the parian porcelain body. This new body was used for many different purposes and for many different styles of hollow wares, but it was originally produced for making figures and it was for this purpose that it was considered ideally suitable. It is said that experiments were being made concurrently at both Copelands and Mintons towards the production of a material of this nature. At Copelands the parian body seems to have been produced in the course of attempts to rediscover with the help of an ex-employee of the Derby factory the formula of the old Derby biscuit body. The potentialities of the new body, and the manner in which it was mainly to be used, were expressed in the first group of parian figures from Copelands which were shown at the Manchester Exhibition of 1845–6. The same body, with slight variations, was soon being made by many factories. Copelands called it 'statuary porcelain', Coalport and Wedgwoods called it 'Carrara', but it was the Minton term 'Parian' which eventually passed into the language. It was a comparatively hard form of porcelain, and as such was markedly different from the bone china which was otherwise in universal use as the standard British porcelain body. A writer in the 1846 *Art-Union* was already praising the 'lustrous transparency' of the surface of the parian figures in comparison with the excess of reflected light in glazed figures and the complete lack of it in the older biscuit figures. Although not immediately apparent, parian was normally given a slight 'smear' glaze, which imparted to it the dull smoothness of polished marble.

Modern taste is not easily reconciled to the use of one material in imitation of another. To the Early Victorians, who were inclined to emphasize imitative rather than original elements in the decorative arts, the resemblance of parian to marble justified the immediate and extensive use of the material for making figures in the style of marble statuary. The traditional rococo base, and the use of colour, suddenly became relatively unfashionable. Porcelain figures came to be called 'statuettes', and contemporary publicists were delighted at the elevating effect of copies of fine sculpture being within the reach of every home. The *Art-Union* of London prided itself upon its early recognition of the medium, and in 1846 commissioned reduced copies of John Gibson's 'Narcissus' and J.H.Foley's 'Innocence' (Pl. 59A) to be made by Copelands as prizes for its subscribers. In 1847 Mintons were producing two parian figures, both after John Bell, which were commissioned by Henry Cole for his 'Summerly's Art Manufactures'. Versions of Hiram Power's much-admired statue 'The Greek Slave' appeared from 1849 onwards from Mintons, Copelands, and Pountneys of Bristol. R.J.Wyatt, William Theed junior (Pl. 59A), Carlo Marochetti, Richard

Westmacott and W.Calder Marshall were among the other contemporary sculptors whose work was represented in parian. Many of the Copeland reductions from large-size statues were effected by the reducing machine of Benjamin Cheverton, and the name of Cheverton on the base of a figure has often been misinterpreted to imply that he was the modeller in the normal sense of the word. Statuary was not, however, the only source for derivative designs. A Minton group of about 1849 was taken from a picture of Ruth and Naomi by Henry O'Neil; and Mintons' Prince of Wales in a sailor-boy's costume, of about the same time, was an adaptation of Winterhalter's picture.

Following the example of the great dessert service made by Mintons for the 1851 Exhibition the use of parian figures in combination with normal glazed porcelain became a recognized mode for factory prestige work. Probably the most distinguished of this sort was the 'Shakespeare service' made by Kerr and Binns for the Dublin Exhibition of 1853, in which Shakespearean figures, modelled by W.B.Kirk, were applied to porcelain pieces decorated with Renaissance motifs (Pl. 61B). Work of such virtuosity could not be considered typical, but the use of parian figures on great occasions was a measure of their popularity and of the extent to which the new medium was adapted to contemporary taste.

GLASS

During the eighteen-thirties and early 'forties clear lead crystal with cut decoration continued to be the characteristic product of the British glass factories. This was largely due to the international success of the English and Irish cut crystal of the earlier part of the century; but it can also be attributed in some degree to the heavy excise duty on glass and the restrictive methods used in its collection which tended to limit experiments in new methods of colouring glass and of decorating it.

The early nineteenth-century version of mitre cutting, with its diaper patterns of deeply cut diamonds arranged predominantly in horizontal motifs, became traditional to British cut crystal work and has survived in its essentials to the present day. In the more fashionable work of the 'thirties and early 'forties, however, a distinctive stylistic development was based upon the use of flat or curved surface cutting, implying the removal of slices from the surface of a vessel, rather than upon the criss-cross of mitre grooves. In this phase straight vertical motifs were preferred, and these were achieved most frequently by broadly hollowed or pillared flutes or more simply by flat vertical facets. The use of such motifs affected not merely the decoration of objects but also their shapes. Perhaps because it was easier to cut the broad flutes or facets on surfaces which curved only in one direction, the shapes tended to be ones with angular profiles. The barrel-shaped decanters of the earlier part of the century became basically cylindrical in shape; whilst the neck rings of the older type tended to disappear, probably because they interfered with a sense of simple vertical pattern. These characteristics can already be seen in the pattern drawings of about 1830 which belonged to Samuel Miller, foreman cutter at the Waterford factory,[4] and their development in the 'thirties and 'forties can be noticed in surviving pattern-books in English factories.

The angular broad-fluted work represented in glassware the last phase of the heavy formal Empire style which had affected all the decorative arts of the early nineteenth century. As such it stood in sharp contrast to the revived rococo style which had already developed by the 'twenties in British porcelain and silverwork as a reaction against the Empire formality. Rococo motifs could scarcely be used directly in cut crystal work, but the accompanying feeling for curving shapes and for curved and often asymmetrical motifs was a minor element in British glasswork during the 'thirties and was to become predominant during the later 'forties and 'fifties. Decanters or water-carafes with globular bodies were beginning to appear in the 'thirties alongside the many straight-sided cylindrical examples. The decanter with a globular body and tall slender neck was a natural glass shape which had appeared at many different times in the history of blown glass; and although

the Early Victorian version of it was often decorated with facet or mitre cutting, it was best produced in comparatively thin glass with decoration of shallow-cut hollows or else of engraving. It is interesting to notice that of the six clear glass decanters which happen to be illustrated in the *Journal of Design and Manufactures* from the display at the Birmingham Exhibition of 1849, five are globular or squat-globular in shape. One of these, by George Bacchus and Sons of Birmingham, has engraved decoration (Fig. 1), another by W.H., B. and J.Richardson of Stourbridge is mainly decorated by a pattern of cut hollows, and the others, by Lloyd and Summerfield of Birmingham and by Bacchus, are decorated by cutting over their whole surface. An analogous curvilinear shape was that of the champagne glass with hemispherical bowl, which was in fashion by the early 'thirties.[5] By the middle of the century wineglasses of all sorts were being made in a variety of curved, and often ogee-curved, forms.

The removal of the excise duty on glass in 1845 was followed by an enthusiastic development of deep mitre cutting on objects suitable for making in thick glass, and the more ambitious of this work included the use of curvilinear motifs such as that produced by Richardsons for the 1851 Exhibition (Pl. 64A). On the other hand, almost immediately after the 1851 Exhibition cut crystal work began to lose its fashionable standing, and during the remainder of the 'fifties, and beyond, new designs of this nature tended to be somewhat unobtrusive, such for instance as over-all patterns of small widely-spaced stars. The profiles of vessels made in the middle and later 'fifties were predominantly globular or curvilinear; and twisted work was beginning to be common, especially as a means of forming the handles of vessels.

Engraving

Throughout the Early Victorian period decoration by engraving was becoming increasingly popular. In the 'thirties engraving was being carried out in Dudley by the Herbert family, and

[4] M.S.Dudley Westropp, *Irish Glass*, 1920, p. 56, etc.

[5] W.A.Thorpe, *History of English and Irish Glass*, Vol. I, 1929, p. 314.

particularly by William Herbert, for the firm of Thomas Hawkes of Dudley. Around the 'forties the Wood family of engravers were working in Stourbridge, and Thomas Wood was among the independent exhibitors at the 1851 Exhibition. Of more specialized and local interest was the engraved work, mostly representing Sunderland Bridge, which was carried out in Sunderland on local glass in the 'thirties and 'forties by Robert Haddock and Robert Pyle. Probably the most outstanding engraved pieces shown at the 1851 Exhibition were the goblets with deep floral motifs designed (and perhaps engraved) by W.J.Muckley for Richardsons (Pl. 63A), and the engraved versions of Greek 'oenochoe' jug shapes which were commissioned and shown by the London firm of dealers J.G.Green and were perhaps made by Bacchus of Birmingham. The latter included a rare example of finely engraved figure-work (Pl. 63B). Flower and plant motifs varied from tight bunches in a style borrowed from porcelain painting to loose over-all running patterns which appeared equally in the late 'forties on pottery and silverwork. Probably in reaction against the excessively deep mitre cutting of the years around the middle of the century and against the cheap pressed-glass imitations of cutting, engraving became by far the most fashionable method of decoration during a long period following the 1851 Exhibition. In the 'fifties engraving was used for a wide range of wares from services with simple patterned edgings to elaborate prestige pieces closely decorated with Renaissance arabesques. The great vogue for engraving began to attract emigrant craftsmen from Central Europe. Prominent among these was J.H.B.Millar, a Bohemian, who towards the end of the 'fifties established in Edinburgh an important firm of engravers which was staffed initially by fellow Bohemian craftsmen.

Engraving by acid etching was used commercially in the 'thirties by Thomas Hawkes of Dudley. It was being used by at least one firm in Stourbridge about the early 'forties, and in the 'fifties further experiments were made by Benjamin Richardson (of the Richardson firm which in the later 'fifties was being operated under his name alone). It was not, however, until the 'sixties that extensive use came to be made of the process in this country.

Colour

The styles of cut and engraved glassware which have been described so far were mostly made in the fine clear lead glass for which the glassmakers of this country had already achieved an international reputation. Contemporary British accounts of the glass in international exhibitions never failed to remark upon the superior quality of the British glass material, and the material was naturally seen to its best advantage when it was used clear and uncoloured. In the Central European glassmaking areas of Bohemia and south-east Germany a reaction against British cut crystal had resulted during the 'twenties and 'thirties in a remarkable development in the use of coloured glasses. The techniques and styles associated with the Central European coloured glasswork, of this so-called 'Biedermeier' period, were taken up by glass factories in western European countries and particularly by those of France. About the later 'thirties coloured glass was being used in British factories for simple cased, or layered, work and as an alternative material for pieces normally made in uncoloured glass. The firm of Thomas Hawkes were producing semi-opaque white glassware with gilt decoration in the mid-'thirties, and glasses engraved through silver stain were being made in Stourbridge about the early 'forties. But it was not until the removal of the excise in 1845 that the British glassmakers suddenly found themselves free to participate fully in the international coloured-glass styles. The leading spirit in this movement seems to have been Benjamin Richardson, and already in the Manchester Exhibition at the end of 1845 the main interest of the big display by the Richardson firm was in coloured, opal, cased and painted glasses.

Other firms followed rapidly to exploit this field of glasswork. Even the Birmingham firm of F. and C.Osler, mainly known for large-scale work in crystal glass, was found showing opal flower vases with relief painted decoration at the Royal Polytechnic Institution Exhibition of 1848.

At the Birmingham Exhibition of 1849 the great majority of the glasses of the Birmingham firms George Bacchus and Sons and Rice Harris and Son, as well as those of Richardsons of Stourbridge, showed the use of colour in one form or another. The fashion reached its culmination at the 1851 Exhibition where almost all the important glass manufacturers in the country were seen to be making plain coloured, cased or opal glassware. In the Exhibition catalogue the longest list of colours is that of Rice Harris, which is given as 'opal, alabaster, turquoise, amber, canary, topaz, chrysoprase, pink, blue, light and dark ruby, black, brown, green, purple, etc.'

Coloured glasses might be used for work in any of the current styles of uncoloured glasswork. Perhaps the most characteristic use of plain coloured glass was for comparatively small objects, toilet bottles and the like, in the sharply angular shapes with broad vertical facet cutting which were associated with the contemporary Bohemian coloured glass. The most dramatic use of coloured glasses, however, was in the cased glass of the period, which was also used largely in styles derived from the Biedermeier glass of Central Europe. In cased glass a semi-opaque white was frequently used as the outer layer, or else as an intermediate layer to give emphasis to the change of colour between, say, clear blue glass on the outside and uncoloured glass on the inside. Such glasses were always decorated by cutting through the outer layer or layers of glass. The cuttings were usually spaced to leave between them undisturbed areas of the outer layer, and cut hollows and hollow flutes were often contrived in a manner which was suggestive of the lights of a Gothic traceried window and which accorded well with the neo-Gothic taste of the period (Pl. 63A). The richness of effect might be further enhanced by painting or engraving on the glass exposed in the cut-away areas, or by gilding on the undisturbed areas of an outer white layer. Another use of cased glass was to give emphasis to engraving. A thin outer layer of clear coloured glass was used as a field through which a pattern was engraved on to the uncoloured body beneath. For this purpose casing had much the same effect as staining, but the depth of the colour

made it more suitable for use with comparatively deep engraving. A notable use of this technique was in some at least of the Richardson engraved work associated with W.J.Muckley, which has already been mentioned (Pl. 63A).

The opalines, or vessels made throughout of semi-opaque glass, appeared mostly in styles which were distinct from those of plain coloured or cased glass. Since this material was both coloured and obscured, there was little to gain by cutting it, and makers tended therefore to use it in natural flowing shapes. A current Central European style of two-colour opalines was represented in the work of Richardsons and probably of other Midland factories. White and green opal glasses were combined in the same vessels, the green being used in shapes suggestive of leaves for overhanging rims and other extruding parts. On the other hand, when the British glassmakers were concerned in producing painted and gilt opal glasses, their attention was attracted by the work of the French factories rather than by those of Central Europe. Large white opal vases with floral painting made by Richardsons around 1851 are scarcely distinguishable in general style from the more ambitious French painted vases of the period (Pl. 62B). Most of the painted opalines were of white opal or of alabaster glass; and some of the most attractive of this work appeared on jugs and vases with low-bellied forms which are reminiscent of contemporary jug shapes in pottery. Richardson examples were often painted with friezes of classical figures or with monochrome scenes; and also printed decoration was often used on opalines of this sort.

The fashion for enamel painting did not necessarily imply the use of semi-opaque glasses. The Richardson firm in particular was responsible for a considerable amount of painting on objects of clear transparent glass; and this was the most favoured medium for the glass designs commissioned by Henry Cole around 1847 for his 'Summerly's Art Manufactures'. The latter included glasses painted with a much-imitated motif of water-plants, which were designed by the painter Richard Redgrave and made by the firm of J.F. Christy of Lambeth (Pl. 62A).

The belated British participation in the coloured-glass styles of the mid-century was momentous in its time, but it was also short-lived. Two other influences upon British glasswork of the period need to be considered – those of Greek pottery and of Venetian glass. Neither of these influences was dramatic in its immediate effects, but both were to be of lasting significance in the developing tradition of modern British glassware.

Greek forms

The somewhat academic Victorian revival of Greek pottery forms was reflected in many of the details of glass shapes and decorations after the removal of the excise duty in 1845. The Greek pinched mouth, for instance, became a common feature of the opal and alabaster glass jugs. About 1847 a London dealer, a Mr Giller of Holborn, was producing (through Thomas Webb of Stourbridge and the London decorating firm of Thomas Battam) painted glassware which was deliberately shaped and decorated in the manner of Greek pottery. Other painted glass versions of Greek pottery were shown at the 1851 Exhibition by Davis, Greathead and Green of Stourbridge. The use of Greek jug shapes in clear glass with engraved decoration has already been mentioned in the instance of the display of the dealers J.G. Green at the 1851 Exhibition (Pl. 63B), and it was from sources such as this that the high-shouldered decanters and claret jugs of the later part of the century were derived.

Venetian influence

The Venetian influence is less easily defined. The word 'Venetian' occurs in the 1851 Exhibition catalogue in descriptions of the work of the Richardson firm, of Davis, Greathead and Green, of Rice Harris, and of Apsley Pellat; but it is difficult to find any common denominator among this work other than a certain freedom or eccentricity of style. Glasses made by Apsley Pellat were described as Venetian in the 1847 *Art-Union* with apparently little reason other than that they were engraved with Renaissance arabesque patterns; whilst the Venetian element in the same firm's 'Anglo-Venetian' glasses at the 1851 Exhibition consisted in their being frosted and gilt.

An important feature in the work of the Bacchus firm about the middle of the century was the use of multicoloured threading in the stems of wine-glasses, and these were often also convoluted (Pl. 64B). At the 1851 Exhibition threaded glass was also shown by Rice Harris, and elaborately convoluted stems were a feature of wine-glasses shown by Lloyd and Summerfield. The style of Venetian glass in the sense of a style using rapidly formed plastic shapes, was strongly advocated by Ruskin in the second volume of his *Stones of Venice* (1853); and this concept was applied by the architect Philip Webb when, around 1860, he was designing table-glasses to be made for William Morris by James Powell and Sons of London.

Novelties

A feature of early Victorian glasswork was the appearance of various sorts of glass novelties, which in effect meant the use of glass for unexpected purposes or the use of unusual glass techniques for the sake of their interest as curiosities. Apsley Pellat's 'cameo incrustations', or small white paste images enclosed within clear glass, were, in this country, a novelty of the early 'twenties, although the knowledge of them survived sufficiently for them to be included in the firm's display at the 1851 Exhibition. Around the middle of the century glass busts were being made by two of the Birmingham firms, F. and C. Osler and Lloyd and Summerfield. These were produced in moulds; and those by Osler, at least, were given a frosted surface by abrading. A novelty of the same period was the double-walled vessels with silvering on the interior surfaces, which gave an opportunity for interesting effects of reflection and colour. The patent for this method of manufacture was taken out in 1849 by F. Hale Thomson and Edward Varnish, and the vessels were apparently made at the factory of James Powell and Sons.

The most striking of the Early Victorian novelties, however, were the glass paper-weights enclosing ingenious coloured patterns. The vogue for paper-weights came to this country from France, where they had been made in great numbers since 1845. A writer in the first volume of the

Journal of Design and Manufactures in 1849 gives a clear indication of the extent of the popular fancy for paper-weights and of the firm which was responsible for developing their manufacture in this country: 'It were to be wished that Messrs Bacchus had been a little earlier in the manufacture of their Glass Paper Weights, for the specimens we have recently seen at their works are quite equal in transparency, colour, skilful arrangement of parts, and ingenuity of make, to the foreign works with which stationers' and fancy shops have been and are so crowded.' Most of the paper-weights which can be presumed to have been made in this country during the mid-century years are of the 'millefiori' variety, whereby an internal pattern was built up by arranging small coloured glass canes in concentric circles; and once acquired, the millefiori technique was used in the same manner for other objects, such as standing inkwells and door-knobs, which offered similar opportunities for the use of thick glass as a means of magnifying the internal pattern.

Pressed glass

Most of the fine glasswork of the period was made, as it is today, by the traditional methods of hand-craftsmanship; although some, such as opaline glasses with relief decoration, would be produced by blowing into moulds. This was a period in which the methods of moulding were greatly extended for the making of cheap glassware, and in particular it was the period in which the process of press-moulding was first developed for the production of dishes and other open shapes. The method of pressing glass between a mould and a plunger appears to have been mainly an American invention. In this country it was being extensively used from the early 'thirties onwards by a number of Midland firms, notably Thomas Hawkes, Bacchus (known during most of the 'thirties as Bacchus and Green), and Rice Harris; it was also presumably used by Apsley Pellat, who patented a small modification to the process in 1831. In America the pressed glass of the 'thirties and 'forties was mostly decorated in the 'lacy' style with elaborate relief patterns on finely stippled grounds, and a somewhat similar free style of relief decoration was used on pressed glass in France. Some of the early British patterns for pressed glass were no doubt of this sort; but it seems probable that the majority were in imitation of cut crystal styles, and this was perhaps natural in the country to which cut crystal was native (Fig. 5). Identifiable pieces of British pressed glass in 'lacy' and similar styles are usually found to belong to a later phase about the 'seventies and 'eighties when much of the British pressed-glass industry was concentrated in the north-east of England.

Fig. 5. Pressed-glass fruit dish made Birmingham, 1850. *Journal of* by George Bacchus & Sons of *Design and Manufactures* (IV, 94).

Domestic Metalwork

Gilt brass bell-pull.

Domestic Metalwork

JAMES MELTON

The period under review is notable for the wide incursions into the home made by metalwork of all kinds. The traditional hand methods of furniture-making were proving far too costly and slow to produce the increasing quantities of goods demanded by the rising population, and the opportunity to replace traditional wooden articles by those of cast-iron and brass was seized quickly by enterprising manufacturers.

Early in the 1830's John Claudius Loudon (1783–1843), editor of the *Architectural Magazine*, was foremost among those who advocated the greater use of metalwork in the home. In a monster volume, *An Encyclopædia of Cottage, Farm, and Villa Architecture and Furniture*, first issued in 1833, he wrote:

'The introduction of iron into the furniture of Farm houses would be attended with considerable economy, at least in the article of dining-tables, sideboards, bedsteads, and Hall, lobby or porch chairs. The sideboards may be formed of slabs of native marble in some districts, and slate in others, supported by enriched cast-iron feet, or by brackets of various kinds. Sideboards of this kind have a massive architectural effect, very suitable for all houses whatever, and especially for houses in the country, where room is not an object. For our own part, we should even prefer slabs of finely polished stone, as sideboards, to wood of any kind; but cast iron may be substituted; and where neither metal nor stone is approved of, wood of some kind is always to be obtained, and may be worked and polished at pleasure. The idea of having iron bedsteads will, we have no doubt, shock those who have been always accustomed to consider mahogany as essential for this piece of furni-

ture: but we can assure them that they are to be found in the houses of people of wealth and fashion in London; sometimes even for best beds.'

As in other instances, the new medium was introduced in the form of the material it intended to rival. The various articles of iron were moulded with bunches of flowers and fruit, rococo curves and other ornament in close imitation of the hand-carved woodwork they were to replace. Before long, an outcry arose and the pendulum of fashion was agitated violently in a reverse direction: away from the naturalistic and the curved line and backwards in time to the severe and medieval. This in turn was pounced upon by the contemporary critics, and their denunciations were in bitter terms. Augustus Welby Pugin (1812–52) wrote, in his *True Principles of Christian Architecture* (1841), of 'the inconsistencies of modern grates, which are not infrequently made to represent diminutive fronts of castellated or ecclesiastical buildings with turrets, loopholes, windows, and doorways, all in a space of forty inches. The fender is a sort of embattled parapet, with a lodge-gate at each end; the end of the poker is a sharp pointed finial; and at the summit of the tongs is a saint. It is impossible to enumerate half the absurdities of modern metal-workers; but all these proceed from the false notion of *disguising* instead of *beautifying* articles of utility. If a clock is required, it is not unusual to cast a Roman warrior in a flying chariot, round one of the wheels of which, on close inspection, the hours may be descried; or the whole front of a cathedral church reduced to a few inches in height, with the clock-face occupying the position of a magnificent rose window.'

Once launched, Pugin's pen sailed relentlessly onward. He attacked 'those inexhaustible mines of bad taste, Birmingham and Sheffield', and described 'staircase turrets for inkstands, monumental crosses for light-shades, gable ends hung on handles for door-porters, and four doorways and a cluster of pillars to support a French lamp; while a pair of *pinnacles* supporting an arch is called a Gothic-pattern scraper, and a wiry compound of quatrefoils and fan tracery an abbey garden seat. Neither relative scale, form, purpose, nor unity of style, is ever considered by those who design these abominations; if they only introduce a quatrefoil or an acute arch, be the outline and style of the article ever so modern and debased, it is at once denominated and sold as Gothic.'

Those who strove to draw attention to the many inconsistencies of contemporary design were themselves no less guilty in their striving after a pointless perfection. Their zeal embraced even the common door-hinge, and they deplored the fact that it was concealed in the jambs of doorways and cabinets, and was no longer the elaborate and decorative article of earlier centuries. Even the heads of bolts and rivets, they said, should not be left plain, but should be in the form of a rosette, quatrefoil or fleur-de-lys.

Altogether the attacks of Pugin and others had little effect on contemporary design. The mass of the people preferred and demanded plentiful ornamentation on everything they bought, and the manufacturers and the designers took care to supply it in quantity and variety. There were very few styles of the preceding centuries that were not incorporated, either singly or anachronistically and haphazardly with others, in the decoration of metal objects ranging from pokers to bedsteads, and from cradles to chandeliers.

Centres of manufacture

The manufacture of metal wares centred on Birmingham and Sheffield. At the latter were made principally articles of steel, but at Birmingham (which may be understood to include the nearby towns of Wolverhampton and Walsall and the numerous adjacent villages) was made a multiplicity of objects of all kinds, in both iron and brass, and of every quality – the latter, when at its lowest, having borrowed the name of its place of origin as a description, and the term 'Brummagem made' adheres to this day to anything of a trashy or counterfeit nature. In fairness, it must be mentioned that while a high proportion of goods from the Birmingham factories certainly were made for the cheaper markets, a considerable amount of high-quality work was done there. The standard set by the Soho Works of Matthew Boulton, who died in 1809, but whose manufactory was continued for a further period of nearly forty years, was not easily forgotten.

Between the years 1810 and 1850 the population of Birmingham increased by no less than 150 per cent, and at the same time the cost of goods made there was lowered by from 60 to 85 per cent. During the same period exported iron and steel wares rose from an annual figure of 5,800 tons to over 23,000 tons; the latter reaching a value of £2,200,000. Brass and copper goods exported in 1849 were worth nearly £2,000,000, and the majority of them went, incidentally, to India. The rapid rise in the population of the British Isles together with the lowering of the cost of manufactured goods continued until long after 1860, and were part and parcel of the competitive inventiveness that characterized the Victorian era.

Much of the manufacturing of metal wares in the Midlands was carried out in factories of a type similar to those universal today, but much was produced under a system peculiar to the district and the hardware trade. Single men, or groups of men, hired small workshops which were part of a large block where the power for turning and other mechanical processes was provided by the owner of the building; the rental paid for the use of the workshop including also the use of the power. The makers of goods under these conditions sold them each week to a merchant who was concerned with the marketing of them, and with the money received they purchased the materials with which to make their quota in the week to follow. The familiar factory slowly superseded this individualistic way of earning a livelihood, but in 1860 there were many 'power-hirers' still to be found.

Metal wares

The coming of the railway during the first decades of the period under review not only increased the speed of travel, but was the creator of an enormous demand for metal. Rails, engines, coaches, stations and every detail of the new means of communication called for increasing quantities of iron, steel, brass and copper. There was every inducement for manufacturers to improve and cheapen metals, and the ironmasters, especially, were striving eagerly to introduce any new method or appliance that would allow them to produce more metal for less money and at the same time increase their own profits. As a result, there was a plentiful supply of raw material available to the makers of domestic metal wares, who were enabled to reap the benefits of advances initiated by the Iron Horse.

The railways were responsible not only for calling forth abundant supplies of metal, but they played a further part by ensuring speedy delivery of the finished article. At the same time, with the increasing tempo of life and the greater rapidity of communications, the spread of ideas was facilitated. What was fashionable in London could be imitated in provincial centres in a matter of hours instead of days or weeks, and the opposite was doubtless similarly achieved.

Zinc, known and used from ancient times but not understood properly until the eighteenth century, came to the fore in the Victorian period. In 1833 Germany was producing about 6,000 tons annually, but then Russia commenced production and added a further 2,000 tons to the world supply. By 1855 England was herself producing some 3,000 tons a year. The metal was a valuable constituent of many alloys, of which brass is the best known. The process of 'galvanizing', by which iron articles are dipped in hot zinc and thereby rendered rust-proof, was patented by a Frenchman, M. Sorel, in the 1840's. Its use became widespread, and the familiar sheets of corrugated-iron for roofing were used by the Admiralty as early as 1850. Under the same authority galvanized iron was used for the lining of coal bunkers in the ships of the Royal Navy.

Britannia Metal, an alloy of antimony and tin with copper, lead and zinc or bismuth, and *German Silver*, an alloy of copper, nickel and zinc, were used in great quantities. Other imitations of silver were perfected, and ingenious methods of replacing the old manual processes were evolved.

These, however, lie outside the scope of this article, and the reader will find them described in detail in the Chapter entitled *Silver and Silver Plate* (p. 72).

Brass or bronze, gilded and known as *Ormolu*, had been widely popular since the eighteenth century. The gilding had been performed then by amalgamating pure gold with mercury, coating the article to be gilded with the amalgam, and driving off the unwanted mercury with heat. New processes which gave passably similar results, but without the use of gold itself, came into use, and the invention in 1832 by G.F.Muntz of *Muntz Metal* (known also as *Yellow Metal* or *Patent Metal*) resulted in the production of a material of a full golden-yellow colour that did not fracture too easily. Further, in the 1820's was discovered a method giving brass wares a 'rich dead gold-like colour'; one that was attained inexpensively by means of numerous baths in acid with a final application of lacquer to prevent tarnishing. Electroplating with gold was used also on occasions; it was found that variations in the strength of the current employed produced different shades of gilding, and that tints of green and red could be obtained by the addition of proportions of silver or copper respectively to the electrolytic solution.

Iron manufacture continued by methods that had been developed in earlier decades, but was being improved constantly in minor ways. It became possible, for instance, to make such things as bedposts in one single length; to make tapered tubes, and to cover tubing with a thin sheet of brass which was polished and lacquered to form the basis of the familiar 'brass' bedstead. Another advance was the joining of the tubes which comprised head and end rails by means of ornamented brackets. These were made in cast-iron moulds modelled with the required ornament in intaglio;

the tubes were placed carefully into the moulds in which entry-holes were left for the introduction of molten metal.

Bedsteads

Loudon, who is a reliable authority for the period 1830–40, states that cast-iron bedsteads made by William Mallet of Dublin were used in Irish farm-houses at that time. An illustration of one shows an uninviting trough-like contrivance with a pierced base which was 'well adapted for the ploughman's room'. Less Spartan in appearance, and doubtless more conducive to providing the average man with a night's rest, is an iron half-tester bedstead 'which, however, does not fold up, but which has the advantage of being remarkably cheap. It is manufactured by Messrs Cottam and Hallen, of two feet six inches in width, for 46s. 6d., and of five feet in width for 68s.; in both cases it is complete, with castors, head board, and curtain rods, and is thrice painted in oil' (Fig. 1).

In the years between 1850 and 1860 the metal bedstead competed seriously with that of wood, and the numerous examples shown at the 1851 Exhibition bear witness to the fact (Pl. 67). They were principally of traditional four-poster pattern, but half-tester, tent and folding-tent types also were exhibited. Their ornamentation generally was elaborate, and while the makers carefully designated their productions as being in some par-

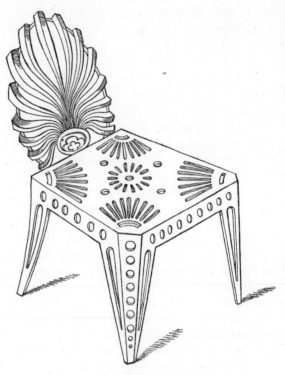

Fig. 2. Lobby chair of Etruscan design.

ticular style – English or Continental – students of the periods named would scarcely recognize any of the attributions. In addition to external embellishments, attempts were made to improve the comfort by using steel laths on which to rest the mattress, and various designs of this kind were registered. Apart from their low price and their appearance, the use of metal bedsteads was encouraged for their undoubted cleanliness when compared with those of wooden construction.

One field in which the metal-bedstead manufacturer was supreme was in the making of folding bedsteads for travelling; principally for the use of Army officers. One such article shown at the 1851 Exhibition was described as an 'officer's portable brass bedstead, to form sofa, with the exhibitor's patent spring mattress and musquito curtains'. The same maker, Henry Pratt, of 123 New Bond Street, showed a brass chaise-longue, and a 'travelling chair in brass, to form couch and bedstead'. Such pieces of furniture were contrived

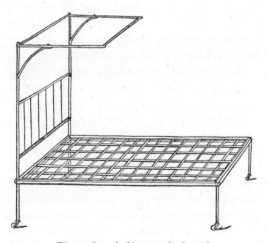

Fig. 1. Iron half-tester bedstead.

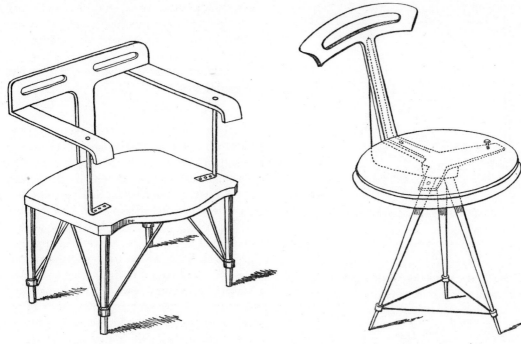

Fig. 3. Iron armchair, the seat of wood.

Fig. 4. Cast and wrought iron cottage chair. From Loudon's *Encyclopaedia*.

ingeniously to be packed for transit into wooden chests fitted with strong carrying-handles; while consideration was given to making the article occupy as small a space as possible, little thought was expended in lessening the weight.

Chairs

Loudon illustrates several examples of chairs, one of which is described as 'a lobby chair of cast iron, suitable for a porch (Fig. 2). The Design is Etruscan; and Mr Mallet, to whom we are indebted for it, says that it may be cast in two pieces. It would therefore, come cheap, and would look exceedingly well in the porch of a cottage in the Italian style. Mr Mallet observes that where carved work, or much ornament, is to be executed in furniture, cast iron will always be found cheaper than wood, even though a small number only of the article were wanting.' A further design from the same source is of a more functional pattern: 'the back and elbows are cast in one piece; the supports for the elbows and also the legs are of gas tubing, screwed into a cross frame of iron, which proceeds from the back of the chair under the wooden seat' (Figs. 3, 4).

In spite of the enthusiasm of Mr Mallet of Dublin, metal chairs did not meet with wide approval, and very few were to be seen twenty years later at the 1851 Exhibition. One maker showed brass-framed rocking- and arm-chairs, upholstered in morocco, but on the whole such pieces do not seem to have been popular and the scarcity of surviving examples confirms the fact that very few were made.

Garden chairs and seats offered a more practical subject for the attention of manufacturers, and the heavy metals then in use were satisfactorily employed in making them in various patterns.

Fig. 5. Invalid's bedside table.

Articles for use outdoors were finished by the application of paints or lacquers, or by the newly-introduced process of galvanizing.

Tables

Loudon shows a circular-topped table, the top of wood and the base of cast-iron resting on ball-castors; and also a metal-based invalid's bedside table with a projecting wooden top (Fig. 5). In the next two decades the metal table would seem to have made little headway, and not a great number of them was to be seen at the Great Exhibition. The most enterprising display was that of the Coalbrookdale Company, of Shropshire, makers of the iron gates that remain in Hyde Park to this day, sited not far from where they were exhibited originally in 1851. This firm showed a number of metal tables, including: 'Cast-iron Chess-tables; Hall, or console-table, in cast-iron, painted in white and gold, marble top; Large table, with cast-iron legs, painted oak; Intricate iron casting, bronzed and marbled, of a hall-table, arranged with pedestals for hats, coats and umbrellas, containing also a pillar for a lamp and looking-glass, with boxes for letters and for brushes, and an inkstand.' (Pl. 68D.)

A table made entirely of wire was exhibited by John Reynolds, New Compton Street, under the description of an 'ornamental flower table'. It was

in the form of three serpents, posed upright and looking very like sea-horses, on the heads of which rested a circular top with a wire gallery. Presumably this article was painted and was intended for use in a conservatory.

Winfield, of Birmingham, showed 'brass tables with marble tops'.

The fireplace

Much patience was expended between 1830 and 1860 in devising satisfactory ways of heating the rooms of a house, and at the same time of making the most efficient use of coal. 'Patent' grates and stoves were innumerable, and each one was claimed by its inventor to be perfect. The majority were made of cast-iron, blacked, but some were of polished steel, and others bore mounts of bronze or of gilt metal. Their form varied with the prevailing fashions, and ranged from Grecian to Gothic, and included numerous essays in the French and Italian styles of preceding centuries. Most of the grates were provided with fenders designed to match them, and with sets of fire-irons *en suite*.

A typical production of the 1850's was described by the makers, proudly and at length, in these words:

'Ornamental chimney-piece and grate, with decorations illustrative of deer-stalking, boar-hunting, and hawking. The figures are of cast-iron, electro-gilt, and the mouldings are marbled. The grate consists of a burnished steel front, and ornaments in bronze, electro-gilt. The decoration connects, in one design, the fender, ash-pan, and grate. The fire-brick for the back is in one piece, including the bottom of the grate, on which the fire rests. The fender, ash-pan and grate remove in one piece to afford greater convenience in cleaning the chimney.

This *tour-de-force* was modelled and designed by B.W. Hawkins, and is described as standing seven feet in height and four feet wide. It was referred to in a contemporary magazine as 'a beautiful example of manufactured Art' (Pl. 66A).

An important fireplace accessory of metal was the coal-scuttle, which was of brass, copper, or, sometimes, of zinc. It was of many shapes, and in the 1851 Exhibition Tyler and Sons, Warwick

A gilt-brass three-light chandelier for burning oil, *c.* 1830.
Saltram Park, Devon. National Trust.

PLATE 65

(A) Chimneypiece and grate exhibited in 1851. The figures of gilt cast-iron, and the mouldings painted to imitate marble; the grate of burnished steel and the rococo ornaments of electro-gilt bronze by Coalbrooke dale Company. *Art-Journal Illustrated Catalogue*, 1851.

(B) A group of candelabra, lamps and a chandelier shown in 1851 by Messrs Salt and Lloyd of Birmingham. *Art-Journal Illustrated Catalogue*, 1851.

PLATE 66

'A four-post brass bedstead clothed in green silk, the metalwork in the Renaissance style, with figures, foliage, and scrollwork introduced.' Exhibited in 1851 by R. W. Winfield of Birmingham and London.

PLATE 67

(A) Japanned iron coal-box,
c. 1850.

(B) Gilt brass paperweight with black silk
tassel, 1855.

(C) An ornamental gas bracket shown
in 1851 by William Potts of Birmingham.

(D) Cast-iron table with white marble
top.

PLATE 68

Lane, showed their latest pattern (Fig. 6), in addition to 'copper coal scoops, exhibiting the changes in their patterns during the last 70 years'. The lidded coal-box, or purdonium, was made most often of japanned tinned-steel (see p. 112), sometimes with a back-painted glass panel inset in the lid (see Pl. 68A).

Light-fittings

During the years between 1830 and 1860 changes in methods of lighting the homes of both rich and poor were taking place. In few preceding periods can there have been more time and thought devoted to the problem of obtaining a greater degree of illumination from a given quantity of illuminant. Experiment was ceaseless, and the foundations were laid for even more spectacular advances to be made in the lifetimes of coming generations. At the commencement of the period, gas-lighting for the home was slowly being introduced, but was still an expensive novelty that often produced no more than an intermittent flicker of light and an unpleasant smell, together with the twin threats of sudden explosion and asphyxiation. The use of the same agent for the cooking of foodstuffs was also little other than an interesting experiment that was more widely mooted than practised.

A company calling itself grandiloquently (and almost incredibly) 'The Patriotic Imperial and National Light and Heat Company' was promoted by a German, Frederick Albert Winsor, and, after Parliamentary opposition, was incorporated in 1810. In spite of Winsor's suggestion that subscribers to his enterprise would be assured of a profit of 10,000 per cent on a capital of £300,000, and the fact that Brougham sarcastically deflated the whole scheme in the House of Commons, the company did manage to prosper. It became later the Gas Light and Coke Company and is now merged in the Gas Board. Opposition to Winsor's company was led by William Murdoch, of Redruth, who had given demonstrations of gas-lighting as early as 1792, and who had commenced six years later to light Boulton and Watts' Soho, Birmingham, engine-works by the same means.

The use of the new illuminant was confined at first to the public highway, large buildings, and to the outdoor celebration of the Treaty of Amiens (1802). Such displays provoked great discussion and interest, but it was not until the decade of 1830–40 that the demand for gas grew large enough to merit the opening of works for its production up and down the country. Although it was not until shortly after the period under review that increased improvement in the efficiency of burners and in the quality of the gas ensured its universal adoption, minor innovations were being introduced continually and attention was paid to the design of wall-lights, chandeliers and other fittings.

While gas was the subject of general wonder, the humble candle continued in general use and was challenged strongly in the public favour by the oil-lamp. The latter, perhaps because of apprehension on behalf of interested parties that the competition of the newly introduced gas might prove disastrous, was constantly being improved. Thus, the *Moderator* lamp embodied a spring to raise the oil to the wick, while some employed clockwork for the same purpose and others increased their power of illumination by the admixture of oxygen or naphtha with the oil. Whale-oil, marketed under the name of *Train-oil*, was the most used,

Coal-scuttle, a pattern introduced in 1851.

Fig. 7. Vine-pattern wall-light for gas.

but many others were tried and achieved a brief popularity. Lard-oil, benzene, camphene, turpentine and others had their devotees, and finally, in 1859, came the discovery of petroleum oil and the promise of ample supplies of paraffin to be realized in the years ahead.

The design of light-fittings during the years 1830–60 varied as widely as did the design of all types of metal wares. Functional efficiency was seldom the first consideration, and was usually disguised by every possible device of ornamentation, which was not always appropriate to the purpose. In the case of chandeliers and wall-lights, bronze chimeras were to be seen spouting flame from the tops of their heads, blameless lilies and cherubic infants were similarly involved, and the illuminant seemed to have been set an impossible task in finding a way through the mass of entwined metal tracery that encumbered the path to the final outlet (Pl. 68c and Fig. 7).

Probably the best-known metal articles of the period are reading-lamps, which have survived in large numbers to this day and seem assured of a further span of useful life when adapted for electricity. The lamps were made usually of bronze, ormolu or electro-plated nickel-silver, and often with base and capital of metal applied to a column of marble, coloured glass or some other suitably decorative material. Many of the columns were modelled on classical originals, and the most popular of all was the pure Corinthian Column, which was made in electro-plate or lacquered brass in great quantities. Other designs were entirely novel in conception; embodying *motifs* from several earlier styles, together with a generous sprinkling of contemporary vine-leaves complete with grapes and tendrils (Pl. 66B).

Kitchen wares

Metal wares continued to hold their place in the kitchen, and there were few notable changes during the period under review. Copper cooking-pans with tinned interiors were popular over the years, but in spite of the highly attractive appearance of a polished and gleaming *batterie-de-cuisine* of this metal, the 1850's saw the introduction and acceptance of the more hygienic and more easily-managed enamelled iron.

The greater number of households employed cooking utensils made from tinned steel, which, while it had neither the good looks nor the lengthy life of heavy-gauge copper, stood up to the rigours of daily usage in both skilled and unskilled hands. Articles made from this material included: basting ladles; coffee-boilers and coffee-pots; colanders; fish-kettles; saucepans; skimmers; slices; soup ladles and tureens; stewpans; and tea-kettles. The range of articles in sheet steel was even wider, and embraced: bed-airers; candlesticks; oval cheese steamers and toasters; chocolate pots and mills; coffee biggins; boilers, filterers and pots; allblaze (fireproof?) steak and fish dishes; covers for plates and dishes; egg-poachers, coddlers and ladles; Etnas, for boiling water; fish-knives; flour-boxes; graters; hot-water dishes and plates; inhalers; pepper-boxes; strainers for milk, gravy and gruel; moulds; 'tea-extractors' (infusers?), kettles and pots; warmers for carriage, for feet and for stomach; and wine mullers and strainers. Many of these things have long since passed out of use and have been discarded, and it needs a long memory to recall their exact appearance or, in some instances, their purpose. It would tax the resources of most to try to distinguish between, say, a strainer for gravy and one for gruel.

Pewter was in use throughout the period, although not by any means on as wide a scale as it had been a century earlier. It was employed, among other things, for the making of complicated moulds for the freezing of ice-puddings, and for the making of jellies and blancmanges. These moulds comprised a top and a base and a hinged central portion, each part being highly embossed with the design to appear in relief on the finished dessert. Although many moulds for these and other purposes were made of tin and copper, soft pewter was unsurpassed for the purpose, and managed to hold its own until the vogue for such edible extravagances grew less common. Ale-tankards of pewter were made and survive in large numbers.

The tea-pot was made often of metal, but it had long been standardized in form and function. Coffee, then as now, was the subject of many inventions designed to improve the flavour of the beverage and to extract the greatest good from the fewest beans. Percolators of various types were on the market, but more ingenious devices were made and used. One of these was *Beart's Patent Pot*, which was described in the 1850's in these words: 'The upper portion of the pot may be considered a cylinder, in which moves the coffee-holder, which consists of a piece of cloth strained over what may be called a piston, the action of raising which, produces a partial vacuum, and the coffee is strained through the sieve-like material of which the piston is composed, by atmospheric pressure.'

General decoration

In no department of metal wares was the demand keener than in that of the general fittings for the decoration of rooms. These included not only door-plates, knobs and escutcheons, decorative bell-handles and handles and mounts for pieces of furniture, but there was a large demand for the fashionable brass-cased cornice-poles with decorated end-pieces from which hung the curtains on large brass rings. Further, when drawn back in the daytime, curtains were held lightly but firmly in the grasp of a hold-back: a U-shaped bracket of metal screwed to the wall and with a decorated side facing into the room. These had been introduced in the early years of the century, and remained popular throughout the Victorian period.

Among the articles in this category that were included by various makers in the Great Exhibition were: 'brass window-cornices and ornaments; poles with ends, rings and brackets; curtains bands and pins; finger-plates for doors, brass and japanned; ornaments for watch hooks; frames for miniatures or pictures; specimens of door-handles, tea-bells, hat and coat hooks and castors, of new and ornamental construction; vases in various styles: bronze, electro-silvered, dead gold and relieved – also [vases] fitted with improved spring igniter for lighting the vesta matches.'

The writing-desk was also the repository of much metalwork, including such things as paper-clips, inkstands and paper-weights (Pl. 68B).

The metal used in making the majority of these objects was principally brass, treated to enhance its resemblance to gold and then lacquered to prevent tarnishing. Whenever possible, for reasons of economy, sheets of the metal were used and stamped with steel dies, in other instances casting was employed. Where extra strength was needed, as with cornice-poles, cast-iron was overlaid with brass. Hand-work was cut down to a minimum, and to produce the greatest quantity of goods to sell at the lowest price was the target; mass-production methods were brought quickly into use as the years proceeded, and hand processes were employed only for finishing. Designers gave full rein to their imaginations, and while many of the results may provoke a condescending smile or a gasp of horror, the majority do not fail to show considerable ingenuity on the parts of both artist and maker.

Mention must be made of the large numbers of bronze figures and groups that were made to adorn mantelpieces and sideboards. Many were the work of contemporary artists, but others were from classical or more recent sources; in the latter category is what is almost certainly the best-known of all – the *Marly Horses*, from the marble originals now in the Champs-Elysées, Paris, executed by Guillaume Coustou (1677–1746).

Japanned wares

Founded during the seventeenth century, the japanned metal industry centred on the Midlands reached its peak in the mid-nineteenth century. Wolverhampton gained a name for goods which showed a high quality of design and finish, while Birmingham and other places continued to supply articles for less discriminating tastes. The range of goods manufactured was very wide, and visitors to the 1851 Exhibition saw, among others, a comprehensive display comprising: 'Baths; bread and cake baskets; boiler fillers; bonnet boxes; botanical boxes; candle boxes and safes; candlesticks; canisters, round and square; cash-boxes; cheese trays; cigar trays; coal scoops, shovels, and vases; date cases; dressing cases; ewers and basins; fire baskets and screen; gunpowder canister; hearing trumpet; inkstands; jugs; knife trays; lamps; lanterns; leg bath; letter cages; music stand; nursery lamps; plate carriers and warmers; sandwich and spice boxes; spittoons; snuffer trays; sugar-boxes; tables; tea-caddies; toast racks; toilette sets; trays; umbrella stands; vegetable warmers; ventilators; waiters; water cans; wax boxes; and writing boxes.' While many of the articles were plainly japanned in black with no more than a line or two of gilding to relieve the surface, others were ambitiously painted with central coloured panels surrounded by elaborate gilt patterns. The better work was all painted and gilded by hand, but a transfer process was employed for cheap wares.

BOOKS FOR FURTHER READING

There are no books devoted specifically to the metalwork of the period as a whole, but most volumes published between the years 1830 and 1860 devoted to the Arts in general mention it, either at length or briefly. The designs current in the year 1851 are described (and, in many instances, illustrated) in the *Official Descriptive and Illustrated Catalogue of the Great Exhibition*, and in the *Illustrated Catalogue of the Exhibition of the Industry of All Nations* published by the *Art-Journal*.

Stamped and gilt brass cornice pole-end.

Textiles

THE VICTORIAN SOCIETY

55 Great Ormond Street, London, W.C.1.

Telephone: Chancery 3672

———————◀◆◆▶———————

THE VICTORIAN SOCIETY has been formed to make sure that the best Victorian buildings and their contents do not disappear before their merits are more generally appreciated.

The Society for the Protection of Ancient Buildings has kindly agreed to take the Society under its wing and to provide it with accommodation at 55 Great Ormond Street, W.C.1. This will enable the work of the new Society to take its proper place as an extension of what the Society for the Protection of Ancient Buildings has done since its foundation by William Morris.

The objects of the Society comprise the study and appreciation of Victorian architecture and associated arts with a view to the preservation of outstanding examples. Such study is an essential step towards discrimination between the thousands of buildings and other products of the Victorian and Edwardian ages. By no means all these are worthy of preservation but some of them are great works of art and some of them are landmarks in our architectural and artistic history. Almost all are insufficiently appreciated at present and for this reason are in danger of neglect and destruction.

THE VICTORIAN SOCIETY hopes to stimulate appreciation and encourage research by means of lectures, exhibitions and privileged visits which will make known the names and achievements of architects and craftsmen between 1837 and 1914. The latter date has been chosen because it represents the end of an era which did not terminate with the century. The Society's programme includes the setting up of sub-committees and the development of regional groups. These will cover in addition to buildings and the fine arts such specialised aspects as furniture, decoration, ceramics, glass, textiles and metalwork.

Substantial funds are needed to carry out the Society's work and this is an appeal for your support issued in the name of the Committee which has been formed in London and whose names are given opposite. Please send a subscription and if possible a donation. The categories of membership are as follows:

Founder-Benefactor (including Corporate Membership in the case of Organisations)....£100

Founder Member £25

Life Member.................£15. 15s.

Member (Minimum Annual Subscription) £1. 1s.

Attention is drawn to the advantage of Life Membership and Ordinary Membership at the above rates, which will be liable to increase after the Society has become established.

Textiles

BARBARA MORRIS

Introduction

'There is no general agreement in principles of taste. Every one elects his own style of art. ... Some few take refuge in a liking for "pure Greek", and are rigidly "classical", others find safety in the "antique", others believe only in "Pugin", others lean upon imitations of modern Germans and some extol the *Renaissance*. We all agree only in being imitators.'

This opening to 'Hints for the Decoration and Furnishing of Dwellings' (*Journal of Design*, 1849) sums up the eclecticism which is characteristic of the Victorian approach to the decorative arts, but it would be wrong to consider the Victorians as mere imitators. While borrowing heavily from the past, the leading designers imbued their work with a new spirit, recreating from their historic prototypes something that was essentially of their own age and could have been produced at no other time. In this way, although the source of inspiration is always apparent, whether 'Gothic', 'Arabesque', or 'Louis Quatorze', to mention only three, there is a certain affinity between all the styles.

The Victorian equation of elaboration with beauty is demonstrated by the use of pattern on all available surfaces – the walls, the carpets, the upholstery and the curtains. Carefully contrived schemes such as the 'Elizabethan' dining-room at Charlecote, where the pattern of the carpet echoes the strapwork design of the flock wallpaper, are exceptions, and a mixture of unrelated patterns was the general order.

Whereas during the Regency there was a pre-ponderance of plain fabrics for curtains and upholstery, during the period 1830–60 patterned materials were most favoured. Until about 1840 fairly light colours predominated, but thereafter darker colours, particularly crimson and bottle green, were most popular, which, when combined with the use of heavier fabrics, such as worsted damasks, velvet or brocatelle, gave a sombre but rich effect. These heavier fabrics were used extensively in drawing-rooms and dining-rooms, and chintz was more or less relegated to the bedrooms, except when used to make 'throw-overs' or loose covers for upholstered furniture. Elaborately patterned machine-woven cotton lace or madras muslin replaced the plain or lightly sprigged muslin of the preceding era. An alternative was semi-transparent blinds, printed with imitations of stained-glass windows, or even with pictorial subjects, including representations of the Royal Family.

Draperies

Thomas King, writing in 1833 as 'an upholsterer of forty-five years experience', states that during this time 'has occurred the entire introduction of French Draperies and Curtains; then the extreme prevalence of massive brass Rods with Large Rings, and at a later period, the universal use of Piped Valances. Now the most modern style blends all three'.[1] (See Figs. 1–3.)

During the 1830's, in fact, very little that was absolutely new was introduced and generally

[1] *The Upholsterer's Accelerator*, 1833.

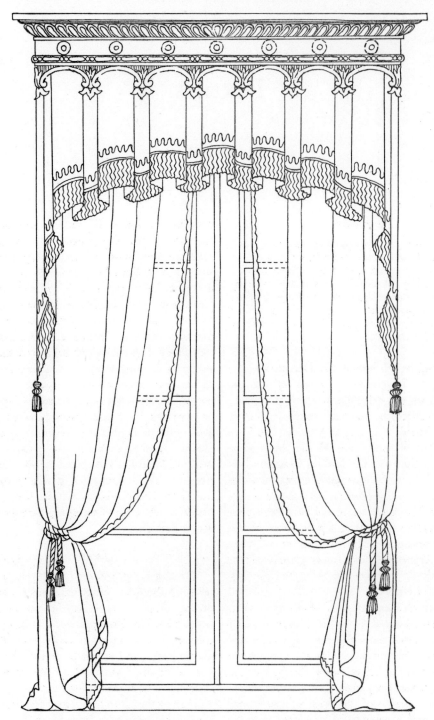

Fig. 1. Drawing-room window curtain from *An Encyclopaedia of Cottage, Farm, &*
Villa Architecture & Furniture by J.C.Loudon, London, 1833.

(A) 'Elizabethan Window Curtains.' Plate 27 from *Furniture with Candelabra and Interior Decoration designed by R. Bridgens*, London, 1838.

(B) Window curtain in the 'François Ier' style. Plate VII from *A Series of Designs of Furniture & Decoration in the Style of Louis XIVth, Francis Ist, Elizabeth & Gothic*, designed and drawn by Henry Wood, London, n.d., *c.* 1845.

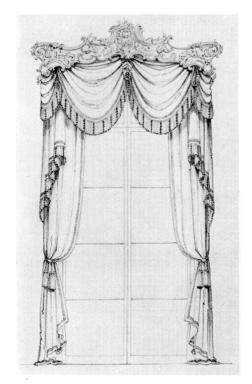

(C) A window curtain in the 'Louis Quatorze' style from *The Upholsterer's Sketch Book of Original Designs for Fashionable Draperies &c.*, by T. King, London, 1839.

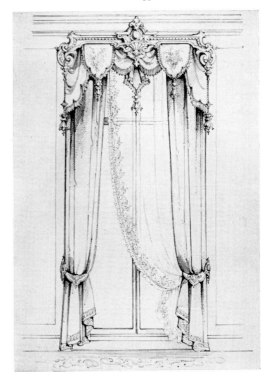

(D) Window curtain. Plate 28 from *Select Designs for 1852. Window-cornices, Valances &c. Devised, Drawn on Stone & Published by Laugher, Dwyer & Greenberry, 17, Poland St.*, London.

PLATE 69

(A) Silk and linen damask with watered ground (tabbinet) woven by J. Stillwell & Co., White Lion Square, Norton Falgate, London, in 1843. *Property of the Patent Office.*

(B) Brocatelle woven by Daniel Walters & Son, New Mills, Braintree, Essex, in 1850. *Property of the Patent Office.*

(C) 'The Queen's Pattern.' Silk brocade designed and woven by pupils of the Spitalfields School of Design for the Great Exhibition of 1851. *Victoria and Albert Museum.*

(D) Silk brocade, purchased by the Victoria and Albert Museum in 1859. *Victoria and Albert Museum.*

PLATE 70

(A) Wool and cotton damask, manufactured by McCrea & Shepherd, Halifax, 1847. *Property of the Patent Office.*

(B) Wool damask designed by A. W. N. Pugin for F. Crace & Son, 1850. *Property of the Patent Office.*

(C) Cotton and wool damask manufactured by John Shepherd & Co., Halifax, 1852. *Property of the Patent Office.*

(D) Wool and silk damask manufactured by James Akroyd & Son, Halifax, 1855. *Property of the Patent Office.*

PLATE 71

(A) Block-printed cotton with machine 'cover'. Printed by Charles Swainson at Bannister Hall, near Preston, 1837. *Property of Stead, McAlpin, Ltd.*
(B) Cotton, roller-printed in two colours, with additional colours printed by surface roller, 1834. The birds and flowers copied from J. J. Audubon's *Birds of America*, Plates 20, 123, 131 and 134. *Victoria and Albert Museum.*

(C) Cotton, roller-printed by Kershaw, Leese & Sidebottom, Ardwick Print Works, Manchester, 1847. The design shows the young Prince of Wales. A Berlin wool-work picture of the same subject is in the Victoria and Albert Museum. *Property of the Patent Office.*

PLATE 72

(A) Cotton block-printed for John Watson & Co., London, 1846.
Property of the Patent Office.

(B) Cotton, block-printed at Bannister Hall for
Swainson & Dennys, 1848. Awarded the Silver
Medal of the Royal Society of Arts in March, 1849.
Property of the Patent Office.

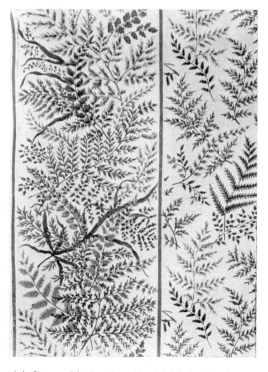

(C) Cotton, block-printed by McAlpin, Stead & Co.,
Cummersdale, 1858. *Property of the Patent Office.*

PLATE 73

(A) Needlework carpet. Wool on canvas; cross-stitch, *c.* 1840–50. *Victoria and Albert Museum.*

(B) Hand-knotted carpet; woollen pile on flax warps. Probably made at Axminster. *c.* 1835. *Victoria and Albert Museum.*

PLATE 74

Hand-knotted Axminster carpet made by Jackson and Graham, Oxford Street, London, 1851 (Plate 132 of *The Industrial Arts of the Nineteenth Century* by M. Digby Wyatt, 1853).

PLATE 75

(A) Cushion. Silk on canvas; cross-stitch. Worked by Mary Anne Redfern (Mrs Hall) *c.* 1848. *Victoria and Albert Museum.*

(B) Stool cover. Wool on woollen cloth; tent-stitch. Worked by Caroline Davies (Mrs Boileau) *c.* 1850. *Victoria and Albert Museum.*

(C) Band of satin, machine-embroidered in ombré silks. Made by Houldsworth & Co., Manchester, and purchased by the Victoria and Albert Museum from the Dublin Exhibition of 1853. *Victoria and Albert Museum.*

(D) Panel. Silk on serge. Designed by William Morris for his own house, Red House, in 1860. *Property of George Howard, Esq., on loan to the Victoria and Albert Museum.*

PLATE 76

speaking most of the draperies were slight modifications of styles already in fashion in the 1820's. This was particularly true of draperies in the 'Grecian' or 'Gothic' style, although in both styles the carved and gilded cornices tended to be more elaborate. In the simplest styles, considered suitable for 'cottages in the Greek or Italian manner', the curtains were suspended by brass rings from a curtain-pole, and a simple fringed valance, gathered into pleats at intervals, was hung either in front or behind the long curtains. Muslin sub-curtains were often used, particularly in drawing-rooms and dining-rooms. More elaborate festoon draperies, with swags of material looped over the curtain-pole, were used with carved cornices in the classic style, particularly for drawing-rooms.

'Gothic' styles were more commonly employed in dining-rooms or libraries. For Gothic windows shaped valances or pelmets were most favoured, consisting either of a simple shape with deep corners which followed the general line of a Gothic arch, or a long straight piece cut into vandykes or other fancy shapes at the lower edge which was piped or edged with a contrasting colour and often further decorated with tassels. Both the valances and the borders of the curtains were often embellished with appliqué embroidery of Gothic ornaments such as oak leaves, fleur-de-lys or other heraldic devices.

By the late 1830's pure classicism had more or less disappeared and even more variety was apparent with elaborate draperies in the prevailing styles of 'Louis Quatorze', 'Elizabethan', 'François 1er', and 'Gothic', together with more fanciful expressions of the upholsterer's invention which bore little relation to any known historic style. By 1840 the elaboration and complexity of the draperies had reached a point where they were criticized not only on their æsthetic merits but also on utilitarian grounds. Pugin in his *Christian Architecture* (1841) writes that 'all the modern plans of suspending enormous folds of stuff over poles, as if for the purpose of sale or of being dried is [sic] quite contrary to the use and intentions of curtains and abominable in taste; and the only object that these endless festoons and bunchy tassels can answer is to swell the bills and profits of the upholsterers who are the inventors of these extravagant and ugly draperies, which are not only useless in protecting the chamber from cold, but are depositories of thick layers of dust, and in London not infrequently become the strongholds of vermin'.

Festoon draperies in the late 1830's and 1840's were especially prevalent in the so-called 'Louis Quatorze' style, having a natural affinity with the curves and scrolls of the elaborately carved 'rococo' cornices. This style was frequently adopted where formerly the 'Grecian' style was considered appropriate. Typical examples are included by Thomas King in his *Upholsterers' Sketch Book of Original Designs for Fashionable Draperies* (1839) (Pl. 69B). King includes not only festoon draperies made of a single piece, but also more complex types, with separate pieces hanging in deep oval swags, lavishly trimmed with fringe and tassels. Although examples of the 'Louis Quatorze' style are found considerably later, it appears to have reached its zenith as far as draperies were concerned in the 1840's; and Henry Whitaker, in his *Practical Cabinet Maker and Upholsterer's Treasury of Designs* (1847), seems to have some justification for his remark that the 'Louis-Quatorze style is going out very fast'.

The 'Elizabethan' style, although equally elaborate, presented a more formal appearance with flat valances cut at the lower edge into curved and angled shapes which echoed the strapwork and cartouches of the carved wooden cornices (Pl. 69A). The bottom of the valance was usually trimmed with a contrasting narrow band and tassels were suspended at regular intervals. These shaped valances were used equally for windows and for four-poster bedsteads in the Elizabethan style, with the curtains hung from poles, by large brass rings, set in front, or, less frequently behind, the valance.

It is not always easy to distinguish the 'François 1er' style from the 'Elizabethan', but generally speaking it was more elaborate and more curvilinear, with human figures and masks introduced into the carving. The window curtain (Pl. 69B) shown on Plate 7 of Henry Wood's *Designs for Furniture and Draperies in the Styles of Louis*

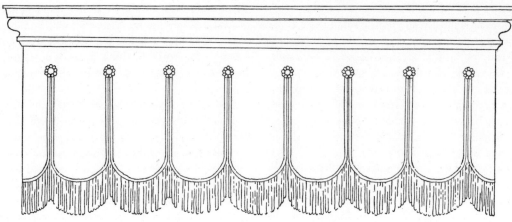

Fig. 2. Piped valance from *The Upholsterer's Accelerator* by Thomas King,
London, 1833.

XIVth, Francois 1er, Elizabeth and Gothic (London, n.d., *c.* 1845) is a typical expression of the style, particularly in the use of festoon drapery behind the flat-shaped valance.

In the 1850's the clear division into styles is often no longer apparent, and the leading upholsterers display an astonishing eclecticism in the selection of detail which includes 'Arabesque', 'Alhambresque', and 'Renaissance' ornament. For example, in the *Select Designs for 1852*, published by Laugher, Dwyer and Greenberry of 171 Poland Street, London, it is possible to attach an appropriate label to most of the cornices, but the draperies beneath them must be considered more or less interchangeable. The complex type of drapery, with looped swags and shaped embroidered panels shown in Pl. 69D with an 'Elizabethan' cornice, appears also, with only slight modifications, with a cornice of realistically carved vines. The same inconsistencies of style are also apparent in the draperies published by Henry Lawford in his *Cabinet of Practical, Useful and Decorative Furniture Designs* (1855) (Figs. 4, 5).

By the 1850's, instead of being held back by cords, curtains were generally fastened by curtain-bands, which were shaped pieces of material, stiffened by a canvas interlining, with a ring at either end which fitted over a hook on the wall.

The band was often decorated with a fringe, or embroidered to match the valance. Both valances and curtain-bands were supplied decorated by machine-embroidery in gold thread or coloured silks, ready to be made up by the upholsterer or housewife.

One of the most characteristic features of the period as a whole is the excessive use of fringes and tassels and fancy braid trimmings. Valances made entirely of cords and tassels were sometimes substituted for those made of stuff. Typical of these were examples exhibited at the Great Exhibition of 1851 by Mr R.Burgh of London (Fig. 6). Cheaper substitutes were made of printed cotton, with fringe and tassels imitated with printed shadows to give a three-dimensional effect. These printed valances seem to have been the speciality of James Burd, of Mount Zion Works, Radcliffe, near Manchester.

Although short muslin curtains were used in 'cottages', during the 1830's until about 1850, as during the Regency, the muslin sub-curtains were used full-length. After 1850, however, they were frequently used only at the lower half of the window, even in formal schemes of drapery. For a simple sash window, the muslin was stretched in taut folds by rings on small rods attached to the top and bottom of the lower half of the window. For

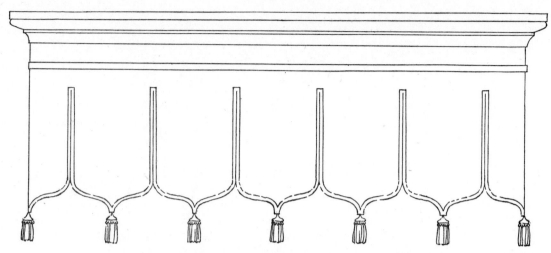

Fig. 3. Piped valance from *The Upholsterer's Accelerator* by Thomas King,
London, 1833.

French windows, two muslin curtains were used, one on each of the opening panes. By the 1840's elaborately patterned curtains of the type known as 'Madras muslins' or lenos were extensively used. These were mainly woven in Scotland by such firms as McLachlan & McLean of Glasgow and W.J. Lowndes & Co. of Paisley. Fancy machine net and lace curtains were also made by J.Heathcoat & Co. of Tiverton and Robert Scott of Leicester.

The styles of bed-draperies parallel those of the window-curtains. Beds for more formal apartments were usually of the four-poster variety, particularly in 'Elizabethan', 'Gothic', and 'Renaissance' styles, with shaped or pleated valances, decorated with fringe and tassels, and four curtains. Half-tester beds with canopies, called 'Arabian bedsteads', by Henry Lawford were also common. Tent beds and French beds are also found, particularly in the earlier part of the period.

Woven fabrics

In the field of woven furnishing fabrics the early Victorian period is characterized by the development of elaborate figured patterns, ranging from abstract designs of strapwork and Moorish arabesques to naturalistic designs of flowers and fruit. The complexity of the figured patterns was facilitated by the increased use, from 1830 onwards, of the Jacquard loom not only in the production of worsted fabrics in the Yorkshire area, but also in the production of silk fabrics in Macclesfield and Manchester and to a more limited extent in Spitalfields and East Anglia.

Immediately after 1826, when the embargo on the importation of French silks was lifted, the sale of English silks was 40 per cent below that of French goods. Contrary to expectations, however, the import of French goods gave an impetus to the English silk industry, and by 1832 the sale of English silks was only 20–25 per cent below the French figure, and English silks were even exported to France. The increase, however, was largely in the manufacture of dress fabrics from Macclesfield, and few English firms were producing furnishing silks that could compete with French articles.

As during the previous period, the main production of Spitalfields was of plain silks and velvets. For example, in 1849, when there were 8,000 to 9,000 weavers employed in the neighbourhood of Spitalfields, the proportion of plain to figured goods was in the relationship of ten to one. Patterned silks were, however, woven in Spitalfields, and their production was encouraged by the establishment about 1840 of the Spitalfields

Fig. 4. Cornice and valance from Plate XCIX of *The Cabinet of Practical, Useful and Decorative Furniture Designs* by Henry Lawford, London, 1855.

School of Design, which was set up by the Government to train designers for the industry. A typical example of the work produced by the students was the 'Queen's Pattern' (Pl. 70C), which was specially woven for the 1851 Exhibition. The leading producer of furniture silks in Spitalfields was the firm of Keith & Co. The *Journal of Design* instances their fabrics as 'conclusive proof that the present London weaver can do anything in silk weaving which the public would pay for'.

One of the most popular furnishing silks was a satin-striped silk known as 'tabaret', with broad alternating stripes of satin and watered material, differing from each other in colour. Originally woven in Spitalfields, the manufacture of silk tabaret was established in Manchester in 1830 by Louis Schwabe, who 'by his ability, ingenuity and excellent taste ... soon rivalled the manufacture of Spitalfields who had previously almost monopolised the manufacture of furniture damasks'. According to Cooke Taylor, writing in 1843, 'the flowers wrought in his silks and satins appear more like the work of the best painter than the weaver'. After the death of Louis Schwabe, the firm was taken over by Houldsworth & Sons (see also section on Embroidery).

Another popular furnishing fabric was 'tabbi-net', a heavy poplin with a silk warp and a woollen or linen weft, with figures woven on a watered ground. Tabbinets were extensively woven in Ireland by firms such as Pim of Dublin, Fry of Dublin and R. Atkinson & Co., but they were also made in the Norwich area and in Spitalfields, notably by the firm of J. Stillwell & Co., of Norton Falgate (Pl. 70A).

The leading producers of furnishing silks, Daniel Walters & Son, were situated not in Spitalfields but at Braintree in Essex. This firm received the Gold Medal of the Royal Society of Arts in 1849 and won prizes at the International Exhibitions of 1851 and 1862. The brocatelle shown on Pl. 70B, which helped to win the Gold Medal in 1849, was described by the *Journal of Design* as 'substantial enough to last as many centuries as the Bayeux tapestry'. The firm was established at Braintree about 1826 and expanded rapidly. By 1861 there were 150 Jacquard looms in operation with over 300 employees.

A type of textile, not hitherto manufactured in this country – a heavy, stamped Utrecht velvet – was introduced by the firm of Bennett and Co. of Manchester. A considerable quantity of this fabric was ordered from Bennett's in 1850 for Windsor Castle, where some of it still remains.

The furniture silks and velvets, however, can

Fig. 5. Cornice and valance from Plate XCIX of *The Cabinet of Practical, Useful and Decorative Furniture Designs* by Henry Lawford, London, 1855.

only be considered as luxury articles, and the most characteristic furnishing fabrics of the period are the elaborately patterned Jacquard and power-woven damasks in a mixture of cotton and worsted, or silk and worsted, that were produced in large quantities in the neighbourhood of Halifax and Bradford. Among the leading firms may be mentioned James Akroyd & Son of Bradford; John Priestley & Son, Wibsey, near Bradford; H.C.McCrea; Hoadley & Pridie; and Brown & Ward, all of Halifax. It is in the production of firms such as these, with their extensive output, that the successive changes in style and taste can be most clearly traced.

In 1830 most of the fabrics were in more or less traditional damask patterns of formalized flowers and leaves, usually woven in one colour, with fairly broad areas of warp and weft brought to the surface to form the pattern. A few designs with small figures, such as a sprig of lily-of-the-valley on broad alternating stripes, are found, and also designs in which vine ornament, trefoils and other Gothic motifs are introduced.

In the 1830's and early 1840's a number of designs of acanthus leaves or 'classical' motifs occur, but these become increasingly rare. The only ornamental style to find favour throughout

the period was the 'Gothic', and several distinct expressions of it are found. Formal patterns, of the type found on fifteenth- and sixteenth-century damasks or velvets, were introduced by designers such as Pugin, who designed fabrics for F.Crace and Son in the 1850's (Pl. 71B). Other designs were based on Gothic architectural details such as tracery, crocketing and cusping. A third type consisted of floral designs, with exaggerated spiky leaves, thistles and other naturalistic details, with a Germanic or Flemish Gothic flavour.

The first 'Elizabethan' designs appear about 1834 and become increasingly popular during the 'forties and early 'fifties. Some are purely abstract, with bands of strapwork, cartouches and bracket scrolls, but more common are patterns in which flowers are introduced. Another variant is designs suggestive of Elizabethan carved woodwork in which, by means of shading, the strapwork is given a three-dimensional effect.

Similarly, the 'Louis Quatorze' style was represented by designs with 'rococo' scrolls and cartouches filled with diaper ornament, combined with curling leaves and sprays of flowers. This style seems to have reached its peak in the mid-1840's, and by 1850 it had more or less disappeared.

Fig. 6. Valance composed of fringe and tassels exhibited by R.Burgh, London,
at the Great Exhibition of 1851.

Although Owen Jones published his *Plans, Elevations, Sections and Details of the Alhambra* in 1842, the 'Moorish' or 'Alhambresque' style does not appear in woven fabrics until about 1853; but by 1855 it had become the dominant ornamental style. Elaborate patterns of interlacing strapwork and asymmetrical scrolls cover the whole surface of the fabric or, alternatively, bands of Moorish ornament alternate with naturalistic floral cascades (Pl. 71D). Purely geometric designs of interlocking tiles are also found.

Floral designs remained in favour throughout the period, but there are marked changes in both treatment and choice of subject-matter. During the 1840's turnover patterns of formalized flowers and scrolling leaves are most common, but about 1848 a fashion for exotic plants arose, a style which reached its culmination in the fabrics shown at the 1851 exhibition. Huge tropical plants, with luxuriant leaves and trumpet-like flowers, often over life-size, sprawled over the fabric. The repeat of the design was necessarily large, and the whole surface was covered with naturalistic detail. Not only exotic plants, but also vines and roses were similarly treated.

During the latter half of 1851, no doubt as a reaction against these sprawling designs, detached motifs of a single flower, or a single leaf, were widely spaced on a plain ground. This fashion

lasted throughout the 1850's. At the same time arborescent designs of blossoming trees were also popular and in 1852 designs of fruit were introduced. Throughout this year sprays of apple, pear, plum and currant remained the most popular subjects.

After 1855, purely floral furnishing damasks were less common, and the introduction of ornamental stripes became general. As with printed fabrics, the designs became increasingly eclectic, with motifs borrowed and adapted from every known historic style, and it is by no means rare to find a Moorish border combined with a naturalistic rose enclosed in a panel of Elizabethan strapwork.

Distinct fashions in colour, no less than in surface pattern, can be traced throughout the period. During the 1830's and 1840's bright, clear colours – scarlet, turquoise, yellow and light green – were used for the ground with the pattern in white or natural-coloured thread. In the early 'fifties the colours tended to become heavier, with crimson replacing scarlet, and a dark bottle green as the dominant colour. It was not until 1855, however, that the heavy sombre colours usually associated with the Victorian period were apparent. Hideous combinations of a dark maroon ground with flowers in bright tan and an ornamental stripe in a heavy green were all too common. Three or four colours were used in one design, where hitherto two had been the general rule.

Printed Textiles

The period 1830–60 saw a gradual decline in the level of design of both wood-block and roller-printed furnishing fabrics, although for the first few years the deterioration was hardly apparent and the high standard of engraving, which had persisted in the 1820's, was still maintained.

Generally speaking, the block-printed fabrics maintained a higher standard than the roller-prints, and the elaboration and naturalism of many of the floral designs have caused the Victorian era to be regarded as the high-water mark of the English floral chintz. These elaborate designs required the skilful cutting and careful registration of many blocks, and their production was virtually the monopoly of two firms, namely Bannister Hall, near Preston (under the successive management of Charles Swainson until 1856 and Thomas Clarkson 1856–93) and McAlpin, Stead & Co., the factory transferred from Wigton to Cummersdale, near Carlisle, in 1835. Since most of the designs printed by these firms were 'engaged' to leading London merchants and linen drapers describing themselves as 'Furniture Printers', the concentration of production is not generally realized. Among these the best known were Miles & Edwards of Oxford Street (taken over by Charles Hindley in 1847), John Watson & Co., Jackson & Graham (established 1836), and Clarkson & Turner, later known as Thomas Clarkson. Clarkson described himself as 'Furniture Printer to Her Majesty' and took over the Bannister Hall Printworks in 1856. In addition, between 1844 and 1856 Charles Swainson of Bannister Hall marketed his own productions in London under the name of Swainson and Dennys.

Large flowers, crisply drawn with the accuracy of a botanical plate and widely spaced on the fabric, were popular for the first five years. The ground was usually white, but a light green ground was also favoured. Machine-printed grounds, or 'covers', which were the speciality of Joseph Lockett (later Lockett, Crossland & Co.), were also employed (Pl. 72A). A simple, all-over pin design, known as a 'Stormont ground', or an all-over vermicular ground were the most popular, and some of the more elaborate grounds were reserved exclusively for the use of a particular firm.

By the 1840's the crisp drawing had been replaced by a looser technique, the petals being drawn without an outline and the shading achieved by the over-printing of light, transparent tones, giving the effect of a water-colour wash. The general use after 1835 of a solid green, which replaced the older method of the over-printing of blue and yellow, altered the appearance of the leaves and, in particular, the stems, which no longer had to have a dark outline to mask misregistration.

In the 1840's scrolls and cartouches were often introduced into the floral designs with the pattern covering the whole surface of the fabric (Pl. 73A). A common variant was carefully drawn bunches of flowers set against an all-over background of more sketchily drawn flowers or leaves, often printed in drab shades, giving the effect of a design in two planes. This idea of two planes was also apparent in abstract designs where a design of scrolls, arabesques or Moorish-tile shapes were printed in strong, flat colours against a subsidiary but unrelated geometric background.

A characteristic style of the late 'forties was a continuous cascade of mixed flowers, usually over-life size, running down the middle or both sides of the chintz, with a filling of small detached sprays. This style was used with considerable effect on challet, which brought out the rich tones of the dyes with an increased brilliance that could not be achieved on cotton. Several of these 'cascade' designs were exhibited by Swainson and Dennys at the Royal Society of Arts Third Annual Exhibition of British Manufactures, March 1849, and won for them the Society's Silver Medal for printed fabrics (Pl. 73B).

Elaborate floral chintzes, with large bunches of flowers, printed in natural colours, were at the height of their popularity at the time of the Great Exhibition of 1851, but it is interesting to note that even at this time they were subjected to severe criticism on the grounds of naturalism by the 'reformers' of the day. Several of the chintzes that won prizes at the Great Exhibition were included only one year later in an exhibition entitled 'False Principles of Design' organized by Sir Henry Cole at Marlborough House, the 'false principle' in question being 'the direct imitation of nature'.

Roses were popular throughout the period, either on their own or combined with other flowers, and ranged from full-blown cabbage varieties to budding moss roses. Other flowers received less sustained attention and remained in fashion for a year or two at most. For example, in 1848 and 1849 convolvulus was much in vogue, also hydrangeas and striped tulips. Although large flowers remained popular throughout the 'fifties, smaller designs of violets, heather and hare-bells were popular about 1855. A fashion for delicate designs based on ferns is found from 1856 to 1860 (Pl. 73C). These years also saw a fashion for diamond trellis designs, with a border of related flowers or leaves. The end of the period saw the introduction of orchids and other exotics, already popular in woven fabrics, which, in the field of printed fabrics, appear to be the result of French influence.

Throughout the period 'Gothic' blinds, first introduced about 1825, remained popular. These blinds, which were intended to be hung flat, were usually printed with designs imitating stained glass in an architectural setting, often on semi-transparent materials so that the light glowed through them. Some of the earlier designs have a certain charm, but most of the later examples are crudely drawn and carelessly printed in harsh colours.

The enormous range and variety of the roller-printed fabrics make it possible to consider only the most significant of the successive styles. Undoubtedly some of the most bizarre and exotic were intended for foreign markets rather than for the home trade, and these must be discounted when dealing with the changes in English domestic taste.

Until about 1835 the standard of engraving remained high, and finely stippled designs, printed from one, two or even three engraved copper-rollers, with additional colours added by surface rollers or block, were produced by the Lancashire calico-printers. Outstanding among these are six designs of birds and flowers copied from plates in Audubon's *Birds of America* (Pl. 72B). The six designs fall into three pairs, dated 1830, 1831 and 1834, and followed quickly upon the publication of Audubon's plates. The birds, and many of the flowers, are almost facsimile copies of his engravings, but no attention has been paid to their natural colouring. The new chemical dyes were exploited to the full, and each design was produced in over twenty-five different colour-ways, ranging from soft pastel schemes to brilliant reds and oranges on magenta grounds. In the same series of pattern-books (now in the possession of the Calico Printers' Association) are floral designs which show the same accurate drawing of large flowers that is found in the block-printed fabrics of the same date. By 1835, however, the standard is noticeably lower, and the introduction of inconsistent motifs, such as Paisley-shawl patterns, rococo scrolls and jewelled effects, combined with an indiscriminate use of colour, produced ill-organized and confused designs.

The last stage of the pictorial chintz, which finally died out about 1853, is manifest in the enormous variety of romantic, historical, commemorative and exotic designs produced mainly by the firm of Kershaw, Leese and Sidebottom of Ardwick Print Works, Manchester. The various scenes were usually vignetted in a floral wreath, and the design of the young Prince of Wales at Balmoral (Pl. 72C) is typical of their style. The subjects range from violent scenes of battles between Crusaders and Saracens to sentimental scenes of children and animals and parallel the subjects found in the contemporary Baxter prints and folios of engravings such as *The Drawing Room Scrap Book*. These Kershaw pictorials were invariably printed in the same colour range, a combination of subdued reddish-browns, purple and orange with a harsh, royal blue.

In the 1850's one of the most popular styles of cheap roller-prints was designs of flowers printed to imitate Berlin wool-work. Towards the end of the period the designers, confused and bewildered by the mass of 'historic ornament' presented to them both by such monumental works as Owen Jones' *Grammar of Ornament* (1856) and by cheaper, more ephemeral publications produced from the 1830's onwards, picked their motifs at random with an eclecticism that knew no bounds. Designs with 'Paisley' and Chinese motifs against a tartan background or naturalistic flowers set in ornamental panels with Renaissance jewels at the intersections are all too common. Although such travesties were severely criticized by the purists and reformers, this confusion of natural and formal details found general favour at the time, and fabrics of this type were awarded medals at the 1862 Exhibition.

Carpets

The carpet industry made great strides during the period 1830–60, particularly in the field of machine-woven carpets. A review of the Exhibition of Industrial Art at Manchester in the *Art-Union* of 1846 devotes considerable space to the industry. 'The carpet manufactory', says the reviewer, 'is in England carried to the ultimatum of excellence – the machine manufacture of carpets of all countries is incomparably inferior to ours. ... In France, those who purchase carpets are the wealthiest class of the community; but in this country every apartment is carpeted; the great consumption is, therefore, in the moderately priced article, for which in France there would be no demand.'

The main centres of the carpet industry were in Kidderminster, Halifax and other towns and villages in Yorkshire; Wilton, Axminster, Bridgnorth, Glasgow, Edinburgh, and Kilmarnock.

The most important centre was undoubtedly Kidderminster. In 1838 over 2,000 looms were in operation in the town and by 1850 the number had almost doubled. Fifteen large carpet factories, of which the leading firms were Henry Brinton (established 1819) and Pardoe & Hooman, were engaged in the production of all types of carpet. The simplest type, produced on an ordinary loom, was known as Venetian carpeting. It was woven in simple stripes or checks, with a woollen warp and the weft of hemp or cotton, and was used mainly for stairs or passages. The most important type of non-pile carpet was the Scotch or Kidderminster, an ingrain all-wool variety. These carpets were originally of double-cloth or two-ply weaving, with both warp and weft contributing to the pattern, and were usually reversible. In 1824 a stronger three-ply version was perfected at Kilmarnock, and the manufacture of this type soon spread to the other centres.

One of the basic types of machine-woven pile carpets was Brussels, with a looped, uncut pile. The Geneva carpet was a modification of Brussels in which parts of the pile were cut to give a velvety appearance. Wilton was a further modification of Brussels in which all the loops were cut to give a uniform pile. Saxony and Super-Saxony were both superior varieties of Wilton with the structure of a thick pile velvet.

The weaving methods of all these types of carpet necessarily imposed limits on the number of colours that could be introduced into the design, and two important innovations were the Patent Tapestry Carpets, originally patented by Richard Whytock of Edinburgh in 1832, and the Patent Axminster, a chenille carpet first introduced by James Templeton at Glasgow in 1839, which overcame this limitation. A full description of the method of manufacture of the Patent Tapestry Carpets can be found in the *Journal of Design*, April, 1850. The basic principle was that the yarn which was to form the pile was printed before weaving with an elongated version of the finished design, the extra length being taken up by the loops of the pile during weaving. The structure was essentially the same as that of the Brussels, and the pile could be cut or uncut.

In the Patent Axminster carpets the pile was formed by chenille thread, previously woven in the required colours. A strong warp and weft of hemp or linen formed the foundation of the carpet, with an extra warp to bind the chenille. Each row of chenille, with its different-coloured tufts, corresponded to one row of knots in a hand-woven carpet. The Patent Axminster made by Templeton's for the opening ceremony of the Great Exhibition of 1851 is now in the Smithsonian Museum, Washington (ill. Tattersall, *History of British Carpets*, Plate XCVII). It is a long, narrow carpet divided into three main panels by ornamental bands and garlands of flowers. The ground of the panels is covered with a damask-type pattern and there is a central cartouche with the date 1851 in Roman numerals.

Such methods, which imposed no limitations in either the number of colours or the complexity of design, led to the production of carpets which were unsuitable for their purpose and repudiated all canons of good taste. Contemporary critics deplored the use of 'shaded architectural ornament, often used very objectionably in carpets, and suggesting impediments and stumbling' and 'Louis Quatorze scrolls, gigantic tropical plants, shown in high relief and suggestive of anything but a level or plane'. A typical example of this type of carpet, with elaborate rococo scrolls and sprawling flowers, is that in the private apartments at Osborne, which have remained unaltered since the death of the Prince Consort in 1861.

Most of our information about the design of machine-woven carpets, however, must be taken from illustrations in contemporary periodicals and the Patent Office Design Registers.

At the beginning of the period most of the designs were 'classical' with acanthus-like leaves, scrolls and flowers. Carpets in the 'Gothic' taste with architectural motifs were produced throughout the 'thirties and 'forties. 'Louis Quatorze' designs first appeared about 1840 and large 'rococo' scrolls tended to replace the more formal classical ornament. A type of design also introduced about 1840 consisted of a diamond trellis of flowers or leaves which covered the whole ground of the carpet. Good examples of this type remain in the Wilton carpets at Charlecote and in the private apartments at Ickworth. The most exuberant designs belong to the 1850's, with huge exotic flowers, ferns and scrolls, elaborately shaded to give a three-dimensional effect. Patterns based on Persian and Turkish models are found throughout the period.

Hand-knotted carpets were made at Axminster until 1835, when the factory was closed down and the equipment transferred to Wilton. The most impressive hand-knotted carpet of the period to survive is that made in 1850 for the Green Drawing Room at Windsor by Blackmore Brothers of Burdensball, near Wilton, to the design of Lewis

Gruner, the Prince Consort's German adviser. The carpet measures 52 ft. by 38 ft., with sixty-four knots to the square inch, and was one of the most admired pieces in the 1851 Exhibition. The design incorporated areas of naturalistic flowers with panels and bands of ornament in several styles. Several less ambitious hand-knotted carpets are in the Victoria and Albert Museum, including one made at Axminster shortly before 1835 (Pl. 74B). Hand-knotted carpets were also made in London by the firm of Jackson and Graham of Oxford Street (Pl. 75).

Needlework carpets were made throughout the period, mostly with floral designs with an affinity to the contemporary Berlin wool-work (Pl. 74A). More spectacular were co-operative efforts, worked in separate pieces and sewn together, such as the carpet (now in the U.S.A.) worked by ladies of the diocese and presented to the Bishop of Gloucester and Bristol in 1843, and that worked by '150 Ladies of Great Britain' from a design by John Woody Papworth for presentation to the Queen in 1851. The former carpet is a chequered design of seventy-seven alternating panels of bouquets and baskets of flowers and exotic and other birds. The Queen's carpet was composed of 150 squares of geometrical and floral ornament enclosed in a heraldic border containing the initials of all the executants.

Embroidery

During the period 1830–60 the craze for Berlin wool-work virtually eclipsed all other types of embroidery. It was in fact so ubiquitous that the terms 'embroidery' and 'Berlin wool-work' were regarded as synonymous. The preface to the *Illuminated Book of Needlework* (1847) by Mrs Henry Owen opens with the words 'Embroidery, or as it is more often called Berlin wool work, has been brought to such a high state of perfection ... the variety of patterns so great, and so well adapted to every purpose to which it can be applied ... that we do not hope here to be able to throw much new light on the subject'.

The first Berlin patterns were published in 1804, and although a number reached England as early as 1805, it was not until 1831, when Mr

Wilks of Regent Street began importing both the patterns themselves and the materials for working them direct from Berlin, that the fashion was fully established. By 1840 no less than 14,000 different patterns had been published and imported into England. The designs were coloured by hand on squared paper so that the design could be copied on to square-meshed canvas, each square of the design representing one stitch. Elaborate pictorial designs, with religious, historical and romantic subjects, were popular for framed pictures and firescreens. Floral designs, however, were even more popular, particularly for upholstery, and smaller domestic articles, such as hand-screens, bell-pulls, travelling bags and slippers. Bouquets and wreaths of flowers, naturalistically drawn, were worked in brilliant, harsh colours, and the height of attainment was reached when, by means of elaborate shading, the flowers appeared to stand out in high relief from the grounds. Birds, particularly parrots, were often introduced into the designs. At the beginning of the period the designs were rather more restrained and delicate, and were often worked in silk instead of wool. The designs were sometimes worked in the scale of petit-point embroidery on a white silk ground, particularly for small articles such as purses and pin-cushions. In the 1830's and early 1840's white or light-coloured grounds were often used, but by 1850 black backgrounds were almost universal, and served to emphasize the enormous flowers, worked in harsh colours of magenta and vivid primary colours, which, together with their veridian leaves, shone forth with all the brilliance of a stained-glass window. Many of the dyes used, however, were fugitive, and not many pieces survive unfaded.

The ubiquitous use of Berlin wool-work for all types of upholstery is apparent from even a cursory glance at the furniture pattern-books of the period. It is emphasized by publications such as that issued by Henry Wood about 1845 entitled *A Useful and Modern Work on Cheval and Pole Screens, Ottomans, Chairs and Settees, for Mounting Berlin Needlework*. The eighteen plates contain fifty designs for all types of furniture in the prevailing styles of Louis XIV, François Ier, Elizabethan

and Gothic, but no attempt is made to adapt the needlework to the appropriate style, and the Berlin designs are, with two exceptions, exclusively floral, with the occasional introduction of rococo scrolls or cartouches.

The true Berlin wool-work was worked entirely in cross-stitch or tent-stitch, in coloured wools which were manufactured at Gotha and dyed in Berlin, but wools spun and dyed in this country were also used. A variety of the work in which beads, silk and chenille were introduced into parts of the design was known as German embroidery. Raised Berlin wool-work was also extremely popular. In this parts of the design, either individual flowers, a bird or an animal, were worked in loops, which were afterwards cut to give the effect of a thick velvet pile. In addition to the more usual cross stitch, other fancy canvas stitches were also used, particularly for geometric patterns. Mrs Henry Owen lists and describes thirty such stitches, including some with such ephemeral names as 'Hohenlinden' or 'Sutherland' stitch.

While most of the designs were worked from the squared Berlin patterns, by the mid-1840's patterns were sometimes printed or painted direct on the canvas, which made for speedier working. Instructions for Berlin wool-work were also issued in letters and numbers, and read like the instructions for a fair-isle knitting pattern.

Although the fashion for Berlin wool-work persisted well into the 1860's, from 1850 onwards it was subjected to increasing criticism, particularly in the 'art periodicals'. The general improvement in the standard of embroidery during the second half of the century was first noticeable in the ecclesiastical field, through the work and influence of leading architects and designers such as Pugin and Street. Some of the most devastating attacks on Berlin wool-work came from religious quarters. The broadside delivered by a clergyman named James in a paper on 'Church Work for Ladies', read to the Architectural Society of the Archdeaconry of Northampton in 1855, is worth quoting:

'They (that is the ladies) revolt at the continual slavery of basting and hemstitch and very properly allow their mind and their fingers to relax in fancy work. And what does it result in? Art must be invoked, the imagination of the worsted shop tasked and there grows under the needle something of this kind (here the Reverend Gentleman paused to hold up a coloured pattern for Berlin wool-work) or better still a Bandit in glowing coloured jacket, looking over a precipice, with a long gun in his hand – one clever dash of blue worsted gives the eye, at once so tender and so truculent, and the work is done. Or a less ambitious picture is a group of gigantic flowers, with pansies as big as pennies [sic], cabbage roses which deserve the name suggesting pickle rather than perfume; gracefully falling fuschia as big as a hand-bell. Is there any real beauty in this, any originality? – it is simply copy, copy, stitch by stitch. Fancy work without the slightest opportunity to exercise the fancy. Dull task work unenlightened by one spark of freedom and grace.'

Apart from Berlin wool-work, all other forms of domestic needlework took the form of 'Fancy-work' rather than true embroidery. An analysis of Victorian needlework books, such as *Treasures in Needlework* (1855) by Mrs Warren and Mrs Pullan, or of the current fashion periodicals, shows little evidence of a need for originality of design or skill in stitchery. Braiding, which required the couching down of ready-made braid in scrolls or arabesques, was the most popular adornment for table-covers, cushions and antimacassars. Another means of achieving effects with the minimum of skill was the use of *ombré* silks or wool, dyed in various shades of the same colour, whereby the effect of elaborate shading could be imitated with simple stitches. Simple appliqué embroidery was used to adorn small articles such as pocketbooks, needle-cases, cigar-cases and smoking-caps. Patchwork was also favoured, often of silk and velvet rather than of cotton; but most of the surviving Victorian quilts are composed of simple hexagonal patches, with little originality or taste in the compilation of the design. Whitework embroidery, as in the preceding period, continued

in favour for costume, particularly for morning dress. The most general type was *broderie anglaise*, a heavy type of open-work with the pattern formed entirely of holes, variously arranged, and worked round in buttonhole stitch.

The period saw the introduction of machine-embroidered fabrics and trimmings. The leading firm in this field was Houldsworth & Sons of Manchester, who produced fabrics with embroidered figures worked by an adaptation of the pantograph (Pl. 76c).[2]

Whereas an improvement in the standard of ecclesiastical embroidery was apparent by the 1850's, as evinced at the 1751 Exhibition, it was not until the 1870's, as the result of the influence of William Morris and the foundation of bodies such as the Royal School of Needlework, that the same improvement was noticeable in the secular field. William Morris's first efforts at embroidery design do, however, just fall within the present period. These were made in 1860 to adorn Red House, the house built for Morris, by his friend Philip Webb, on his marriage in 1859. The Red House embroideries, which were worked by Jane Morris and her sister, were of two types. The most ambitious (Pl. 76D) were large figure panels, almost life size, representing 'illustrious women'. The figures, which were designed by Morris himself, are evocative of medieval stained glass, and are worked in wool and silk with fairly elaborate stitchery and fine detail. The other Red House embroideries were much simpler, and were worked with sprigs of flowers in coloured worsteds on a coarse serge ground. One of the patterns was of clumps of 'daisies', and foreshadows the 'Daisy wallpaper', the first paper produced by the Morris firm, established in 1862.

[2] For a detailed description of the process see W. Cooke Taylor, *Handbook of Silk, Cotton and Woollen Manufacture*, 1843, and Ure's *Dictionary of Manufacture*.

Costume

Costume

ANNE M. BUCK

WOMEN'S COSTUME

The changing style

Between 1830 and 1860 women's dress was dominated by the movement of its skirt which, for thirty years, without interruption or reversal, steadily grew larger. This increasing dome gave to the dress of the whole period a fixed, though constantly enlarging form.

The movement was already well begun in 1833, when 'skirts both of pelisses and robes, are of a still more extravagant width than last season'.[1] In the next year a rather sharp pen wrote, 'the diameter of the fashionable ladies at present is about three yards'.[2] Although in 1834 it was the circumference, not the diameter, which was between three and four yards, Mrs Carlyle's comment was almost prophetic of the size to come. Every year the spread of the skirt made a slightly larger circle, 'those skirts whose enormous and ungraceful width we had strong hopes would be at least partially curtailed ... their size is even a little augmented'.[3] Throughout the 1840's and 1850's it went on: 'amplitude of skirt still remains one of the leading features in dresses of all kinds',[4] until by 1860 a fashionable woman needed an area of twenty to twenty-five square feet in which to stand comfortably without compression.

The main feature of dress in 1830 was still its enormous sleeves. They lost some of their fullness, 1831–3, in forms which, like those at the beginning of their growth, were tight in the lower arm; but there was no change in their billowing line until 1834, when a new line appeared at the shoulder, from the ornament of deep lapels which passed over the shoulder to the centre waist, and from the muslin pelerines, deep collars which spread over the shoulders, curved over the front of the bodice and ended in points or lappets at the waist (Pl. 77). These gave to the fullness at the shoulder a new declining curve, and by the following year the fullness of the sleeve was broken: 'They are not now one third of the extravagant size they were a year ago ... some are made to fit the arm and tight to it from a little below the elbow to the wrist, with the top disposed in two small bouffants ... there are also some tight at the top and bottom, but full in the middle.'[5]

This change pervaded the whole dress, changing its character and creating the early Victorian style. The dress of 1834 in fashion plate, portrait or surviving example clearly belongs to the years before; the dress of 1836 as clearly to the years which follow. The new downward curve at the shoulder into the tightening sleeve was repeated at the waist (Pls. 79, 80). The lapel trimming, which had helped to smooth down the fullness at the shoulder, and another bodice trimming – flat folds of material curving over the bust from shoulder to waist – both made a triangular shape on the bodice which foreshadowed its new shaping.

[1] *Court Magazine*, Nov. 1833.
[2] Carlyle, *Jane Welsh, Letters*, 1834.
[3] *La Belle Assemblée*, Jan. 1836.
[4] *Ladies Treasury*, Jan. 1858.
[5] *La Belle Assemblée*, May 1836.

Bodices with a pointed waistline had appeared on evening dresses by 1833, and within a few years were, for evening, the general form, 'pointed corsages decidedly the mode ... indeed no others are worn'.[6] This waistline, curving down to its centre point, continued to lengthen during the 1840's, 'now drawn down as low as possible',[7] and until 1855. The new tapering bodice, above the spreading curves of the skirt, remained the constant form of the next twenty years, showing elaboration and variation, but no major change.

Its line was loosened and softened in the 1850's by the development of the jacket bodice with basque (a continuation of the bodice) over the hips; and by the opening of the sleeves at the wrist over full, frilled undersleeves of muslin and lace. In evening dress the softening came at the neckline. This was worn low throughout the period, 'excessively low, far too much so for strict delicacy to approve'.[8] During the 1830's and 1840's it was trimmed with flat folds of material, horizontal or making a slight point at the centre (Pl. 80). By 1843 deep collars of lace, enclosing the arm and the short tight sleeve, fell straight from the low neckline, suggesting the style of 300 years before (Pl. 79). The drapery of flat folds disappeared by 1850, but the deep collar remained to be gathered up in a lighter drapery of lace, net and flowers, and the neckline rose a little on the shoulders to a wide shallow curve.

Double and triple skirts and flounces carried the skirt out to its ever-increasing width during the 1840's. In the 1850's the printing or weaving of flounces in their own patterns and their trimmed edges, which distinguish the flounces of this decade, add a more luxuriant character and a new horizontal emphasis to the widening curves of the skirt: an elaboration and emphasis repeated in the trimmings of the bodice.

Fabric and colour

In 1817 there had been a premature attempt to revive figured silks resembling those of the eighteenth century, 'The antique robes of our grand-mothers, as far as relates to their texture, are again in revival; brocaded silks, small coloured sprigs on a white ground, have made their appearance.'[9] Neither the style of the dress nor the mood of fashion was then quite ready for a return to this more recent past, but after 1830, as the style drew nearer to that of a hundred years before, the revival came, 'In reviving the fashions of the seventeenth century (sic) we have also revived the superb silks and brocades that were then employed.'[10]

Silks now appeared in all their former richness. The light crapes and gauzes remained for ball dress, but for other evening wear there were rich brocades, 'that might vie with the stand-alone silks of our grandmothers and of very similar patterns'.[11] The brocades in dresses 1835–45 show fine examples of the silk-weaver's skill, and, as they often revived earlier patterns, are sometimes difficult to distinguish from those of the eighteenth century. The fashion for brocaded silks of eighteenth-century patterns was so strong that some eighteenth-century dresses which had been kept to this time were now remade: enough of these renovations survive in museum collections to show that this must have been a not uncommon practice. Printed satins, watered silks (plain or with satin stripes), velvet, and lighter silks (figured, checked, striped, plain or 'changeable'), were all worn. They were worn not only for evening and more formal day dress, but by 1840 were beginning to take the place of white cambric and printed muslin even in summer morning dress. 'Changeable' or shot silk, in delicate and subtle shadings, either plain or figured, is particularly characteristic of dresses of the 1840's. Silks *à disposition* – that is, woven with patterns as skirts or flounces, not as a continuous length of fabric – distinguish the dresses of 1851–60. This fashion was not limited to woven fabrics, but was carried out also in printed designs.

An increased use of wool, either alone or mixed with silk, appeared in dress fabrics of the 1830's, mixtures 'of silk and wool, quite as light as jaconot

---

[6] *World of Fashion*, March 1838.
[7] *Ladies Cabinet*, June 1844.   [8] *ibid.*, Feb. 1842.

[9] *La Belle Assemblée*, Feb. 1817.
[10] *World of Fashion*, Feb. 1839.
[11] *La Belle Assemblée*, Nov. 1835.

Detail of The Grosvenor Family, 1832 (exhibited). By C. R. Leslie.

This shows women's dress just before change came to the sleeve. The standing figure is in outdoor dress, pelisse robe with wide lapels, wide-brimmed bonnet, with a spray of flowers beneath the brim, and parasol. The seated figure at the piano wears an elaborate dress cap and a muslin pelerine. The younger woman at the harp, who does not wear a cap, has 'jockeys' over the top of her full sleeves. The men, who have dark coats over light trousers, show three styles of neckwear, a white cravat, a black cravat, and a black cravat with long ends, filling the opening of the low-fastening waistcoat of figured silk. *The Executors of the late Duke of Westminster.*

PLATE 77

Pelisse robe, purple silk, figured in blue, 1830–3.
The sleeves, very full at the shoulders, tapering slightly to the lower arm,
remain the dominating feature of dress until 1835. The figured silk shows the
growing fashion for fabrics resembling those of the eighteenth century. *Victoria
and Albert Museum.*

PLATE 78

Portrait Group, 1844. By FORD MADOX BROWN.

The dress and hairdressing of the older woman is still in the fashion of the late 1830s. She wears a sleeve still retaining part of its fullness in the lower arm and an elaborate cap of the 1830s shape. The younger women wear their hair in the smooth style of the 1840s, and all have the low neckline with the deep collar of lace which had just become fashionable. The bodice shaping of the 1840s and its deep-pointed waist-line can be seen in the dress on the extreme right, which also shows the sleeve beginning to open over white muslin undersleeves. The men both wear dark cravats, one black, the other dark blue spotted in white, above a shirt with plain front and button fastening. Their coat sleeves are open at the wrist, fastening with one or two buttons, a detail of the 1830s and 1840s. *Manchester City Art Galleries.*

PLATE 79

Evening dress, blue and white striped silk, 1841–3.

This dress, which has an alternative, long-sleeved bodice for day wear, shows the short, tight sleeve set low on the arm. The trimming at the neck, flat folds of material, draped with a point at the centre, called 'à la Sevigné', appeared on bodices throughout the 1830s and 1840s. The hair is dressed in the ringlet style of the 1840s with a headdress of Honiton lace and flowers. *Manchester City Art Galleries*.

PLATE 80

James Ramsay, Marquess of Dalhousie, 1847. By J. WATSON GORDON. The double-breasted coat buttons high and the full skirts cover the upper part of the legs. The trousers show the narrow-legged form fashionable in the 1840s and 1850s. The black cravat makes a wide band covering the neck and is tied low, in a neat bow. *National Portrait Gallery.*

PLATE 81

Family Group. Photograph.

The younger woman shows the style of bodice worn from about 1843 into the early 1850s, with draped fullness on the shoulders, gathered together at the centre waist. She wears a ribbon waist-band and a ribbon round her neck, crossed in front and fastened by a brooch, a favourite ornament, 1845–55. The older man keeps the earlier style of a white cravat; the younger shows the narrower band and large bow which had now developed; and in the wearing of his coat, follows a custom of the 1850s and 1860s of fastening the top button only. *Manchester City Art Galleries.*

PLATE 82

Three styles of bonnet, 1835–58.

(*Above*) A silk bonnet, over a stiff foundation, with cone-shaped crown, set at an angle to the wide brim, 1835–8.

(*Below, right*) A drawn bonnet of shot silk, gathered over a framework of cane, the brim in a straight line with the crown, the style of 1840–50.

(*Below, left*) A bonnet of split straw and horsehair plait, with the brim and crown in a line which slopes towards the back of the head, 1853–8.

All have the curtain, shading the neck at the back. *Manchester City Art Galleries.*

The Empty Purse, 1857. By JAMES COLLINSON.

She wears the fashionable bonnet of the mid-1850s, which slopes towards the back of the head leaving the front uncovered. The brim is trimmed inside and a small bonnet veil, now thrown back, is worn. On the stand at her side is a newly fashionable hat. The sleeve of the dress is in the 'pagoda' form, with lace-trimmed, ribbon-threaded undersleeves. The flounces of the skirt are woven with horizontal striping 'à la disposition'. The gloves are very short-wristed and the empty purse of the title is one of the netted, beaded purses which survive in large numbers from this period. *Tate Gallery, London.*

PLATE 84

muslin'.[12] One of the most popular of these was chaly or challis, a fabric of silk warp and worsted weft, which in 1832 'has now retained its vogue for eighteen months',[13] and was to remain in fashion until 1840. It was usually printed, and sometimes woven with a silk stripe, and was used for all dresses except full evening wear. Very fine woollen fabrics appeared in the 1840's, like balzarine, 'of that exquisitely soft and fine cashmere wool ... and half transparent, is as light as muslin',[14] but there was also an increased use of the closer woollen fabrics, cashmere, and merino, 'certainly the material best calculated of all others for walking dress, and is also from the warmth of its texture, admirably fitted for winter costume in so variable a climate as ours'.[15]

The printed muslins which had been fashionable during the 1820's continued in fashion for morning dress in the summer months, 1830–40, but then lost their predominance, as silks, which now included washing silks, became more generally worn. Their patterns in the 1830's grew more complex in colour and design and the muslin was often woven with stripes or checks as a background for the printed pattern, 'quadrilled cambrics, muslins and ginghams are much in favour ... among the prettiest those with a small flower in the centre of each square'.[16]

Dresses of white cambric with embroidery also grew fewer in the 1830's, but much muslin and net, finely embroidered, appeared in the pelerines which fell over the shoulders, or canezous which covered the back and front of the bodice but not the sleeves. This embroidered muslin had its fullest display while the sleeve still spread widely at the shoulder, 'in truth a costly simplicity, for the lace and embroidery ... are much more expensive than the stiff brocades'.[17] (Fig. 1.) After 1845 the muslin lessened in area, and went beneath the dress in the chemisette worn with an open bodice, and in the undersleeves beneath the widening sleeve opening.

Fig. 1. Half-dress pelerine of worked muslin. *La Belle Assemblée*, May 1835.

In the 1830's the mingling of black with bright colours brought a new aspect to dress. Patterns in many colours were woven, printed or embroidered on a black ground, 'shawls of French cashmere, with black grounds, flowered in rich bouquets of very vivid colours',[18] and in the silks of the late 1850's, black made the pattern with a single deep colour. Flounces of black lace were worn over pale silks from 1840 to the end of the period, 'black lace will be as much worn as ever over the light silks'.[19] In the black gauze bonnet veils, which were popular during the 1830's, in the black gauze and lace shawls and black silk mantles, the contrast of black was replacing the ever-recurring white of the previous generation. The decorative aprons which were a fashionable addition to morning dress, 1830–50, were also often of black satin, embroidered in bright colours.

The black lace was a silk bobbin lace, black blonde, which, with the cream silk blonde, fashionable since about 1815, was worn during the 1830's and 1840's. After 1850 black lace is usually Chantilly or Maltese. About 1840 there was a revival of the point and bobbin laces of seventeenth-century pattern in the deep falling collars. Machine-made laces developed during the period and hand-made laces after 1850 lost much of their quality.

Apart from the flounces and collars of lace of

[12] *La Belle Assemblée*, May 1831.
[13] *ibid.*, March 1832.   [14] *Ladies Cabinet*, July 1844.
[15] *ibid.*, Jan. 1842.
[16] *La Belle Assemblée*, June 1835.
[17] *ibid.*, July 1836.

[18] *Court Magazine*, Oct. 1836.
[19] *World of Fashion*, Jan. 1858.

the 1840's, the trimmings of the dress, 1830–50, were not elaborate. A contrast of texture only was characteristic of the restrained ornament of the 1840's, when silk dresses were often trimmed with velvet bands of the same colour. More elaborate trimming came after 1845 in silk fringes on dresses and outdoor garments, but by 1860 plain surfaces were again returning, and flat trimming, in bolder outline and contrasting colour, was being applied to them.

Towards 1860 colours deepened and were used in more striking contrasts than the subdued shadings of the 1840's, although pale colours still appeared in the heavier watered silks. Aniline dyes were being developed after 1857.

Forms and construction

From 1830 the skirt was usually lined in silk dresses and sometimes, though more rarely, in cotton dresses. It was set on to the bodice in pleats with gathers at the centre back, but as skirts grew wider a method of stiff gathering, in which the edge of the fold only was attached to the bodice, appeared in 1841, 'a new method of setting on the skirt by gauging it round the top as far as the points of the hips: by this means that excessive fullness which would be otherwise disposed in gathers or plaits, is formed exactly to the shape, but on the other hand this method lengthens the waist excessively and gives an air of stiffness to the figure'.[20] The lengthening of the waist, the stiffness of the 1840's style, were thus a technical consequence of the growth of the skirt. The lengthening continued until the spread of the skirt was supported by the crinoline frame. The earlier method of setting on the skirt with pleats, now double or triple box-pleating, was then resumed, with a raising of the waistline.

The growing width of the skirt was supported at first by petticoats, stiffly piped at the hem, then, as the spread became a matter of the whole skirt, not of the hem only, a series of waistlength petticoats accumulated beneath, over a stiff underpetticoat of horsehair, the crinoline petticoat.

Other devices gave the desired fullness to the

skirt in the 1830's, bustles, crescent- or bag-shaped, or of stiff frills, 'their bustles (false bottoms) are the size of an ordinary sheep's fleece, the very servant girls wear bustles'.[21] To support her fashionable skirt of 1842, Lady Aylesbury, who 'wears 48 yards of material in each of her gowns', wore a petticoat made of down instead of the usual horsehair one.[22] From 1855 the still-widening skirt was supported on a framework, as the skirt of the eighteenth century had been supported by hoop petticoats and the skirts of the late sixteenth century by a farthingale. This nineteenth-century hoop petticoat, at first hoops of whalebone in a petticoat, developed into light and flexible constructions of covered steel wire, taking from the stiff petticoat which it superseded the name of crinoline. Its lightness, compared with the weight of many petticoats, made it, in spite of its size, an advance in comfort and ease of movement. From this time drawers became an essential piece of underclothing, and these and the remaining petticoats were embroidered at the hem in white openwork embroidery, known as broderie anglaise. During the 1850's the stitching of the new sewing-machines begins to appear.

From 1836, bodices, which fastened at the back, were increasingly 'of the corset kind, cut in three pieces, sitting close to the shape'[23] (Pl. 79). Their corset quality was increased by their boned lining and by the corsets worn beneath them. During the 1840's this tight-fitting, back-fastening bodice was the usual form, 'the majority tight to the shape, but several are full in the shoulders, draped before and terminate somewhat in the fan form under the ceinture'.[24] This alternative form appears more often in photographs and in dresses surviving in English collections from the 1840's, than in fashion plates (Pl. 82). The pelisse robe, with a front fastening, was still worn, mainly as an outdoor style, in the 1830's (Pls. 77, 78), becoming less worn during the 1840's. After 1845 a

[20] *World of Fashion*, Feb. 1841.

[21] Carlyle, *Jane Welsh, Letters*, Nov. 1834.
[22] Clive, Caroline, Diary, 29 April 1842 (*Diary and Family Papers*, 1949).
[23] *Court Magazine*, Nov. 1836.
[24] *Ladies Cabinet*, June 1843

bodice open on the bosom over a chemisette was much worn. Small basques appear on bodices in the late 1840's, the beginning of the development of the separate jacket bodice which was the characteristic form of the 1850's. In 1859 a plain bodice was again appearing, and this became the form of the 1860's, retaining the front fastening of the jacket form.

Sleeves, while still at their climax of fullness, were supported by swansdown puffs. After the sleeve tightened to the arm it was set so low that it hampered the movement of the arm above the shoulder. The sleeve opened at the wrist from the mid-1840's, widening to the 'pagoda' sleeve of the 1850's, 'sleeves are worn of various forms, but pagoda is decidedly the most elegant with the beautiful engageantes below it'[25] (Pl. 84). The widening reached its climax in the wing-like sleeves of 1857–9, completely open, 'a square of material pleated into the armhole',[26] but the open forms were then being superseded by the full bishop sleeve with a closed wrist which had appeared as an alternative form from 1855.

The fitted forms of outdoor garment, the full-length pelisse, and the spencer, the short jacket ending at the waist, were passing out of fashion in the 1830's, although the spencer had a brief revival, 1839–40.

The sleeves of the pelisse opened out to take the large sleeves of the dress, changing the pelisse into a fitted mantle with open sleeves. This and the cloak, often wadded and with a deep cape added to it, were, for most of the period, the wear for cold weather, 'neither novel nor dressy, but exceedingly comfortable and appropriate'.[27] In the late 1850's cloaks of wadded silk or the thinner woollen fabrics were joined by those of heavier materials, 'vecuna and those thick warm materials'.[28] Full length cloaks were more general in the 1830's, and three-quarter length or less after 1840, with still shorter versions from 1854.

Fig. 2. Jacket mantle, for which a paper model was given in the *Ladies Gazette of Fashion*, April 1857.

The mantles bore a great variety of names and many slight differences of shaping, but most of them fell loosely over the upper part of the body so that the waist, so clearly defined in the dress, was, out of doors, obscured. The scarf mantelet was one of the most persistent forms. Shaped to fall as a cape or shawl over the shoulders, with long scarf ends to the knee in front, it appeared in white-embroidered muslin, 1830–45; in black silk from about 1835, sometimes lined with light silk and edged with black lace, resembling the black silk cloaks of the eighteenth century; and in the 1840's in 'changeable' silks, with ruched frills and fringed trimmings instead of lace. By the end of the period, jacket forms of outdoor garments, with sleeves, closed or open, were returning (Fig. 2).

Scarves were summer wear, 'they supersede for the moment both shawls and pelerines'.[29] They were of silk crape, of transparent gauze, of silk or silk and wool, of black lace or net. They were embroidered at the ends, 'cachemire de Thibet ... embroidered in palmettes',[30] or had woven borders. The scarf was worn less after 1845. The

[25] *World of Fashion*, May 1852.
[26] *ibid.*, Oct. 1857.
[27] *Ladies Cabinet*, Dec. 1843.
[28] *World of Fashion*, Jan. 1854.

[29] *La Belle Assemblée*, Aug. 1836.
[30] *ibid.*, June 1832.

shawl, a more enveloping and warmer wrap, even before 1830, when it was still a small square, increased in size. A more informal covering than a mantle, a cashmere or crape shawl was worn with muslin dresses for walking. The fashionable cashmere shawl was Indian or French: 'French cachemire, which both in colour and pattern come very near the Indian shawls. ... It may however be doubted whether one half, perhaps more, of those sold under the names of French cachemire are not really the produce of British looms'.[31] Very large rectangular shawls, which showed increasingly elaborate patterns based on the Indian cone design, were much worn over the large skirts at the end of the period. There were also shawls of printed satin, of plaid or shot silk, of damasked crape, and muslin, gauze, net, and lace.

Hats and headdresses

As the skirt of the dress grew larger, the bonnet, still large in 1830, grew smaller, diminishing rapidly after 1855. Soon after 1830 the crown became cone shaped – a cone with the top cut off – although the crown of drawn bonnets, those with the material gathered over a framework of cane or wire, had a horseshoe shape. The brim was still wide, encircling the face, but in 1832, 'bonnets of the small, close-fitting cottage shape ... coming more into favour with walking dress',[32] were a hint of the shape to come. By 1838 the new form, with brim and crown in a straight line, was established, and by 1841 no other shape was worn. It remained with little change for the next ten years, 'it is now a settled thing that the horizontal form will retain its vogue'[33] (Pl. 83). The only difference was between its close and open styles.

By 1850 the open form was appearing more often than the close, and from the open form came the new style of the 1850's. The brim spread more openly round the face and the crown grew lower and smaller, and was worn back on the head, revealing the face, 'it is the peculiar form of crown which gives this appearance, by

being made low and sloping towards the back'[34] (Pls. 83, 84). By 1858 the sides were receding a little further and the top of the crown tapered forward.

The hat, which had not been fashionable for a generation, returned in 1857. Hats were worn by children and had occasionally appeared as informal seaside or country wear (Fig. 6); they were now being worn by young women, 'of course they are not suited to elderly ladies'[35] (Pl. 84).

Winter bonnets were of velvet, in summer they were of watered silk, crape, straw, or the white rice straw, 'or as we call it in English chip'.[36] Fancy straws, openwork braids of split straw and horsehair, appeared in the 1830's, but were more popular after 1845 (Pl. 87). Felt appeared in 1849, but although it had been used in riding-hats, it did not come into fashionable use until the return of the hat.

Trimmings in the 1830's were of flowers, feathers and ribbon, with blonde lace and bows of ribbon inside the brim. The bird of paradise plume was the most fashionable 1835–45, but feathers were 'dressy or plain to suit the bonnet',[37] and trimmings generally became lighter after 1830. As the brim opened in the 1850's, trimming again appeared on the inside. Large veils were worn over bonnets in the 1830's, black gauze or lace being particularly fashionable for them, 1833–40, 'black veils are so generally adopted ... you see them upon nine ladies out of ten'.[38] Veils lessened in size and use after 1850. A small curtain frill was worn at the back of the bonnet, shading the neck.

In evening dress the turban and the beret were still worn, but these also were smaller by 1832, and by 1834 'berets so long in favour are now no longer seen in evening dress'.[39] Turbans continued to be worn for a few years longer, twisted into shapes from lace and gauze scarves. Probably many of the lighter scarves which survive from

[31] *La Belle Assemblée*, April 1832.
[32] *ibid.*, Jan. 1832.
[33] *Ladies Cabinet*, June 1845.

[34] *World of Fashion*, Nov. 1853.
[35] *ibid.*, June 1857.
[36] *Ladies Cabinet*, July 1844.
[37] *World of Fashion*, May 1841.
[38] *La Belle Assemblée*, Dec. 1834.
[39] *Court Magazine*, Feb. 1834.

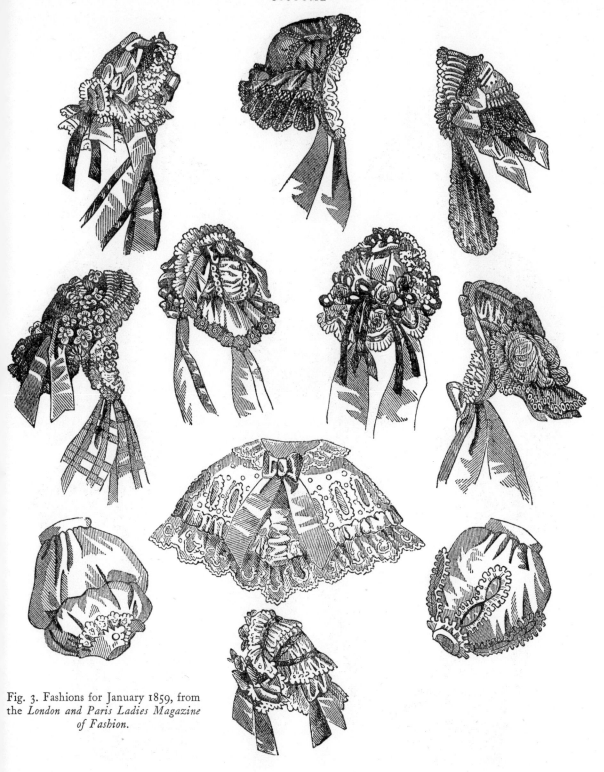

Fig. 3. Fashions for January 1859, from
the *London and Paris Ladies Magazine
of Fashion.*

Fig. 4. Fashions for May 1859, from the *London and Paris Ladies Magazine of Fashion*.

these years were so used, but by 1836 'turbans have lost a little of their vogue',[40] and by the early 1840's they were little worn.

The cap of the 1830's was still round, its brim, like that of the bonnets, rising from the face (Pls. 77, 79), but by 1840 it followed the new bonnet line and lay close to the head. Morning caps were of net, muslin and lace, and evening caps of lace and gauze. The hair was generally worn uncovered with ball dress or ornamented with flowers. Although in 1838–40 there was 'a fashion of covering the head ... even by very young married ladies',[41] for evening, the wearing of caps by younger women was lessening.

Shoes and stockings

Shoes, which were invisible under the long, full skirts, were flat and heel-less, often with ribbons or elastic crossing over the instep. They were usually black or white, 'dark coloured shoes are in general to be preferred to bright',[42] in silk for evening wear, and silk, cloth or kid for day wear. Half boots, just covering the ankles and lacing on the inside, with a single thickness of leather for a heel, were worn for walking. These were usually of cloth in shades of fawn or drab, with a toecap of kid in matching or contrasting shade. Dress boots of silk were also worn. Elastic insets at the sides appeared instead of lacing from the 1840's and heels reappeared during the 1850's. All boots and shoes show a long, narrow shape with squared toes.

Silk stockings were worn, the silk usually ending in cotton tops, well below the knee, and cotton stockings. The cotton ones were usually white, but the silk ones sometimes pale pink or mauve. By 1860 colour began to appear in some stockings, matching the magenta woollen petticoats which were then being worn, 'stockings made in the same colour ... or striped with black'.[43]

Gloves and mittens

Evening gloves became shorter after 1830, and between 1835 and 1845 were ornamented at the

top with ruchings or flowers, 'gloves are worn so short in evening dress that there is space enough between the trimming which finished them at the top and the bend of the arm for three or four bracelets'.[44] By the middle of the 1840's they were wrist length. Evening gloves were usually of white kid, but when the mingling of black with colour was fashionable, black net gloves and mittens were also worn, embroidered in chenille, coloured silks and gold and silver thread, 'as to appear enriched with precious stones'.[45] Black and white mittens were also worn with day dress, and short, wrist-length gloves of pale kid were constant day-time wear (Pl. 84).

Bags, fans and parasols

Bags or reticules appeared in flat forms, hanging from the belt in the 1830's and early 1840's, but they became less used and necessary as the full folds of the skirt gave space for pockets in the seams. Tubular purses of knitted or netted silk, ornamented with steel beads, were made in large numbers and much used (Pl. 84).

Fans of the eighteenth-century style, with ivory sticks, carved and gilt, and painted, pictorial leaves, were carried in the 1840's and 1850's.

Parasols, like hats, grew smaller and shared the woven and watered silks, silks 'à disposition', and the fringed and lace trimmings of the dresses. There was a fashion for feather parasols in 1838. The handles were of wood, bone or ivory, often finely turned or carved; and usually hinged so that they could fold, on the small parasols carried from about 1838.

MEN'S COSTUME

As women's dress was dominated throughout this period by the increasing fullness of its skirt, a new character was given to men's dress by the skirted frock coat. The cut-away coat, which had been the style of the beginning of the century, disappeared only gradually, particularly for country wear, and remained as the style for evening dress, but for formal day-time wear its place was now

[40] *Court Magazine*, Feb. 1836.
[41] *World of Fashion*, Feb. 1839.
[42] *Art of Dress*, 1839, p. 45.
[43] *Englishwoman's Domestic Magazine*, Dec. 1860.

[44] *World of Fashion*, June 1837.
[45] *ibid.*, Oct. 1839.

taken by a full-skirted coat, which, single- or double-breasted, fastened over the front of the body and covered the legs to the knees or just above them (Pl. 81). The forms of men's dress were now as much influenced by the occasion of their wearing as by the period in which they were being worn. The relation between occasion and form, between the garment and its function, was, however, an arbitrary rather than a practical one; the form which had come into dress from the hunting-field and horseback remained for the ballroom, and the tendency was for new styles to pass from informal wear to general wear, and to end as the garments of formal ceremony.

The frock coat, with its full skirt, showed a long-waisted line a few years before the lengthening of the bodice gave the same emphasis to women's dress. In the 1840's, 'If a man be well made about the waist and hips ... a long-waisted frock or great coat which has the waist seam below the hips may be worn to advantage'.[46] The cut-away coat showed a similar lengthening of the waistline. The low fastening and the deep lapel of the coats of the late 1820's remained, but after 1840 the fastening rose higher and closed the coat over the chest in short lapels (Pl. 81). In the 1850's shorter coat-forms with narrower skirts, slightly curving away at the front, began to appear. Throughout the period coats were usually of dark cloth, particularly black or dark blue.

In contrast to the dark coat, trousers were light, drab fawn, grey or white cloth, although for evening wear they were black, matching the coat. For more informal wear during the 1840's trousers of checked cloth were popular, and plain ones often had a broad stripe down the outer leg in the 1850's. By 1860 dark trousers matching the coat were increasingly worn. The legs were very narrow during the 1840's and 1850's, and from 1850 the strapping under the foot was disappearing (Pl. 81).

Between the dark coat and the light neutral shades of the trousers was the last refuge of colour

in men's dress, the waistcoat. For evening this was usually white, but for day wear coloured silks figured in floral or formalized patterns were worn, and, less formally, fabrics in bright checks. At the beginning of the period it usually had an open front with low fastening and deep curved lapels. Here, as in the coat, the fastening rose and the low curved lapels were replaced by shorter pointed ones, but the two styles overlapped, the earlier line still remaining in the 1850's. The base of the waistcoat was already curving to a point at the centre in the 1830's, and this line generally appears throughout the period. In the 1850's the fronts were cut away slightly, making a small triangular gap at the centre front (Pl. 82). Between 1830 and 1850 the backs were laced, or still retained the earlier tape ties, but after 1850 lacing was generally replaced by a buckle fastening.

Shirts in 1830 still had a high collar and a frilled front opening. The frill remained on evening shirts until about 1850, when it was gradually replaced by a front section of vertical tucking or pleating, with button or stud fastening, which had been worn on day shirts from the 1830's (Pl. 79). A small frill sometimes remained round the vertical band containing the button-holes. The collar of the shirt still reached the ears and chin in 1830, but during the period became lower, and in the 1850's began to turn down over the cravat. Detachable collars which could be fastened to a narrow neckband were also worn. Shirts were of white linen, 'Gentlemen's shirts are usually made of fine Irish linen or lawn, and sometimes of long-cloth. Some gentlemen wear striped calicoes, but seldom unless engaged in sporting, boating or fishing.'[47]

The cravat of 1830 was still a triangular piece of muslin, folded into a band, which was wrapped round the neck, and knotted in front. But during the 1830's black silk became increasingly worn for day-time and coloured silk cravats, striped or figured. These seem at times to have penetrated even into evening wear, where white still remained the main fashion, 'Already the young men of fashion have renounced black cravats for even-

[46] Good, T. and Barnett, G., *Scientific Cutting Simplified*, 1845, p. 109.

[47] *The Workwoman's Guide*, 1838, p. 142.

ing. The coloured are only used in the morning. At this I rejoice, never having been able to reconcile myself to them for dinner.' [48] The cravat was sometimes worn with long ends, crossed but not knotted, spread out into the space left by the opening of the waistcoat, and held in position by an ornamental pin. As the collars of the shirts grew lower, 1840–60, the cravat became a narrower band, tying in a wide bow; by 1860 the band had become still narrower and the bow smaller.

Out of doors, the cloak was, with varying length, still worn for evening. The frock-coat form was worn as an overcoat, and another overcoat was the Chesterfield, which was not seamed at the waist, although during this period it was shaped for the waist. This was sometimes worn not as an overcoat, but instead of a frock coat. The box coat – a much looser overcoat, a cloak with sleeves and cape – was also worn. Another cape with sleeves, 'much worn by London Fashionables for driving', was 'made of short milled cloth (either brown or drab) and has long been in wear as a "Macintosh" for driving, that is to say made of Macintosh's India Rubber cloth.' [49]

The tall cylindrical hat in silk, felt or straw, black or in pale shades of grey and fawn, was the only style worn except a low-crowned, broader-brimmed style for country and sporting wear.

Shoes and boots, which were now short, were of leather with long, narrow foot and square toe.

[48] Elizabeth, Lady Holland to her Son, 1821–45, (1946), 30 June 1840

[49] Good, T. and Barnett, G., *Scientific Cutting Simplified*, 1845, p. 55.

Fig. 5. The fashions for enormous crinolines, in *Punch*, November 22nd, 1856.

Fig. 6. The fashion for large hats, as observed by John Leech in
Punch, October 6th, 1855.

Jewellery

Jewellery

J. F. HAYWARD

The history of the applied arts in the nineteenth century presents a complex picture; fashions changed with such rapidity that it is difficult to trace any logical and continuous course of progress. In discussing the earlier periods dealt with in the preceding volumes of this work, it has always been possible to recognize some *leitmotiv* in taste; but in the nineteenth century style in the applied arts was at the mercy of an irresistible desire for novelty, a desire which involved an ever-increasing tempo of change. This constant search for something different was particularly strongly manifest in a minor art such as jewellery, which was affected not only by changes in the main stream of taste, but also by a host of minor fashions dictated by the course of feminine clothing fashion.

The effect of such changes in fashion was stressed in the Illustrated Catalogue to the Great Exhibition of 1851 published by the *Art-Journal*, a document of the greatest importance as a source of information concerning mid-nineteenth-century taste:

'The business of the manufacturing jeweller has undergone a great change during the last few years, for there is a fashion in the works of his hands, which, perpetually changing, compels him to seek new methods of exhibiting his taste and skill. We may instance, as an example, the manufacture of watch-seals, a branch of their art that is now rarely called into exercise. And again, in such objects as ladies' ear-rings which are almost wholly out of date, except as worn on what may be termed "state occasions". These alterations in the style of ornamental dress have compelled the manufac-turer to devote his attention chiefly to bracelets ornaments for the head, and brooches. The last-mentioned objects, though of distant origin, have assumed a totally varied form and feature from even their more immediate predecessors. Here we have now imitations of flowers, either singly or in groups, in which not only their forms are closely followed, but oftentimes successful attempts are made to produce natural colours by the introduction of precious stones.'

Revivalism

The basic trend in jewellery fashion in the period 1830–60 was one of revivalism; revival not of one particular style or period, but of styles drawn from different periods and cultures. The interest in reviving earlier styles of jewellery had already been apparent in the earlier decades of the century, but no great importance had been attached to achieving exactness in their reproduction. The spirit which inspired the *style cathédrale* of the 1820's was not so far removed from that which had created the 'Gothick' fantasies of the mid-eighteenth century. Subsequently towards the middle of the century we find an attitude of almost excessive piety towards medieval art associated with the name of Augustus Pugin, and exact reproductions of earlier pieces were made – exact, that is, in design, but inevitably lacking the life and spirit of the original. In the case of the Gothic jewellery, which Pugin sought to re-create, the originals no longer survived, and his pastiches were based not on actual jewels but on representations in medieval manuscripts and paintings. The taste for romantic Gothic was not immediately banished by Pugin's purism, and even as late as the 1851 Exhibition the leading French jeweller, François Froment-Meurice, exhibited a number of frankly romantic Gothic jewels. Pugin was not the only protagonist of the purist movement in the first half of the nineteenth century, for the Roman goldsmith, Fortunato Pio Castellani, was until his death in 1865 producing the most careful copies of Etruscan jewellery, with its delicate granulated enrichment, the secret of whose manufacture he had himself re-discovered.

When considering the rapidity of fashion changes in the first half of the nineteenth century, it must be remembered that, in spite of ever-improved industrial techniques, costume jewellery was only in its infancy. Most jewellery was still composed of precious or of semi-precious materials and was, therefore, comparatively expensive, and could not be replaced, as can modern costume jewellery. Whereas fashion magazines announced new trends with regularity, it was not a practicable proposition to purchase new jewels to keep up with all the vagaries of taste. Types of jewellery which, according to the journals, were no longer fashionable continued, therefore, in use among all but the very rich. These same magazines do, however, give us much information concerning the details of the feminine *toilette*. As always, a distinction was made between jewellery suitable for daily and for evening wear. In her book entitled *Female Beauty*, published in 1837, Mrs Walker gives the following advice on suitable jewellery:

> 'In promenade or carriage dress jewels are out of place. Nothing should be worn round the neck but a plain or watered ribbon, about half an inch broad, or a chain of silver or gold, as a guard to suspend the watch, or eyeglass if the wearer be short-sighted, for wearing an eyeglass without occasion for it is a piece of impertinent affectation. ... The ball dress requires a union of beauty, elegance, lightness and magnificence. All the resources of the toilet must be lavished upon it. No trivial embroidery or ornaments of gold or silver must glitter there: their place is supplied with pearls, diamonds and other jewels.'

Among other points which are stressed in Mrs Walker's book is the fact that young ladies should prefer flowers to precious stones, leaving the latter to their elders: 'Flowers decorate the system of life which is exuberant only in the young; jewels decorate the system of mind, which excels in the old.' Again, 'Young ladies should never wear rings on their fingers, unless they desire to seem older.'

Fashions in the 1830's were dominated by the same trends as the preceding decade, that is, romantic Gothic and Renaissance. Alongside these fashions there was continuing production of the cheaper jewellery, composed of semi-precious stones with the elaborate filigree settings made of gold wire twisted in various forms known as *cannetille*. The later examples of this latter type of jewel became somewhat larger and coarser and were enriched with coloured enamel instead of having settings of tinted gold. The importance of the Gothic fashion is illustrated by the following extract from the *World of Fashion* for January 1839:

> 'The forms of our *bijous* are now entirely borrowed from the style of the Middle Ages; massive gold pins, with the heads richly chased, or composed of coloured gems set in small flowers, *couronnes* or *guirlandes* of gold and diamonds, or else of gold set with coloured gems. All our ornaments, in short, are *moyen age*.'

Gothic jewellery

The Gothic revival did not, however, exercise an influence on jewellery design comparable with the predominant role it played in the development of Victorian architecture. The most popular form of Gothic jewellery was that produced in cast iron, first made in Berlin, but subsequently in Paris and elsewhere (Pl. 85A). It was still to be seen in the 1851 Exhibition and, to judge by the numerous examples which are to be found in this country, it must have enjoyed considerable popularity here. Though the production of castings of such lacelike fineness was a considerable technical achievement, the poverty of the material renders them dry and uninteresting. Even the designs of Augustus Pugin, which were based on details copied from fifteenth-century Italian and Flemish paintings, lost most of their charm when they were

Fig. 1. Brooch, shown at the Great Exhibition by Messrs C.Rowlands. Enamelled gold with a carbuncle and diamonds.

The Rococo taste

More lasting in effect than either the Gothic or the Renaissance revivals was that of the 'rococo' taste, which enjoyed an almost uninterrupted run of popularity from the second quarter of the century onwards until its end. While silver plate had been made in the neo-rococo style as early as the second decade of the century, the typical nineteenth-century rococo jewellery appears somewhat later, though the fashion was certainly established by the 1830's. It cannot be claimed that much of the Victorian rococo jewellery bore any marked resemblance to what it was supposed to be emulating (Fig. 4). The Victorian taste for massive-looking settings and strong colours was fundamentally opposed to the light and frivolous spirit of eighteenth-century rococo, and only in one field – that of floral jewellery – can the revival be said to have been successful in producing anything more than a parody of the original. The complex settings which had been so carefully constructed by the eighteenth-century jeweller were now usually die-stamped by machine from thin metal. The play of delicate contrasting scrolls which is the basis of much eighteenth-century jewellery design could not be reproduced in the coarse and obese scrolls of which the Victorian versions were composed (Pl. 86A).

Floral jewellery

The revived rococo fashion gave a new impetus to the production of floral jewellery. The taste for diamond sprays had never ceased to be effective ever since the mid-eighteenth century, but in the 1840's the demand for them became stronger, and at the same time efforts were made to render such jewels even more naturalistic (Pl. 86B, c). Among the features which helped to give greater realism to the floral spray was the use of green enamel on the leaves (Pl. 86B, 88B) and the addition of butterflies or insects perching on the blossoms. This was commented on in the *Art-Journal* Catalogue of the 1851 Exhibition: 'the taste for floral ornament in jewellery has been very prevalent of late; and it is a good and happy taste, inasmuch as the brilliant colouring of an enamelled

made up through the inability of the nineteenth-century jewellers, in spite of their technical skill, to catch the spirit of the Middle Ages.

Renaissance jewellery

The revived Renaissance jewellery consisted for the most part of expensive pieces made by a small number of high-class jewellers, such as Froment-Meurice (Pl. 85c) or Castellani; some of it followed Renaissance prototypes very closely, to the extent even of being made after engraved designs by Renaissance artists. Like the Gothic jewellery, however, the cold precision of workmanship of these reproductions differentiates them completely from their Renaissance prototypes (Fig. 1, Pl. 85D).

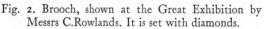

Fig. 2. Brooch, shown at the Great Exhibition by Messrs C.Rowlands. It is set with diamonds.

Fig. 3. Brooch, shown at the Great Exhibition by Messrs Watherston and Brogden. Enamelled gold set with diamonds and pearls.

leaf or floret is an excellent foil to a sparkling stone.' An effective feature which seems to have appeared first in Paris during the 1840's was the application of falling cascades of diamonds which hung down from the sprays like brilliant rain. Examples of jewels with these cascades were shown in the 1851 Great Exhibition (Fig. 2), where indeed a large variety of jewels of naturalistic floral character was to be seen. Among them was a tiara of sapphires and diamonds, made for the Queen of Spain, the points being composed of diamond leaves, and having bands of diamonds falling in loops at the sides.

The most admired English jewel in the Exhibition was a diamond and ruby stomacher composed of naturalistic flowers by the firm of J.V.Morel. This jewel, which included a rose, a tulip and a morning glory, 'was originally intended and designed as a bouquet ... moreover, it was so constructed as to separate into several distinct pieces of jewellery, according to requirement. The setting was contrived with springs, resulting in a waving or slightly oscillating motion when in use, which displayed to the fullest extent the brilliant colours of the stones.' The most popular form of flower-spray in the mid-Victorian era was composed of wild roses in diamonds set in silver with a gold backing, or, after the middle of the century, in platinum.

In the eighteenth and early nineteenth cen-

(A) Bracelet of Berlin cast-iron work in Gothic Revival style, c. 1830.

(B) Bracelet of gold, ornamented with designs copied from an Assyrian relief in the British Museum. By John Brogden, London. Mid-19th century.

All the Jewellery illustrated on plates 85–88 is in the Victoria and Albert Museum.

(c) Enamelled gold pendant by François Froment-Meurice. Mid-19th century. (D) Pendant in revived Renaissance style, enamelled gold set with rubies, pearls, a diamond and a sapphire intaglio. By Castellani, c. 1860. (E) Brooch with locket, enamelled gold and diamonds, c. 1850/60.

PLATE 85

(A) Brooch and pair of ear-rings. Peridots in stamped gold settings. Mid-19th century.

(B) Brooch, enamelled gold with glass paste. Mid-19th century. (C) Hair ornament, two-colour gold set with amethysts, turquoises and foiled crystals, c. 1840.

PLATE 86

(A) Diamond spray brooch, *c.* 1830–40.

(B) Convolvulus brooch, gold set with turquoises and pearls. Mid-19th century.

(C) Brooch, gold set with diamonds, emeralds, and rubies, *c.* 1840.

(D) Spray brooch, turquoises and diamonds, set in silver with gold backing, *c.* 1860.

PLATE 87

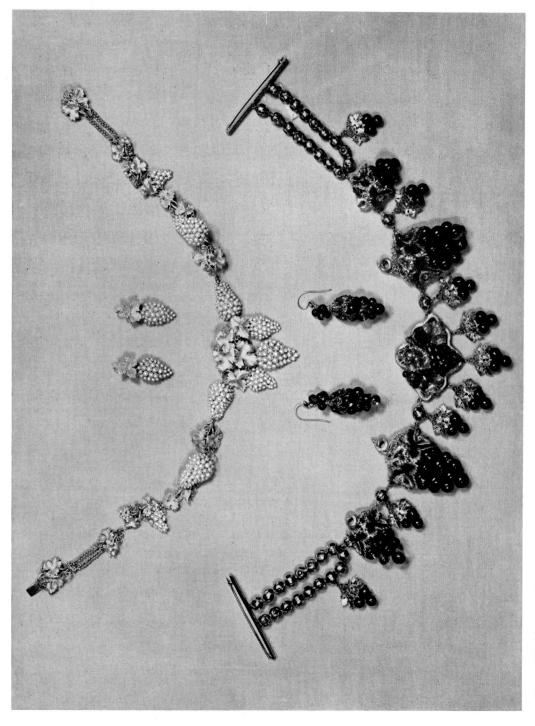

Above. Necklace and ear-rings. Two-colour gold and seed pearls, *c.* 1840. *Below.* Necklace and ear-rings. Enamelled gold and amethysts, *c.* 1840.

PLATE 88

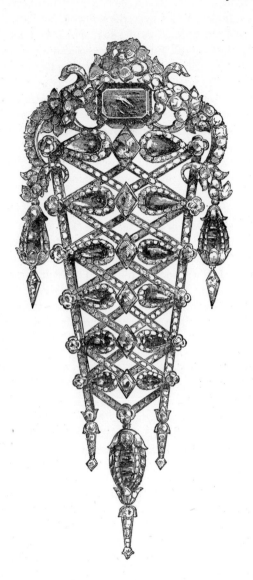

Fig. 4. Brooch, shown at the Great Exhibition by Messrs C.Rowlands. Gold set with rubies and diamonds, the design is based on an eighteenth-century stomacher.

Fig. 5. Brooch, shown at the Great Exhibition by Messrs Watherston and Brogden. Enamelled gold set with diamonds.

turies diamonds had always been set in silver, as it was considered that a coloured setting detracted from the effect of the stones. In the Victorian era silver was thought to be an insufficiently precious material in which to set valuable stones, and a laminated setting was used, the front being of silver and the back of gold (Pl. 87D). These laminated settings gave way in turn to platinum.

Two other floral details that were unfamiliar to the eighteenth-century jeweller, but were particularly favoured in the mid-nineteenth century, were ivy leaves (Fig. 3) and the convolvulus flower

L

Fig. 6. Breast ornament, shown at the Great Exhibition by Messrs Watherston and Brogden. Enamelled gold and pearls.

naturalistic fashion was the spray of lilac shown in the Paris Exhibition of 1867, which was bought by the Empress Eugènie. Its astonishing naturalism was said to have been due to the fact that the craftsman who produced it had a spray of real lilac on his bench while working on it. Naturalistic flower jewels were not necessarily made of precious materials. For the bourgeois taste there were brooches or necklaces composed of sprays of semiprecious stones set in two-colour gold or pinchbeck, such as the attractive example in the Victoria and Albert Museum (Pl. 86B).

As an alternative to flowers, we find jewellery based on fruit or even nut forms (Fig. 6). In 1837 the new brooches for evening were 'composed of pearls and turquoises; the pattern is a hazel nut placed on a branch of foliage. The fruit, which is of a tolerable size, is formed of a single pearl, the leaves, tastefully grouped, are of small turquoises placed very close together.' Another fashion journal of the same year informs us: 'The most novel form of setting diamond ear-rings is a grape between two vine leaves, the grape is in brilliants, the leaves and the stalk in small diamonds.' Such jewels were also produced in inexpensive versions for the bourgeois pocket. A popular form was made in imitation of grape-vines with the bunches of grapes of seed-pearl or amethyst and the foliage of gold tinted in various colours (Pl. 88A, B). The manufacture of the leaves by means of stamping and the use of alloys to tint the gold made it possible to sell such pieces at moderate prices.

As an alternative to pearl, beads of coral were much used to imitate berries; set in gold, they achieved a most attractive effect. Less pleasing were the brooches, and even tiaras, composed of coral branches in their natural state. Such was the importance of the fashion for coral jewellery in England that the London jeweller, Robert Phillips, who showed collections of carved coral at the various international exhibitions of the mid-nineteenth century, was decorated by the King of Italy for his work in developing the Naples coral trade. At the 1851 Exhibition Messrs Hunt and Roskell showed a coral branch tiara ornamented with leaves of enamel and gold enriched with diamonds.

and foliage. The great collection of nineteenth-century jewellery bequeathed to the Victoria and Albert Museum by Lady Cory contains examples both in diamonds (Pl. 87A) and in *pavé* set turquoises (Pl. 87B). The preference for turquoise, which had already manifested itself in the 1820's, became even stronger in the mid-Victorian period, and we find floral brooches and necklaces or bracelets made in the form of snakes profusely set with this stridently coloured semiprecious stone. The presence of the ivy or convolvulus can be accepted as fairly definite evidence of mid-nineteenth-century or later date.

Floral jewels were made in most of the European capitals, and it is not possible to determine their national origin. A typical expression of the

Enamelling

Enamelling returned to fashion as a form of enrichment for jewellery during the second quarter of the nineteenth century; the following quotation from the *World of Fashion* of September 1844, besides giving us full information about bracelet fashions, makes two references to their enamelled enrichment:

> 'Bracelets are now considered indispensable; they are worn in the following manner; on one arm is placed the sentimental bracelet, composed of hair, and fastened with some precious relic; the second is a silver enamelled one, having a cross, cassolette, or anchor and heart, as a sort of talisman; the other arm is decorated with a bracelet of gold net work fastened with a simple *noeud*, similar to one of narrow ribbon; the other composed of medallions of blue enamel, upon which are placed small bouquets of brilliants, the fastening being composed of a single one; lastly a very broad gold chain, each link separated with a ruby and opal alternate.'

A favourite combination in the mid-nineteenth century was to set small brilliants and half pearls against a ground of dark blue enamel; many gold pendants and lockets enriched in this way are still to be found (Pl. 85E). Lockets were the most popular form of mid-nineteenth-century sentimental jewellery; they were usually worn suspended around the neck by a chain or a ribbon, but were also hung from brooches, or even bracelets. The standard relic, as is indicated in the passage from the *World of Fashion* quoted above, was a lock of hair, plaited or arranged in the form of the dear one's initials. Memorial lockets were of similar form, but were enamelled black instead of blue. The recognition of the locket as the sentimental jewel *par excellence* drove out the mourning ring, which became obsolete during the 1840's. Hair-work, which was a natural corollary to sentimental jewellery, was still greatly in favour about the middle of the century, and among the more grotesque objects shown at the Great Exhibition was 'a large vase, most ingeniously composed of human hair, executed by J. Woolley'. Bracelets were also plaited from human hair, secured by a large and usually rather coarse gold clasp. Much ingenuity was shown in devising different ways of plaiting the hair, but the fashion for jewellery made entirely or almost entirely of human hair did not survive the period under review.

Cameos

Cameos had also retained their popularity until the middle of the century and later. Shell cameos, imported, like the carved corals, from Naples and the neighbouring towns along the coast, were much used for the cheaper jewellery, but cameos of onyx, agate or coral were recognized as suitable for wear by the socially ambitious, as is indicated by the following extract from a fashion note of 1857: 'A parure of these cameos (coral and onyx) is altogether aristocratic, and wholly unlike the cameos with which all the world is acquainted. They are pure works of art, modelled and cut by artist gravers, and mounted and ornamented by artists in bijouterie.' A number of cameos were exhibited at the Great Exhibition, mostly by Parisian jewellers, but a Mr Brett of London was amongst the exhibitors.

Minor fashions

Apart from the main course of fashion, there were many other minor fashions that were taken up for a while and dropped when the novelty had worn off. It would not be practicable to attempt to describe all the vagaries of fashion between 1830 and 1860, but the following are the most important. The excavations at Nineveh, an account of which was published in 1848, led to an Assyrian fashion (Pl. 85B), and in that year we read that flexible bracelets set with Assyrian rosettes or lotus flowers in precious stones were popular. Among the peculiarities exhibited at the Great Exhibition were the ear-rings of emeralds, diamonds, carbuncles, etc., based upon the sculptures from Nineveh, which were shown by Messrs Hunt and Roskell. The firm of Watherston and Brogden, who made the jewels shown in Figs. 3, 5 and 6, also showed examples of Assyrian jewellery at the Great Exhibition.

The campaigns fought by the French in

Algeria in the 1840's were followed by a fashion for elaborate knots and tassels copied from North African jewellery; and a Celtic phase was well represented at the 1851 Exhibition, where numerous reproductions of ancient Irish brooches were shown by Waterhouse of Dublin. Queen Victoria's pride in her Stuart ancestry led in turn to a fashion for traditional Scottish jewellery set with cairngorms and polished pebbles. Finally, after the Great Exhibition, increased interest was shown in Greek revival jewellery of the type that the firm of Castellani had been producing since the 1820's.

In considering Victorian jewellery as a whole, it has to be remembered that it was designed to be set against heavy fabrics of sombre colouring. The massiveness of the settings, now so apparent, must have been far less oppressive when seen in conjunction with contemporary clothing styles. The best of Victorian jewellery has been sacrificed to changes in taste and been broken up for re-setting. Unfortunately much of what remains is of the cheaper type, gaudy in colour and meretricious in design, with coarsely stamped settings of low-grade gold. Most of the Victorian reproduction jewellery failed in its purpose, owing to the impossibility of adapting the precise and altogether mechanical technique of Victorian craftsmanship to the spirit of earlier styles.

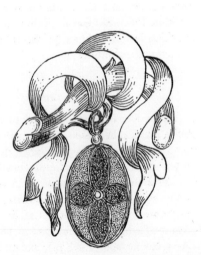 

Fig. 7. Two water-colour designs for brooches with lockets. Mid-nineteenth century. *Victoria and Albert Museum.*

Figs. 1–6 have been reproduced from the 'Art-Journal Illustrated Catalogue', 1851.

Music and Musical Instruments

Music and Musical Instruments

ROBERT DONINGTON

The old dominance of Handel

Music in eighteenth-century England had fallen under the spell of the great, but also very astute Handel to an extent which it is hard to credit now that his deserved reputation, as a genius of massive rather than ecstatic inspiration, has found its natural proportions.

In Early Victorian England the spell of Handel did not in the least diminish. He ruled undisputed, and there can have been few musically-inclined early Victorians who did not cherish the *Messiah* as the probable summit of musical achievement. A society known as the Handel Society 'for the production of a superior and standard edition' flourished from 1843 to 1848, and the publication was continued commercially until 1855, the year before the great German Handel Society was founded. In 1833 the Sacred Harmonic Society (founded the year before) was launched, with a programme almost entirely of Handel's music. Its criterion of a good Handelian performance included a considerable emphasis on volume, and by 1837 its combined orchestra and chorus numbered 500 – the chorus far outweighing the orchestra. North-country singers were brought to London to augment the ranks. They were amateurs, but they were found work in London for the purpose.

This emphasis on large forces, and on the grandiloquence of performing style inseparable from large forces, was somewhat typical of the period. It was not merely that the numbers were large, however; for that there were precedents, as in the commemoration of the centenary of his birth, that is to say in 1784 (actually a year early, since he was born in 1685). There was then a choir of 274 but an orchestra of 251, being both strong in the bass sections and with some chance of reasonable balance. The Early Victorian renderings started half a century later in 1834 with the balance quite upset in favour of the choir: 365 singers against 222 players. This was a mere beginning. For the centenary of his death in 1859 (there was a preliminary Festival in 1857) 2,396 performers were assembled in the only building large enough to contain them, the Crystal Palace, inherited from the Great Exhibition of 1851; and it seems almost unkind to relate that this apocalyptic array was subsequently outnumbered, the total rising to 3,500 in 1874 (in the proportion of six singers to each player) and to 4,000 in 1923.

This was a piece of musical ineptness and spiritual inflatedness, partly foreshadowed, it is true, before the Victorian Age, and continued long afterwards, that received its chief impetus from something in the times which we cannot help thinking of as characteristic of one of the many strains in that great, yet contradictory period. It argues a certain element of grossness and a certain ability to mistake the trappings for the reality. It was an inflation which collapsed with remarkable suddenness and appropriateness at the total destruction of the Crystal Palace by fire in 1936, by which time a movement was preparing to return, as many musicians are by now returning, to the small forces and crisp transparency of execution of Handel's own original performances.

Bad imitation Handel, mostly in the shape of

oratorio, came still more infelicitously from Early Victorian than from Regency imaginations; and the Victorian cantata was a new rival to the oratorio in weighty dullness. What partly saved this unfortunate situation, though at the price of a further servitude not much more wholesome than the old, was the fact that a rival was now found for Handel. He was not dethroned; there was still a majority to echo Stafford Smith's opinion of a short generation ago (in 1812) that 'the superior knowledge of instrumental effect possessed by Haydn, Mozart, Beethoven, and others, by no means compensates for the want of that manly, open, clear, vocal melody which characterised the work of Mr Handel'. But though not pushed from his throne, he had to share it as never previously in England, and share it with a visitor who was, like himself, a German and was, like himself, a man of sound business instincts as well as musicianship. This visitor was Mendelssohn.

The new influence of Mendelssohn

Mendelssohn came to London in 1829 on the first of a series of frequent visits throughout the remainder of his short life (he died in 1847, aged thirty-eight). As a young virtuoso of twenty he was welcomed as 'one of the finest piano-forte players in Europe ... supposed to be better acquainted with music than most professors of the art' (*Harmonicon*, 1829, p. 116). He was handsome and well-off (his father was a leading Hamburg banker); he had a precociously abundant talent and most winning manners; he was both artistically and socially more than acceptable. The friend of Goethe in Germany and later of Queen Victoria in England, he appeared to have every gift of fortune in his favour; but appearances were deceptive in one respect. He lacked one ingredient for lasting greatness: he knew very little about human suffering.

Mendelssohn's advance to popularity in England, at first as an executant but almost as rapidly as a composer, was little short of meteoric. He was soon worshipped almost to idolatry; and the influence of his genuinely inspired and readily attractive music swept the country. A new sect was formed that was not so very different from that of the Handel-worshippers. A new sect rather than a new religion, however; for in spite of their obvious differences of style and period, the two composers have an element in common which goes far to account for their common influence over Early Victorian musicianship. This element has to do with a certain unvarying optimism, imperturbable in the case of Handel, just perceptibly forced in the case of Mendelssohn, but in both of them unleavened by that sad wisdom which is an essential ingredient in every artist of the profoundest quality. Both composers had real greatness to substantiate their success; it was the uncritical reception of them which was its unhealthy aspect. They did not merely influence the Victorian musical scene; they imposed on it unnaturally. It is impossible to give any account of Early Victorian music which does not give these two foreigners pride of place.

Composers of talent but not of genius

We have first, paradoxically, to take one of those palpable exceptions which prove the rule concerning the dominant influences in early Victorian music. Robert Lucas Pearsall (1795–1856), a leisured amateur, worshipped neither Handel nor Mendelssohn; instead, his work reveals an intense interest in the one period least recognized by the average Handelian and Mendelssohnian, namely the golden age of the Jacobean madrigals. He wrote imitations of them which are so excellent that we are almost tempted to forget that they are in fact imitations, with the barest suspicion of Victorian sentiment to give the game away and to add at least a touch of originality. Unfortunately there is no law of nature and of art more inexorable than the law which prevents imitations, however excellent, from having the effect of originals.

Michael William Balfe (1808–70) was a composer of a very different stamp. An Irishman, the son of a dancing-master and brought up in a highly professional, not to say diversified environment, he was the very opposite of a cultured amateur, and the word leisure scarcely entered his vocabulary. He was playing the violin for a dancing-class at six and composing at seven. By eleven

Papier mâché upright Pianoforte by A. Dimoline, Bristol.

PLATE 89

Two artists' impressions of a grand Pianoforte with inlaid ebony decoration and ornamental gold relief work by Broadwood of London.

PLATE 90

(A) A square Pianoforte by Collard and Collard of London.

(B) A carved horizontal grand Pianoforte by Collard and Collard of London.
Art-Journal Illustrated Catalogue, 1851.

PLATE 91

A grand Pianoforte and harps by Erard.

PLATE 92

he had achieved public success in both directions. At fifteen he lost his energetic father, but earned his living without difficulty, including singing on the operatic stage among his professional successes – under the exacting Rossini, one of his patrons. By twenty he was an accepted Continental figure.

At a period when opera in London virtually spelt Italian opera, Balfe scored an immediate success with his first English opera, *The Siege of Rochelle*, first produced at Drury Lane in 1835. Others followed, but not all were successful. He lives now (and until quite recently lived very actively indeed) in his enormously popular *The Bohemian Girl* of 1843. His vein is tuneful, his style is catchy, his appeal is immediate – but indubitably shallow. Talent could hardly go farther, and very enjoyable talent it is in a certain mood. But genius, which is certainly not too strong a word for Gilbert and Sullivan in later Victorian England, is hardly in question with the facile Balfe. At least, however, he was not a post-Handelian, nor much of a Mendelssohnian; he shares these rather negative virtues with his fastidious opposite, Pearsall.

Samuel Sebastian Wesley (1810–1876) was the natural son of the great Samuel Wesley, and grew up in an equally professional atmosphere, though of a very different character. His background was ecclesiastical, and so is the bulk of his most important music. Though not quite a genius, he was more nearly so than any of his English contemporaries; he certainly seemed to be one to his own age, and it may be that the change in our tastes has been a little unfair to him. Spohr's testimony to him as candidate for the professorship of music at Edinburgh in 1844 is a fair and by no means unduly flattering description:

> His works show, without exception, that he is master of both style and form ... not only in sacred art, but also in glees and in music for the pianoforte. His sacred music is chiefly distinguished by a noble, often even an antique, style, and by rich harmonies as well as by surprisingly beautiful modulations.

In other words, he was Handel crossed with Mendelssohn: but that is not in itself an adequate summary of his achievement. In the first place, a

further and valuable influence was the Tudor church music, with which he was more familiar than most Victorians. In the second place, like Pearsall he had a certain individuality of his own, and in a far more versatile and fluent form. His sentiment is decidedly Victorian, and the Mendelssohnian ingredient falls rather strangely on our modern ears in this religious context; but he kept on the right side of dignity. He was also evidently a most impressive executant on the organ. As a master of the rank just short of genius, he commands respect, and he might well for those in sympathy with his Victorian mood command affection too.

Sir George Alexander Macfarren (1813–87) had the force of character to overcome the handicap of a blindness which became total early in his career, and this force and the integrity which went with it are evident in his music. Handel and Mendelssohn are both hard at work in it, however, and the mixture in his sacred music is ponderous rather than explosive. But his secular works are far more lively; it is an unexpected coincidence that this very worthy man, like the volatile Balfe himself, had a dancing-master for a father, and we can only wish that this ingredient in his development had been a little more influential than it evidently was. He had the enterprise to edit Purcell's *Dido and Aeneas* for the Musical Antiquarian Society; but his editions of Handel Oratorio, as the Handel Society's secretary from 1843, are somehow more typical of the man. He wrote a number of operas, some, such as his *Robin Hood*, successful in their day; but that day is gone, while Balfe's more vulgar but robuster *The Bohemian Girl* may even yet be not quite finished.

Heinrich Hugo Pierson (1815–73) was born plain Henry Hugo Pearson, the son of an Oxford clergyman and don – an environment from which he appears to have reacted with little gratitude. He had some small success in England as a young man, and thereafter a very notable success in Germany, where he became increasingly acclimatized both in disposition and in composing style. Though on terms of quite close relationship with Mendelssohn, he never accepted him undiluted, as did most English musicians: he was more critical in his appreciation, and he was equally well acquainted with Spohr, Meyerbeer and above all Schumann, who took a favourable view of his talent. Indeed, German musical circles in general did so to an extent which it is difficult to justify today, since his music, though ambitious and by no means without the divine spark, was marred by incorrigible amateurishness of technique. The spark was there, and in a form more original, potentially, than in his English contemporaries; but it flickered too fitfully to survive the winds of time, and he is entirely neglected by now both in Germany and elsewhere.

There was another Englishman of much sounder talent who also aroused the high hopes of the most influential German musicians, Schumann and Mendelssohn among them. This was Sir William Sterndale Bennett (1816–75), the most substantial of the Early Victorian composers, and with no deficiency in his technical equipment to hamper him. The son and grandson of professional musicians, he had the thorough grounding which comes best from growing up in practical musical surroundings from the earliest age. He was something of a prodigy, but not an extreme one: he was accepted at the newly founded Royal Academy of Music, with a free place there, as a boy of ten. In 1832 he had his first public success as a composer, and this success was repeated a year later in the presence of Mendelssohn, who took him up at once and invited him to Germany. The influence was all too successful, and Bennett never really escaped from it.

That would not necessarily have been fatal – no contemporary influence is harmful to a strong talent, and at least Bennett did not seriously succumb to Handel and the lure of the glorious past. But for no obvious reasons, Bennett's talent, which really was strong at the start of his career, soon weakened, and at last dwindled to virtual impotence. His German friends could not conceal their disappointment – not excluding the generous Schumann. His case was one of those which cannot be accounted for by the musical historian, and which only a psychologist can understand. There is no question that the gift was there, and that it was by nature more substantial than that which

any of his English colleagues showed. But there was an inner resistance to it in his own soul which slowed down the flow and eventually brought it to a standstill. His general influence as a teacher and administrator was wide and admirable.

Italian opera in London

If Mendelssohn's arrival in London aroused all too profound a response in the English musical world, there was another foreign body which the Victorians seemed to tolerate, and indeed enjoy, with no organic reaction of significance whatsoever. This was the Italian opera, which more than a century since its first advent was still the sacrosanct institution it had always been and was to go on being for a further half-century, when German opera, in the formidable person of Wagner, made some inroads.

The Haymarket, Drury Lane and Covent Garden competed for social and financial support with fluctuating fortunes. Mozart and Rossini provided the staple repertory; Weber, Donizetti, Meyerbeer and Bellini became scarcely less popular. Italian was the normal language, though German originals and English translations were not unknown. The English opera proper was so much lighter in style that it remained in a separate artistic class: which is presumably why it was so little susceptible to the influence of its more pretentious rival.

The history of internecine quarrels and financial crises which marked Italian opera from its early eighteenth-century acclimatization showed no sign of abating. In 1846 the conductor at Her Majesty's, Michel Costa, deserted to Covent Garden with most of his principals, to open there as the 'Royal Italian Opera House' in 1847. The singers presently assembled were of legendary variety and excellence; the opening night gave Rossini's *Semiramide* with Grisi, Alboni and Tamburini. A young and controversial addition to the list of composers was Guiseppe Verdi. In 1856 the building was for the second time destroyed by fire (1808 had been the first occasion); it was replaced by 1858 by the beautiful and acoustically admirable building which is still the main centre of London opera.

The Italian opera itself flourished in full vocal glory until the disruption of the first World War, after which the art of singing fell into a decline which has by now become catastrophic. The greatest German singers, like the Italians, were trained on Italian methods productive of feats of singing which can no longer be effected. The style passed with the glittering social order which supported it; but while it lasted, Covent Garden remained one of its greatest centres.

The contralto, a Victorian speciality

There was, indeed, one Early Victorian contribution to the art of singing of considerable, though not unreservedly beneficial, consequence. This was the popularization, by the phenomenal Madame Sainton (Charlotte Dolby), of the female contralto voice. There had always been traditional male altos, but the female of the species, though known, was something of a rarity. This is, however, a story which concerns oratorio rather than opera.

In opera, the second female line had traditionally been the mezzo-soprano, a tessitura much lighter than the contralto, much more ringing in quality and much more brilliant in execution. Only the very best contraltos avoid a certain fruity richness which may have been to the Early Victorian taste, but more because of its natural fitness to the heavier brands of oratorio than from any tonal charm. Since the purity of Madame Sainton's vocalization is the attribute most stressed in contemporary descriptions, there can be no doubt that she was one of the admirable exceptions; but her popularity opened the way for a lesser breed whose influence still helps to weight our performances of oratorio with that sense of leaden after-dinner discomfort peculiarly associated with this form of art.

The climax of Madame Sainton's career was also the climax of Mendelssohn's, and, in a sense, of Early Victorian music itself. This was the celebrated first performance, at Birmingham on 26 August 1846, of the only oratorio to have established itself in our English affections on an equality with the *Messiah*: namely Mendelssohn's *Elijah*. Mendelssohn wrote to his brother the

same day that 'a young English tenor' – it was Charles Lockey– 'sang the last air with such wonderful sweetness that I was obliged to collect all my energies not to be affected and to continue beating time steadily'. The work was given next year in London, in four performances of which the third was attended by the Queen and the Prince Consort, to their great delight. Within a few months, Mendelssohn was dead, the news being received with particular grief in England.

Musical instruments

No major developments occurred in the manufacture of musical instruments at the hands of Early Victorian craftsmen, but a steady stream of small improvements continued, especially in the making of pianos. The most crucial English contributions to the latter had already been made in the previous generation, when the famous 'English action' had been evolved among other developments; but English pianos maintained their progress on an equality with those of continental design, and were indeed preferred by some distinguished continental performers.

The flourishing Regency school of violin-makers declined a little in the early years of Victoria, but there were still a number of good makers whose instruments are well regarded today – including a flourishing school in Aberdeen. Their work, however, was based on an excellent reproduction of the best Italian models rather than on original design. The English school continued to take its share in the evolution of wind instruments, with the same tendency to growing mechanization as is found on the Continent; but in some directions we were unusually conservative. The trumpet, for example, was in transition from Early Victorian times until the present century – possibly it is still; but at that period English players and makers held conservatively to the slide-trumpet, which had always been mainly an English variety, and for a time resisted the continental adoption of the valve trumpet. Kohler and Pace were both making valved F trumpets in England by the 1880's, but these were slow to take a hold. And on the whole the same obtains with other wind instruments. The century saw great changes, but not many of importance originated in England.

On the other hand, so far as quantity is concerned, the English makers held their own. The number of pianos produced by the leading firms was surprisingly large when their considerable cost is taken into account. Flutes were in quite astonishing demand, the more expensive having keys up to eight in number, the cheaper being less well provided in this respect: whole operas were transcribed for amateur performance on the flute. The harp was another instrument which flourished remarkably in Early Victorian England: it was the acknowledged adornment of ladies of good breeding, and graced many drawing-rooms with its romantic and by no means diminutive presence. But even the piano was thought in some circles to be a rather effeminate accomplishment, and a case is on record of a young male pianist being hissed off the platform on this account – by the undergraduates of Oxford, so the story runs.

The appearance of Victorian instruments

The mood of Victorian musicianship was closely reflected in the appearance given to those musical instruments whose appearance is in fact capable of considerable modification without interfering with their functions.

Of these, the organ and the piano are the most conspicuous. It is, of course, possible to show the working pipes of an organ, and when, as in the new Royal Festival Hall organ, this policy is adopted, the result can have genuine functional beauty. But that has never been usual with large organs, and we should not expect it in the Victorian age. It has always been, and was then, usual to set a screen of ornamental dummy pipes in front of those actually producing the sound. The screen fronts of Victorian organs tended to be neo-Gothic in style, and more than ordinarily ornate.

The shape of the piano is determined by the arrangement of its strings, which range from a few inches to perhaps seven feet in length; and there are only a few arrangements which are mechanically and acoustically satisfactory. The Victorian taste here made its appearance mainly in the decoration of the legs and sides. The legs,

which must in any case be extremely robust to sustain the weight of a full grand piano, were ornamented with carving, often in very deep relief. Their main girth has to be in the upper portion where they meet the frame; their lower portion can be narrower without undue weakening. Hence where the harpsichord, and the earlier pianos of lighter weight, have no more than a slight tapering down from top to bottom, such as the universal principles of good design suggested, the very weighty Victorian pianos have a high degree of tapering, from wide top to narrow bottom. To avoid a clumsy appearance, the section, instead of being rectangular, normally became circular. The most popular materials were rosewood and ebony. The overall effect is rich and massive, but this effect is well in keeping with the structural and musical character of the instrument itself.

The musical character of the English pianos of the Victorian age, in common with those built on the Continent (to which the English makers had given the lead in certain respects since the last decades of the previous century), was determined by the use of very thick, heavy and tense strings, and by an action and a framework conditioned by this weight and tension (it might be well over two tons, a single string accounting for a pressure of perhaps 150 lb.). The resulting tone is somewhat deficient in the upper partials, but extremely powerful in the first six partials or so of the natural harmonic series. It is, therefore, of a less colourful quality than either harpsichord tone or early piano tone, but louder and more massive than either. It is this massiveness of tone which is so well conveyed visually by the weighty construction and heavy ornamentation which meet the eye in the illustrations to the present chapter.

The massiveness of tone in its turn corresponded, and was indeed produced in answer to a genuine musical demand. The music for which the harpsichord had been so well suited was largely contrapuntal, and even when not contrapuntal had been of a kind to need, above all other qualities, a certain clarity and transparency of tone at which the harpsichord excels. But the music of Mendelssohn, Schumann and other German favourites of

Fig. 1. A selection of Signor A.B.Ventura's string instruments exhibited at the Great Exhibition. *L. to r.,* the new British Ventura, the newly invented English Cetra, the Venturina, the Harp Ventura, and the Lyre Ventura. *Official Illustrated Catalogue of the Great Exhibition,* Vol. 1.

the Victorian musical salon and concert hall, together with the English piano music more weakly composed in imitation of these great romantics, does not require and would not tolerate the quality of clarity. The Victorian piano is capable of building up far more sonority than the early piano, and a totally different kind of sonority from the harpsichord. By the skilful use of the damper raising pedal, a surge of high partials is allowed to accumulate which adds to the tone that colourfulness and poetry which it is otherwise too neutral to possess. Cascades of arpeggios and runs intensify this colourful and atmospheric flow of sound – but at the almost total expense of clarity. This is precisely what piano music of the more romantic schools requires, and it was in this direction that the Victorian makers served their clients so well. The decorative exteriors, which were carried to their extreme development in the examples here shown from the Great Exhibition of 1851 (Pls. 89–91), have the undeniable merit of matching the musical idioms with which they were associated. Their artistic quality in itself, however, will probably be judged inferior to the best of the music, though their mechanical and acoustic virtues were on the highest level.

Most other instruments are so closely determined by their mechanical and acoustic necessities that even the Victorian taste for decorative exteriors could hardly affect them. The front pillar of the orchestral harp (then a fashionable instrument in the drawing-rooms of good society) took on an unmistakable neo-Gothic appearance, which it has never since lost. An occasional experiment was made in the outline even of the violin; but though such experiments have occurred before and since, they have never been permanently successful. A Victorian family settling down to play string quartets in its richly furnished drawing-room used instruments no different virtually from those of the classic period, or indeed of today. Yet the early nineteenth century had seen internal changes in the bass-bar of the violin, and an overall increase of tension, which somewhat changed the tone in the same direction (indeed for the same reasons) as that taken by the piano, though not to the same extent.

Such chamber-music playing was to become an increasing feature of domestic life. Neither in this period nor subsequently did it attain the range and popularity so conspicuous in nineteenth-century Germany, but it took a certain hold, and it did so in direct imitation of the German fashion. Here, as elsewhere, it is impossible not to detect and admire the influence of the Prince Consort. A genuine lover of music, and a most practical patron, Prince Albert left perhaps a clearer mark on the musical life of this country than on any other single activity.

The prominence taken by Victorian instruments of music at the Great Exhibition he did so much to further, paid a graceful tribute to his influence.

The spread of choral singing

But the most striking feature of early Victorian amateur musicianship was its enthusiasm for large-scale choral singing. The Georgian delight in glees and other part-songs diminished a little, though it by no means vanished. But the delight in great choirs grew beyond bound and reason. No glee or part-song could satisfy this mighty appetite: oratorio was its staple diet; cantata, as understood in those stalwart days, filled the gaps. The Sacred Harmonic Society of 1832 found speedy imitators. From 1840, recruits were trained in systematic classes pioneered by John Hullah and others. Hullah's 'Fixed *Do*' system of notation was one of the sources (for a time it attracted more attention as one of the rivals) of what

was to become a much more important system – John Curwen's famous 'Movable *Do*' tonic solfa system.

Although it was not immediately apparent, a movement had been launched in these developments which was to become one of the most influential in Early Victorian music, not, it is true, for the profession, but for the larger and less specialized body of those to whom music is important, and even necessary, without being a means of livelihood. When this did become apparent, a reaction followed which may seem ironical enough in the light of after events: for there were professional musicians who took genuine alarm at the prospect of thus bringing great music within the reach of so many whose understanding of it must inevitably be limited in extent, though not inevitably in depth of feeling. In fact, the consequences were certainly beneficial both to music and to the profession. There can be little doubt that it was this spread of musical enthusiasm which prepared the ground for the subsequent harvest which we are enjoying in the renaissance of English music begun by Elgar in later Victorian England. The German critic who dismissed England as 'the land without music' did not allow enough for the possibilities of new growth latent in this widening of the field under cultivation.

Fig. 2. A pianoforte by M.Pape of London which can also be used as a table when the top is shut down. *Art-Journal Illustrated Catalogue*, 1851.

Bookbinding and Printing

(B) Mosaic binding by J. W. Zaehnsdorf, c. 1856. Kâlidâsa, *Sâkoontalâ*, tr. M. Williams, Hertford, 1855. Brown gold tooled morocco, with a sunk panel of cream leather with onlays of various colours. Exhibited at the International Exhibition of 1862 in London. *British Museum.*

(A) A design blocked in blind on dark blue cloth (repeated front and back). Marryat, *The Pacha of Many Tales*, London, 1835.

PLATE 93

THE EARLY VICTORIAN PERIOD

(B) A 'Yellow back' binding, 1856. Maria Edgeworth, *Vivian*, London, 1856. Colour-printed yellow paper over paper boards. *British Museum*.

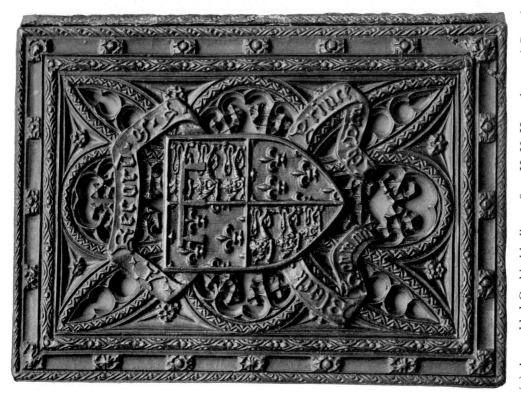

(A) A moulded Gothic binding, 1849. H. N. Humphreys, *A Record of the Black Prince*, London, 1849. Black moulded papier mâché covers ('in imitation of carved ebony') over a red ground, with a plain leather spine. The papier mâché covers were manufactured by Messrs Jackson & Son and the binding was the work of Jane & Robert Leighton, Harp Alley, both of London. *British Museum*.

PLATE 94

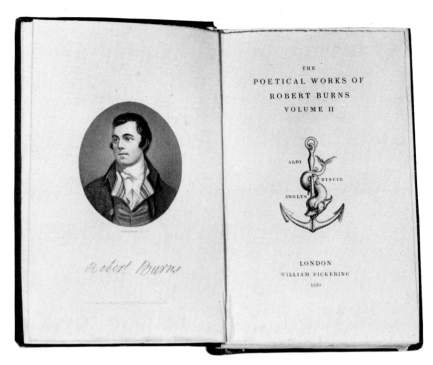

(A) The title-page opening are of Pickering's Aldine editions of the British Poets, 1830; page size $6\frac{1}{2} \times 4$ in.

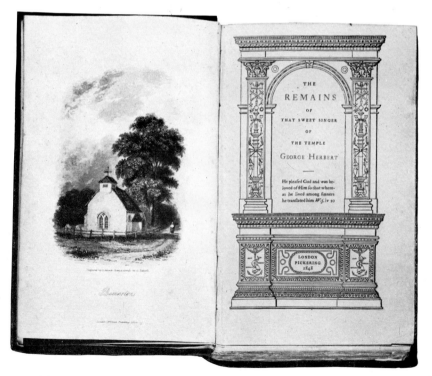

(B) A Pickering title-page in red and black of 1848; page size $6\frac{1}{2} \times 4$ in.

PLATE 95

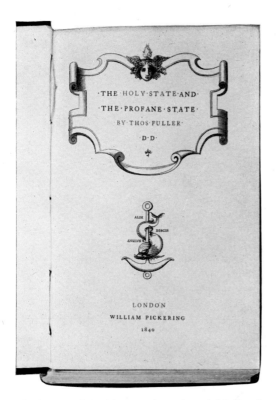

(A) A Pickering title-page in red and black of 1840, $6\frac{1}{2} \times 4$ in.

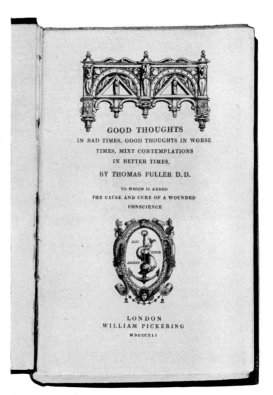

(B) A Pickering title-page in red and black of 1841, $6\frac{1}{2} \times 4$ in.

(C) An early chromolithograph title-page. *The Musical Bijou*, edited by F. H. Burney, London 1847.

(D) Title-page of Pickering's Prayer-Book of 1844; page size $14 \times 9\frac{1}{4}$ in.

PLATE 96

Bookbinding

HOWARD M. NIXON

By 1830 the 'extra' leather bindings produced by the 'West-end' section of the London bookbinding trade had begun to show a depressing lack of originality. For the next fifty years they tended to be beautifully tooled pastiches in the 'Grolier', 'Harleian', or 'Eve' styles – 'faultily faultless, icily regular, splendidly null'. Until his death at the age of fifty in 1836, Charles Lewis remained at the head of this branch of his profession. Francis Bedford, his foreman, carried on the business for five years for Mrs Lewis, then went into partnership with John Clarke, and finally set up on his own in 1850. He speedily succeeded to Lewis's former position and carried on his tradition of admirable technique and sad lack of invention. John MacKenzie, 'bookbinder to their late Majesties, King George ivth and King William ivth', Wickwar and Hayday were other leading West End binders whose firms had a comparatively short life. Hayday produced some strikingly original bindings for J.W.K.Eyton in the 1840's. On the other hand, Robert Rivière and Joseph Zaehnsdorf (a native of Budapest) each founded a business which was to carry their name for over one hundred years. Both were capable of some originality. Pl. 93B shows a binding executed by Zaehnsdorf in the late 1850's which was ostensibly an imitation of the Oriental style, but is so far removed in both style and technique from the work of any Eastern craftsman that it may be appreciated as a new and imaginative design.

The developments that took place in commercial binding, as the publisher took over the responsibility of having his books bound, were far more interesting. The mechanization of the trade proceeded speedily, with Archibald Leighton, who had introduced book cloth in the middle of the 1820's, playing a leading part. By 1832 the problem of rapid commercial gold-blocking of book cloth had been overcome and blocking in blind was also mastered so successfully that five years later Saunders and Otley were able to commission the splendid binding shown on Pl. 93A for their illustrated editions of some of Captain Marryat's novels. Blocking was also revived on leather for such work as the 'illuminated bindings' of J.S.Evans. These were first blocked in blind, parts of the design were then coloured by hand, and finally the remainder was blocked in gold. Inferior leathers, such as skiver, generally maroon or black, were frequently used both on Bibles and prayer books and also on annuals such as *Friendship's Offering* in the 'thirties. The plates used for these skiver bindings were often very finely engraved. Some of the best are signed by De la Rue and Co. and other good examples come from the shops of Remnant & Edmonds and Westley & Clarke.

Binders such as these firms, together with Bone, Burn and the various Leightons, also did much cloth work, the most elaborate specimens of which were the table books, indispensable objects in the properly overcrowded Victorian drawing-room with their lavish gilding and colour. The printing of coloured inks on cloth was not mastered completely until after 1860, and on most of the earlier examples coloured paper onlays were ingeniously used to produce polychrome effects.

M

The decorative effect of early cloth bindings was by no means invariably the result of the lavish application of gold and colours, but was often inherent in the designs of the fabric itself. 'Watered' cloths were being produced by De la Rue at the suggestion of Archibald Leighton in 1831 and were followed by a particularly elegant series of 'ribbon-embossed' fabrics which unfortunately proved too expensive for general use. In addition, the passion for pictorial blocking in the 'forties encouraged the use of cloth with simple grainings, although about 1845 striped cloths flourished briefly and between 1851 and 1855 there was a vogue for marbled cloth.

As the distribution of novels was largely in the hands of wholesale booksellers, who supplied the circulating libraries of provincial towns and the larger country houses, and was not carried out by the publishers, cloth did not become the standard covering of novels for long after it was *de rigueur* for most other types of books. Even in the 'fifties novels were still being bound in paper-covered boards with printed paper title-labels. Another style in which many cheap novels were to be found was the 'Yellow-back' binding, developed about the middle of the century for display and sale on railway bookstalls. The essential features of the yellow back were the use of a glazed coloured paper (most frequently yellow, but sometimes pink, green, blue or grey) over thin strawboards, a pictorial design (often printed in several colours) on the upper cover, and advertisements on the lower cover (Pl. 94B).

The bindings of the period, however, which have most in common with other early Victorian applied art were neither of leather, cloth nor paper-covered boards. They cover a number of works written by H.N.Humphreys, or with illuminations by Owen Jones, all of which date from within two or three years of the Great Exhibition of 1851. Some have covers of carved wood, but several of the Humphreys books have most elaborate Gothic moulded designs usually built up in black papier mâché over a metal framework. One has six oval medallions in relief representing miracles of Christ; another has the Black Prince's arms, with titles and mottoes on a scroll, adapted from a panel on the prince's tomb at Canterbury (Pl. 94A); a third, covering *The Origin and Progress of the Art of Writing*, has a decorated Gothic T enclosing the rest of the short title. All have Gothic borders in high relief and were very clearly intended to lie on drawing-room tables rather than to jostle with other books on library shelves.

One interesting feature of the period is that quite a high percentage of the bindings are signed. Lewis, Mackenzie and the other West End binders usually used a name pallet impressed in gold or blind on the turn-ins of the leather, or in ink at the top of the fly leaf. In addition, the 'forties and 'fifties witnessed in cloth books a revival of the binder's ticket, which had been popular in leather work at the end of the eighteenth century. But whereas the earlier examples had generally been oblong and pasted on the verso of a fly-leaf at the beginning of the book, the new ones were customarily square (often printed lozenge-wise) and were pasted on to the pastedown at the end of the volume. One or two of the artists who designed the blocks also signed their work, and the initials of Luke Limner, the pseudonym of John Leighton, are frequently to be found on the best blocked work of the period.

HOUSES OF PARLIAMENT

Fig. 1. Elongated roman type, *c.* 1838.

Printing

RUARI MCLEAN

This period saw an enormous increase in Britain's population and a corresponding expansion of the printing and publishing trades. The average yearly number of new books (not including reprints and pamphlets) rose from about 850 between 1802 and 1827 to about 2,530 in 1853; [1] the sale of *The Times* rose from 6,000 copies daily in 1817 to about 65,000 copies in 1861.[2]

Among the many newspapers and magazines born during this period were *Punch* (1841), *The Illustrated London News* (1842), and *The News of the World* (1843).

It was the period of a new reading public, who devoured Dickens' and Thackeray's novels as they came out in parts, and the period of the first great popular illustrators, such as Cruikshank, 'Phiz', Leech, Tenniel and Doyle. The work of these artists was printed either by etching, lithography, or wood-engraving. The period also saw a proliferation of decorative type-faces for advertising, the displacement of leather balls for inking by composition rollers (patented by Cowper in 1818), and the commercial introduction of cloth for binding editions of books. Mechanical type-founding came in by about 1860, after much opposition from the type-founders, and by about the same time stereo plates for newspapers were in universal use; although Earl Stanhope had perfected the necessary process as early as 1802. During all these years attempts were being made to find a satisfactory method for setting up type mechanic-

ally, and for the photographic engraving of illustrations, but neither process was perfected till well after 1860.

During the whole of the nineteenth century the energies of nearly every progressive printer were directed to speeding and cheapening production, so that fine printing became increasingly rare; but our period includes the career of William Pickering, perhaps the first publisher to base a publishing policy consciously on design.

William Pickering

Pickering, said to have been the illegitimate son of 'a book-loving earl and a lady of title', was born in 1796, and started business as a bookseller in 1820. In the same year he began publishing, by launching a series of 'Diamond Classics', beginning with the works of Horace. Being set in 'diamond' type (equivalent to $4\frac{1}{2}$ point), they could not be read except with a magnifying glass; but the series was evidently successful, for it was continued and eventually included Shakespeare (1825), Milton (1828), and Homer (1831). The early titles were all printed by Corrall, of Charing Cross, but later titles were printed by other printers and were not all in diamond type. This series also made publishing history because it included the first books sold in cloth bindings. It is not certain which title was the first; but it is certain that the young Pickering was dissatisfied with paper boards, which were then the only alternative to morocco, and asked his binder to suggest 'some neater mode' (Pickering's own words): the binder showed him some music

[1] Marjorie Plant, *The English Book-Trade*, 1939.
[2] *The History of The Times*, vols. 1 & 2, 1935–9.

bound in light blue glazed calico which had been bought to line curtains; and some time, perhaps early in 1825, this revolutionary binding material was used for 500 copies of one of the 'Diamond Classics'.[3] By 1830 the idea had been widely adopted by other publishers. The description 'extra boards' in contemporary publishers' advertisements almost certainly meant 'cloth'.

After the 'Diamond Classics', Pickering published books in more normal formats, at the same time continuing to maintain a large antiquarian bookselling business. Most, but not all, of the books he published before 1830 were printed by Thomas White, whose work for Pickering is his chief claim to fame. In 1825 began the 'Oxford English Classics', a series published by Pickering in association with Talboys and Wheeler of Oxford, and printed at Oxford, but showing clearly Pickering's influence on the design. The whole series, which included Smollett's *History* and Gibbon's *Decline and Fall*, consisted of forty-four volumes, and fifty or seventy-five copies of each work were printed on large paper.

In 1825 came the first example of Pickering's well-known wreath ornament on a title-page, which became one of his characteristic and most charming styles, though not used for more than about thirteen books. It was not until 1828 that he first used the dolphin-and-anchor device of Aldus, the great Venetian sixteenth-century printer, combined with the motto 'Aldi Discipulus Anglus'. This was cut in various forms and became Pickering's most famous title-page device; it underlined his chief aim as a publisher, which was, like Aldus, to produce the classics in cheap and handy formats.

In 1828 he met Charles Whittingham, the printer and nephew of the founder of the Chiswick Press. A friendship began which lasted till Pickering's death in 1854. Whittingham the younger – born in 1795, the year before Pickering – had just separated from his uncle and set up on his own in Took's Court, Chancery Lane. The first book he printed for Pickering appears to have been *The Carcanet*, an anthology selected by Sir Nicolas Harris Nicolas (the editor of Nelson's Letters), dated 1828. From 1830 onwards nearly all Pickering's books were printed by Whittingham. The nephew, like his uncle, was a fine printer, but his typographic style before he met Pickering was undistinguished.

In 1830 Pickering began his 'Aldine Edition of the British Poets', a series of small volumes ($6\frac{1}{2}$ in. × 4 in.) which set a completely new standard in British book design, and which are still most agreeable books in which to read the included authors. The first poet was Burns (Pl. 95 A): the simplicity of the title-page was in contrast to the normal style of the time, which still tended to overburden title-pages with lengthy sentences. The series ran to over fifty volumes, all printed by Charles Whittingham the younger, and selling at 5s. each in cloth or 10s. 6d. in morocco. The cloth bindings were dark blue, with a paper label on the spine.

Pickering's friendship with Whittingham brought him into contact with Mary Byfield, the Chiswick Press wood-engraver, and it is probable that most of the decorations in Pickering's books after 1830 were cut by her. Elaborate frames and cartouches were designed for the title-pages of the works of George Herbert, Thomas Fuller, Francis Bacon, Jeremy Taylor and others (Pls. 95 B, 96 A, B), in a style of intelligent archaism.

Perhaps the most important books Pickering ever published were his series of liturgical histories and reprints of the Prayer Book. The first was William Maskell's *The Ancient Liturgy of the Church of England*, 1844. Seven further works of Maskell's were published by Pickering, of which the most important was *Monumenta Ritualia* (1846–7), 'the scientific value of which was confirmed nearly forty years later in 1882, when it was reprinted at the Clarendon Press. From Maskell ... English liturgical scholarship has gone from strength to strength.'[4] The reprints of the Prayer Book consisted of six magnificent folio volumes printed in black-letter, rubricated and

[3] John Carter, *Binding Variants in English Publishing 1820–1900*, 1932.

[4] S. Morison, *English Prayer Books* (3rd edition), 1949.

bound in vellum. Another fine piece of printing was Keeling's *Liturgiae Britannicae*, 1842, with complicated comparative settings and rubrication throughout. From a visual point of view, perhaps the most attractive book of all was the edition, in 1853, of Queen Elizabeth's Prayer Book of 1569. It was Mary Byfield's as well as Whittingham's and Pickering's masterpiece, for every page was ornamented with her wood-blocks. She cut over one hundred, based on those in the original edition, themselves based on designs of Holbein, Dürer, Tory and others. The blocks were designed in the style of the marginal borders of the old manuscript Books of Hours, and were in strip form. They could then be used again and again in different combinations, so that no two pages were identical.

Many of the designs for the decorative blocks cut by Mary Byfield were drawn by Whittingham's daughters Elizabeth and Charlotte. The Chiswick Press, which exists today, although no longer at Chiswick, still possesses, and shows in its specimen books, many of Mary Byfield's wood-cut decorations and initial letters.

Pickering, it is sad to relate, died in bankruptcy, having backed a friend's venture which ended in failure. He was buried in the Whittingham family ground at Kensal Green Cemetery. His work, in his lifetime, was appreciated by the discriminating few, and then forgotten. Interest in him was not revived until the publication of Sir Geoffrey Keynes' admirable monograph, *William Pickering, Publisher*, in 1924.

Charles Whittingham the younger

Charles Whittingham, his printer friend and collaborator, was the finest printer in Britain and probably in Europe during the whole period. Whittingham became a partner with his uncle (also called Charles Whittingham) in the Chiswick Press in 1824, but set up on his own in 1828, and did not return to the Chiswick Press until, on his uncle's health failing in 1838, he resumed control of it. In 1840 his uncle died. Like his uncle, the nephew specialized in the printing of wood-engravings, and never installed presses for copper-plate printing or lithography. It is interesting to note that hand-presses only were used at the Chiswick Press until 1860, although the rotary steam press had been in use (for newspapers) since 1814, and for books since at least 1837.[5]

In 1833 Whittingham printed and Pickering published *Illuminated Ornaments selected from Manuscripts and early printed Books*, by Henry Shaw, F.S.A., which contained forty-nine colour plates of medieval lettering. These were drawn by Shaw in facsimile, printed from etched plates, and hand-coloured. The effect was superb, but such lavish use of colour could clearly not be economic. After producing one or two other books with a few coloured plates, Shaw issued in 1843 *Dresses and Decorations of the Middle Ages*, also printed (the letterpress pages only) by Whittingham and published by Pickering. This work in two volumes is illustrated on every page, nearly always in colour, either from hand-coloured etchings or wood-blocks printed in colour: the monochrome illustrations are wood-engravings probably by Mary Byfield. The effect is extremely rich and the work as a whole is one of the highlights of mid-Victorian book design and production. In *Alphabets Numerals and Devices of the Middle Ages*, which followed in 1845, and in *The Decorative Arts Ecclesiastical and Civil of the Middle Ages* (1851) Shaw introduced some colour-printing by lithography, as well as hand-colouring and printing in colour from wood blocks.

Shaw financed his own publications, and they were not, according to Warren (in *The Charles Whittinghams, Printers*), financially successful; but they represent a notable achievement in craftsmanship. Technically, their greatest interest lies in the use of colour-printing from wood blocks. This method, which dates back to the very earliest days of printing, had been demonstrated in 1822 by William Savage in his *Practical Hints on Decorative Printing*, in which one illustration was printed in thirty colours from twenty-nine blocks; in several others Savage successfully imitated hand-coloured aquatints or etchings with between three and ten printings from wood.

[5] Cf. J. Southwood, *Progress in Printing and the Graphic Arts during the Victorian Era*, 1897.

Henry Cole, one of the prime movers in the Great Exhibition, used Whittingham's skill in colour-printing from wood-blocks for his 'Felix Summerly' series of children's books, which from 1841 onwards were the most elegant and charming books of this kind that had yet appeared.

Whittingham's leading position in the printing trade was marked by his appointment as secretary of the jury in the section of printing and allied trades in the Great Exhibition of 1851. He died in 1876.

The Colour-printing of Edmund Evans

Colour-printing from wood-blocks at the Chiswick Press has been mentioned above. The development of this art is chiefly associated with the firm of Edmund Evans, and although his greatest artistic triumphs were the illustrations of Kate Greenaway, Doyle and Caldecott after 1860, his early work requires mention here.

Edmund Evans (1826–1905) was a wood-engraver who had been apprenticed to Ebenezer Landells, himself a pupil of Bewick and the chief originator of *Punch*. Evans set up on his own in 1847 and subsequently cut colour blocks for various Birket Foster illustrations. In 1853, after cutting pictorial colour blocks to be printed on the wrappers of Mayhew's *Letters Left at the Pastry Cook's* (itself a novelty), 'Evans had the [as it transpired] sensational idea of using yellow glazed paper and of mounting it on board. It is therefore certain that Evans was the first man to see the possibilities of coloured pictorial printing on coloured paper, and that to him more than to anyone else was due the establishment of the yellow-back in popular favour.' [6]

Yellow-backs, which became a tremendous industry and were a revolutionary new idea in publishing, were essentially books bound in printed paper-covered boards and sold at 2s., as against the 5s. or 6s. of the current and till then highly successful cloth-bound Standard Novels of Bentley, Colburn and Blackwood. The first series was the Parlour Library of Simms and McIntyre, which

began in 1847: it was followed by numerous imitators, of which the first and perhaps the most successful was Routledge's *Railway Library*, from 1849 onwards. In their heyday, during the 'fifties and 'sixties, yellow-backs were, as Sir Michael Sadleir points out in his essay quoted above, well-edited, well-printed, and adventurously and attractively designed. According to the same authority, 80 per cent of the yellow-back covers produced between 1855 and 1865 were the work of the firm of Edmund Evans: his early ones were signed in one of the bottom margins.

Pictorial yellow-back covers, from which the modern book-jacket is directly descended, were themselves anticipated by the cover designs of novels issued in parts, although these were not printed in colour. The publication of books in monthly parts was not a new idea in the nineteenth century, but it was not applied to fiction until the success of *Pickwick Papers* in 1836 pointed the way; [7] after that most of the major novels of Dickens, Thackeray, Marryat, Surtees, Trollope and many others were so issued. The parts were nearly always illustrated with etched plates and the covers (usually green, grey, red, blue or yellow cartridge paper) carried a pictorial design printed in black from a wood-block. Sometimes these designs were retained for the title-page of the book when it was later issued in bound form. Notable designs in this manner were made by George Cruikshank and 'Phiz'.

Another aspect of the same design problem was magazine covers, and indeed several magazines, such as *Bentley's Miscellany* and *Ainsworth's Magazine*, existed to publish novels in monthly parts. An example is provided by *Punch*, which started in 1841 with a cover designed by A.S.Henning and had four more covers until Richard Doyle, with his second attempt, produced in 1849 the famous design which survived so long. Doyle

[6] Michael Sadleir, 'Yellow-backs', in *New Paths in Book Collecting*, 1934.

[7] '*Pickwick* started slowly, sales of the first number (probably 1000) being so discouraging that only 500 of the second were printed. With the appearance of Sam Weller, popularity began and increased by leaps and bounds, so that first printings of the later parts ran well into five figures.' John Carter, *Victorian Fiction*, N.B.L. Catalogue, 1947.

FRANCE &

MUSIC

HUMBER

BRIGHTON

MARGATE

THE CONCERT

ROSE

Fig. 2. Early Victorian decorative type faces. All (except 'France &') are in *The Specimen Book of Types Cast at the Austin Foundry by Wood & Sharwoods*, c. 1838, but may have been cut earlier.

(1824–83) was an illustrator with a genuine, if highly individual, feeling for lettering, and in his title-pages for Ruskin's *The King of the Golden River*, 1851, and *The Scouring of the White Horse*, 1859 (and in his *Punch* cover), the lettering is completely, hauntingly, integrated with the illustrations.

Chromo-lithography

While experiments in colour-printing from wood-blocks were being made at the Chiswick Press in the 'forties, experiments were also being made by other printers in colour-printing by lithography. These soon led to success and to an immense new branch of the printing trade: many, if not most, colour posters today are still printed virtually by the same process.

Lithography had been discovered by the German, Senefelder, in 1798, and was soon introduced into England, but for some years its artistic potentialities were not understood, and it was despised as an inferior substitute for etching. The person who did most to pioneer and popularize lithography in Britain was Charles Joseph Hullmandel (1789–1850), an artist of German parentage born in London. He made several important technical innovations leading up to 'chromalithography', as it was then called, whereby the effect of a painting in oils, or water-colour, could be achieved by the superimposed printing of a number of lithographic plates. *Sketches at Home and Abroad*, by J.D.Harding, printed by Hullmandel and published in 1836 by Tilt, was one of the earliest books of tinted lithographs, with one tint only: Thomas Shotter Boys' *Picturesque Architecture in Paris Ghent Antwerp Rouen*, also printed by Hullmandel, and published by Boys in 1839, had four tints, and was perhaps the earliest masterpiece of colour lithography. *Original Views of London as it is*, 1842, also by Boys and printed by Hullmandel, was another early lithographic masterpiece in two colours, and an important record of London for this period.

Some magnificent colour-printing by lithography was also designed by the architect Owen Jones, who was responsible for the painting and interior decoration of the Crystal Palace in 1851.

Whereas Hullmandel and Boys were chiefly concerned to reproduce representational paintings, Jones used large numbers of flat colours usually in juxtaposition. Among his most interesting works are *Plans, Elevations, Sections and Details of the Alhambra*, 1841–5, *The Book of Common Prayer*, 1845, *The Illuminated Books of the Middle Ages*, 1849, and *The Grammar of Ornament*, 1856. They are triumphs of elaborate chromo-lithographic printing, but they do not make as pleasant books as Henry Shaw's collaborations with Whittingham and Pickering; and they certainly fathered much of the most tasteless decorative printing that followed.

Mention must also be made of the books designed and illustrated by Henry Noel Humphreys. *A Record of the Black Prince*, 1849, is an exquisite small book, printed by Vizetelly in black letter and illustrated with both wood-cuts and chromo-lithography. Another very pretty book of his is *The Gold, Silver, and Copper Coins of England etc*, 1846; with wood-cut borders and initials, and plates chromo-lithographed in gold, silver, copper and royal blue.

Baxter and Kronheim

George Baxter, whose first colour prints were made in 1834, did not use lithography, but 'used an engraved metal plate, usually aquatint, as a key-plate for the subsequent wood-engraved colour impressions'.[8]

J.M.Kronheim, a German who came to London in 1846, became a prolific colour-printer who used wood-blocks for the key and printed the colours from metal plates.

The primacy in cheap commercial colour lithography passed later in the century to Germany, with the result that the colour pages of many British books and magazines were imported from that country.

Type faces

During the Regency period the English type-founders had already invented fat faces, sans-serif

[8] See Michael Oliver's notes in J.R.Abbey's *Travel in Aquatint and Lithography*, 1956.

(sometimes confusingly called 'Egyptian', 'grotesque' or 'Doric'), 'Egyptian' (i.e. slab-serif, also known as 'Antique' or 'Ionic') and shadowed letters, both in roman and black-letter. The so-called 'Tuscan' had also already appeared, whose body and extremities were bifurcated and curled, forming types of great jollity which had their most appropriate use in circus and theatre printing, although they were by no means confined to that.

The way in which the types produced during the 'thirties, 'forties and 'fifties reflect the intellectual and spiritual moods of the period have been acutely described by Nicolette Gray in her *Nineteenth-Century Ornamental Types and Title-pages*, 1938. She traces a sudden change from Regency joviality to Victorian social conscience: a change also reflected in the difference between Dickens' first novel, *Pickwick Papers*, 1836, full of drinking and kissing, and his next book, *Oliver Twist*, 1837, devoted to reform of the Poor Laws. In the elongated romans (Fig. 1) which came in about 1838, Mrs Gray finds a face which has 'caught the symbolism of the Gothic spire'; and she points out that the sans-serif, although invented earlier, was in 1847 first produced in a normal form and was 'the letter *par excellence*, of the 'fifties' – the typographic counterpart of the architecture of the railways and the Crystal Palace.

Besides the types already mentioned, an increasing number of new decorated faces was being produced during the whole period, including outline letters, letters set on decorated backgrounds, and 'perspective' letters. These types were used in jobbing and commercial printing, not in books, except for labels and covers of part-issues.

The more startling aberrations of Victorian ingenuity in both type and book design fall, happily, outside our period.

A SELECT LIST OF CONTEMPORARY PUBLICATIONS MENTIONED

Architecture of Country Houses, The (Downing) (1850), 45.
Art-Journal, 82, 83, 90, 145, 147, 162.
Art-Union, 78, 89, 90, 91, 93 *and* fig. 3, 94, 95, 99, 125.
Attempt to Discriminate the Styles of Architecture in England, from the Conquest to the Reformation (Rickman) (1817), 21, 31.

Belle Assemblée, La, 131, 132, 133 *and* fig. 1, 135, 136.
Builder, The, 30, 32 fig.

Cabinet-Maker's and Upholsterer's Guide,

Drawing-Book and Repository (Smith), 38.
Cabinet-Maker's Assistant (Blackie) (1853), 41, 44.
Cabinet of Practical, Useful and Decorative Furniture Designs (Lawford) (1855), 118, 120–1 *and* figs.
Contrasts (Pugin) (1836), 24, 31.
Court Magazine, 131, 133, 134, 136, 139.

Designs for Carving and Gilding (King) (1834), 39.
Designs for Furniture and Draperies (Wood) (c. 1845), 117–8.

Designs for Gold and Silversmiths (Pugin) (1836), 81.

Elizabethan Furniture (Fildes) (1844), 39.
Encyclopaedia of Cottage, Farm, and Villa Architecture and Furniture (Loudon) (1833), 37, 39, 103, 106–7 *and* figs., 116 fig. 1.
Englishwoman's Domestic Magazine, 139.
Exemplars of Tudor Architecture and Furniture (Hunt) (1829–30), 39.

Female Beauty (Walker) (1837), 146.